Modern Operating Systems

Modern Operating Systems

Edited by
Kate Summers

www.willfordpress.com

Published by Willford Press,
118-35 Queens Blvd., Suite 400,
Forest Hills, NY 11375, USA

ISBN: 978-1-68285-478-5

Cataloging-in-Publication Data

Modern operating systems / edited by Kate Summers.
    p. cm.
Includes bibliographical references and index.
ISBN 978-1-68285-478-5
1. Operating systems (Computers). 2. Systems software. I. Summers, Kate.
QA76.77 .M63 2018
005.43--dc23

For information on all Willford Press publications
visit our website at www.willfordpress.com

Contents

Preface

Computers have become an inevitable part of our daily lives, be it for office work or personal use. They have enabled us to do tasks in a quick and efficient manner. Operating systems are the most vital part of any computing device. They are the software which makes the device function. The different types of operating software include embedded software, real-time software, single and multi-tasking software, distributed software, etc. The topics covered in this book provide the readers with in-depth insights in the field of operating systems. The textbook is appropriate for those seeking detailed information in this area.

A short introduction to every chapter is written below to provide an overview of the content of the book:

Chapter 1 - The system software that manages software and hardware together to run a computer program is called an operating system. An operating system performs several functions like helping a program connect to the CPU, and saving the user's data. A few types of operating systems are macOS, Linux, Microsoft Windows, Chrome OS, etc. This is an introductory chapter which will introduce briefly all the significant aspects of operating system; **Chapter 2 -** The information stored in the non-volatile secondary memory amounts to files in a system. Since all information regardless of its type is a file, the storage system of a computer can contain huge number of files. File system does the needful in handling this problem. It controls the way data is stored and recovered. This chapter has been carefully written to provide an easy understanding of the varied facets of file system and management in an operating system; **Chapter 3 -** Owing to time constraint in some data processing applications, it becomes necessary that system responses reach within the stipulated time. This time period, however, can be generalized as it depends on the application and its urgency. These data processing application include online banking, tele-ticketing, online stock trading, etc. and are known as real time systems. The major components of real time operating systems are discussed in this chapter; **Chapter 4 -** In the age where the Internet has become a part of the daily human lives catering to many needs such as booking tickets, socializing, buying and selling products, etc., information needs to be protected. Since the operating system is the resource regulator of a computer system, it should also be the security service provider. This section elucidates the crucial theories and principles related to computer security.

Finally, I would like to thank my fellow scholars who gave constructive feedback and my family members who supported me at every step.

Editor

Understanding Operating System

The system software that manages software and hardware together to run a computer program is called an operating system. An operating system performs several functions like helping a program connect to the CPU, and saving the user's data. A few types of operating systems are macOS, Linux, Microsoft Windows, Chrome OS, etc. This is an introductory chapter which will introduce briefly all the significant aspects of operating system.

Operating System

Operating System (or shortly OS) primarily provides services for running applications on a computer system.

Need for an OS

The primary need for the OS arises from the fact that user needs to be provided with services and OS ought to facilitate the provisioning of these services. The central part of a computer system is a processing engine called CPU. A system should make it possible for a user's application to use the processing unit. A user application would need to store information. The OS makes memory available to an application when required. Similarly, user applications need use of input facility to communicate with the application. This is often in the form of a key board, or a mouse or even a joy stick (if the application is a game for instance).

Keyboard

Mouse

Joystick

Monitor

Printer

The output usually provided by a video monitor or a printer as some times the user may wish to generate an output in the form of a printed document. Output may be available in some other forms. For example it may be a video or an audio file.

Let us consider few applications:

- Document Design

- Accounting

- E-mail

- Image processing

- Games

We notice that each of the above application requires resources for

- Processing information

- Storage of Information

- Mechanism to inputting information

- Provision for outputting information

- These service facilities are provided by an operating system regardless of the nature of application.

The OS offers generic services to support all the above operations. These operations in turn facilitate the applications mentioned earlier. To that extent an OS operation is application neutral and service specific.

User and System View

From the user point of view the primary consideration is always the convenience. It should be easy to use an application. In launching an application, it helps to have an icon which gives a clue which application it is. We have seen some helpful clues for launching a browser, e-mail or even a document preparation application. In other words, the human computer interface which helps to identify an application and its launch is very useful. This hides a lot of details of the more elementary instructions that help in selecting the application. Similarly, if we examine the programs that help us in using input devices like a key board – all the complex details of character reading program are hidden from the user. The same is true when we write a program. For instance, when we use a programming language like C, a printf command helps to generate the desired form of output. The following figure essentially depicts the basic schema of the use of OS from a user stand point. However, when it comes to the view point of a system, the OS needs to ensure that all the system users and applications get to use the facilities that they need.

Also, OS needs to ensure that system resources are utilized efficiently. For instance, there may be many service requests on a Web server. Each user request need to be serviced. Similarly, there may be many programs residing in the main memory. The system need to determine which programs are active and which need to await some form of input or output. Those that need to wait can be suspended temporarily from engaging the processor. This strategy alone enhances the processor throughput. In other words, it is important for an operating system to have a control policy and algorithm to allocate the system resources.

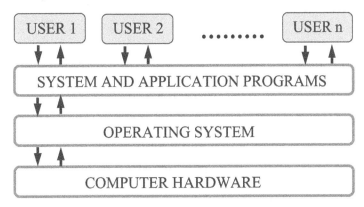

The Evolution

It would be worthwhile to trace some developments that have happened in the last four to five decades. In the 1960s, the common form of computing facility was a mainframe computer system. The mainframe computer system would be normally housed in a computer center with a controlled environment which was usually an air conditioned area with a clean room like facility. The users used to bring in a deck of punched cards which encoded the list of program instructions.

The mode of operation was as follows:

- User would prepare a program as a deck of punched cards.

- The header cards in the deck were the "job control" cards which would indicate which compiler was to be used (like Fortran / Cobol compilers).

- The deck of cards would be handed in to an operator who would collect such jobs from various users.

- The operators would invariably group the submitted jobs as Fortran jobs, Cobol jobs etc. In addition, these were classified as "long jobs" that required considerable processing time or short jobs which required a short and limited computational time.

Each set of jobs was considered as a batch and the processing would be done for a batch. Like for instance there may be a batch of short Fortran jobs. The output for each job would be separated and turned over to users in a collection area. This scenario clearly shows that there was no interactivity. Users had no direct control. Also, at any one time only one program would engage the processor. This meant that if there was any input or output in between processing then the processor would wait idling till such time that the I/O is completed. This meant that processor would idling most of the time as processor speeds were orders of magnitude higher than the input or output or even memory units. Clearly, this led to poor utilization of the processor. The systems that utilized the CPU and memory better and with multiple users connected to the systems evolved over a period of time as shown in Table.

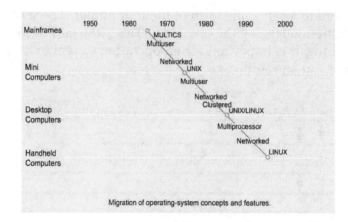

Migration of operating-system concepts and features.

At this time we would like to invoke Von - Neumann principle of stored program operation. For a program to be executed it ought to be stored in the memory. In the scheme of things discussed in the previous paragraph, we notice that at any time only one program was kept in the memory and executed. In the decade of 70s this basic mode of operation was altered and system designers contemplated having more than one program resident in the memory. This clearly meant that when one program is awaiting completion of an input or output, another program could, in fact, engage the CPU.

Late 60's and early 70's

Storing multiple executables (at the same time) in the main memory is called multiprogramming. With multiple excutables residing in the main memory, the immediate consideration is: we now need a policy to allocate memory and processor time to the resident programs. It is obvious that by utilizing the processor for another process when a process is engaged in input or output the processor utilization and, therefore, its output are higher. Overall, the multiprogramming leads to higher throughput for this reason.

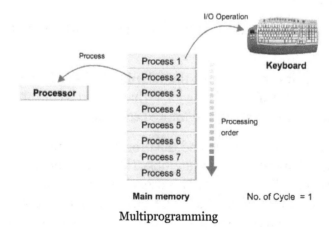

Multiprogramming

1980's

In late 70s and early part of the decade of 80s the system designers offered some interactivity with each user having a capability to access system. This is the period when the timeshared systems came on the scene.

Basically, the idea is to give every user an illusion that all the system resources were available to him as his program executed. To strengthen this illusion a clever way was devised by which each user was allocated a slice of time to engage the processor. During the allocated time slice a users' program would be executed. Now imagine if the next turn for the same program comes quickly enough, the user would have an illusion that the system was continuously available to his task. This is what precisely time sharing systems attempted – giving each user a small time slice and returning back quickly enough so that he never feels lack of continuity. In fact, he carries an impression that the system is entirely available to him alone.

Timeshared systems clearly require several design considerations. These include the following: How many programs may reside in the main memory to allow, and also sustain timesharing? What should be the time slice allocated to process each program? How would one protect a users' program and data from being overwritten by another users' program? Basically, the design trends that were clearly evident during the decade of 1970-80 were: Achieve as much overlapping as may be feasible between I/O and processing. Bulk storage on disks clearly witnessed a phenomenal growth. This also helped to implement the concept to offer an illusion of extended storage. The concept of "virtual storage" came into the vogue. The virtual storage essentially utilizes these disks to offer enhanced addressable space. The fact that only that part of a program that is currently active need be in the main memory also meant that multi-programming could support many more programs. In fact this could be further enhanced as follows:

1. Only required active parts of the programs could be swapped in from disks.

2. Suspended programs could be swapped out.

This means that a large number of users can access the system. This was to satisfy the notion that "computing" facility be brought to a user as opposed to the notion that the "user go to compute". The fact that a facility is brought to a user gives the notion of a utility or a service in its true sense. In fact, the PC truly reflects the notion of "computing utility" - it is regarded now as a personal productivity tool.

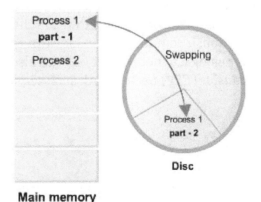

Main memory
Swapping of program parts main memory - disc, vice-versa

It was in early 1970s Bell Laboratory scientists came up with the now well-known OS: Unix. Also, as the microcomputers came on scene in 1980s a forerunner to current DOS was a system called CP/M. The decade of 1980s saw many advances with the promise of networked systems. One notable project amongst these was the project Athena at MIT in USA. The project forms the basis to several modern developments. The client-server paradigm was indeed a major fall out. The users could have a common server to the so called X-terminals.

The X windows also provided many widgets to support convenient human computer interfaces. Using X windows it is possible to create multiple windows. In fact each of the windows offers a virtual terminal. In other words it is possible to think about each of these windows as a front-end terminal connection. So it is possible to launch different applications from each of the windows. This is what you experience on modern day PC which also supports such an operating environment.

In our discussions, we shall discuss many of the above issues in greater detail as we move to later chapters. On the micro-computer front the development was aimed at relieving the processor from handling input output responsibilities. The I/O processing was primarily handled by two mechanisms: one was BIOS and the other was the graphics cards to drive the display. The processor now was relieved from regulating the I/O. This made it possible to utilize the processor more effectively for other processing tasks. With the advent of 1990s the computer communication was pretty much the order of the day.

CP/M based computer

Networking topologies like star, ring and general graphs, as shown in the figure, were being experimented with protocols for communication amongst computers evolved. In particular, the TCP/IP suite of network protocols were implemented. The growth in the networking area also resulted in giving users a capability to establish communication between computers. It was now possible to connect to a remote computer using a telnet protocol. It was also possible to get a file stored in a remote location using a file transfer (FTP) protocol. All such services are broadly called network services.

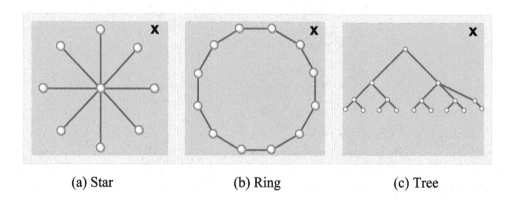

(a) Star   (b) Ring   (c) Tree

Let's now briefly explore where the OS appears in the context of the software and application.

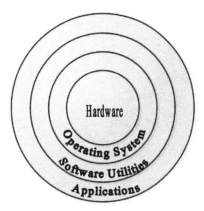

Let's consider a scenario where we need to embed the computer system in an industrial application. This may be regulating the temperature of a vessel in a process control. In a typical process control scenario

- Monitoring – initializes and activates the hardware.

- Input – Reads the values from sensors and stores it in register.

- Decision – checks whether the readings are within the range.

- Output – responds to the situation.

- Scenario: A temperature monitoring chemical process.

- What we need: A supervisory program to raise an alarm when temperature goes beyond a certain band.

- The desired sequence of operational events: Measure input temperature, process the most recent measurement, perform an output task.

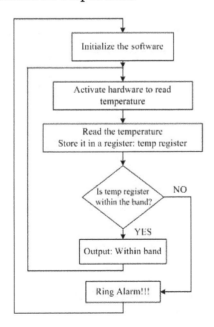

The computer system may be employed in a variety of operational scenarios like a bank, airlines reservation system, university admissions and several others. In each of these we need to provide the resources for:

- Processing

- User access to the system

- Storage and management of information

- Protection of information against accidental and intentional misuse

- Support for data processing activities

- Communication with I/O devices

- Management of all activities in a transparent manner.

Let's now review what an OS does.

- Power On Self Test (POST)

- Resource management

- Support for multi-user

- Error Handling

- Communication support over Network

- (Optional) Deadline support so that safety critical application run and fail gracefully.

Operational View

Let's briefly look at the underlying principle of operation of a computer system. Current systems are based on The Von-Neumann principle. The principle states that a program is initially stored in memory and executed by fetching an instruction at a time.

The basic cycle of operation is

- Fetch an instruction (Fetch)

- Interpret the instruction (Decode)

- Execute the instruction (Execute).

Modern systems allow multiple users to use a computer system. Even on a stand alone PC there may be multiple application which are running simultaneously. For instance, we have a mail program receiving mails, a clock to display time while we may be engaged in browsing a word process.

In other words OS need to schedule the processor amongst all the application simultaneously without giving an impression that the processor time is being divided and scheduled per an application.

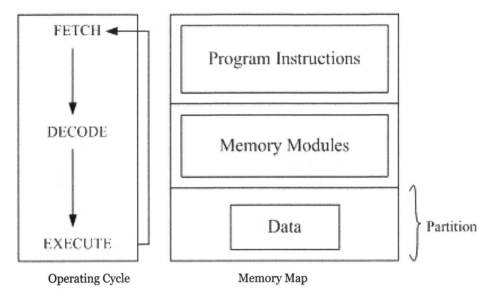

Operating Cycle   Memory Map

An Operational Overview:

- Processor – schedule and allocate processor time

- Memory – executes program and access data

- Input output devices

- Communication with devices

- Mutual exclusion – schedule the usage of shared device and fair access

- Shell of an OS

- Human computer interface (HCI/CHI).

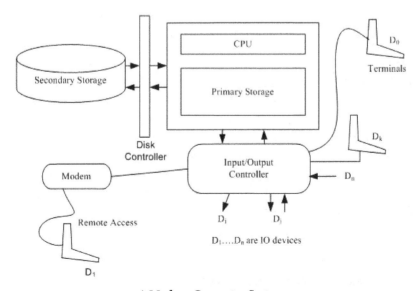

A Modern Computer System

The peripheral devices communicate in a mode known as interrupt mode .Typically human input is considered important and often uses this mode. This is so because human desire to guide the operation. For instance, we use a mouse click or a key board input. These require immediate attention by needing an appropriate interruption service.

An operating system (OS) is system software that manages computer hardware and software resources and provides common services for computer programs. All computer programs, excluding firmware, require an operating system to function.

Time-sharing operating systems schedule tasks for efficient use of the system and may also include accounting software for cost allocation of processor time, mass storage, printing, and other resources.

For hardware functions such as input and output and memory allocation, the operating system acts as an intermediary between programs and the computer hardware, although the application code is usually executed directly by the hardware and frequently makes system calls to an OS function or is interrupted by it. Operating systems are found on many devices that contain a computer – from cellular phones and video game consoles to web servers and supercomputers.

The dominant desktop operating system is Microsoft Windows with a market share of around 83.3%. macOS by Apple Inc. is in second place (11.2%), and the varieties of Linux is in third position (1.55%). In the mobile (smartphone and tablet combined) sector, according to third quarter 2016 data, Android by Google is dominant with 87.5 percent and a growth rate 10.3 percent per year, followed by iOS by Apple with 12.1 percent and a per year decrease in market share of 5.2 percent, while other operating systems amount to just 0.3 percent. Linux distributions are dominant in the server and supercomputing sectors. Other specialized classes of operating systems, such as embedded and real-time systems, exist for many applications.

Types of Operating Systems

Single- and Multi-tasking

A single-tasking system can only run one program at a time, while a multi-tasking operating system allows more than one program to be running in concurrency. This is achieved by time-sharing, dividing the available processor time between multiple processes that are each interrupted repeatedly in time slices by a task-scheduling subsystem of the operating system. Multi-tasking may be characterized in preemptive and co-operative types. In preemptive multitasking, the operating system slices the CPU time and dedicates a slot to each of the programs. Unix-like operating systems, e.g., Solaris, Linux, as well as AmigaOS support preemptive multitasking. Cooperative multitasking is achieved by relying on each process to provide time to the other processes in a defined manner. 16-bit versions of Microsoft Windows used cooperative multi-tasking. 32-bit versions of both Windows NT and Win9x, used preemptive multi-tasking.

Single- and Multi-user

Single-user operating systems have no facilities to distinguish users, but may allow multiple programs to run in tandem. A multi-user operating system extends the basic concept of multi-tasking with facilities that identify processes and resources, such as disk space, belonging to multiple users, and the system permits multiple users to interact with the system at the same time. Time-sharing operating systems schedule tasks for efficient use of the system and may also include accounting software for cost allocation of processor time, mass storage, printing, and other resources to multiple users.

Distributed

A distributed operating system manages a group of distinct computers and makes them appear to be a single computer. The development of networked computers that could be linked and communicate with each other gave rise to distributed computing. Distributed computations are carried out on more than one machine. When computers in a group work in cooperation, they form a distributed system.

Templated

In an OS, distributed and cloud computing context, templating refers to creating a single virtual machine image as a guest operating system, then saving it as a tool for multiple running virtual machines. The technique is used both in virtualization and cloud computing management, and is common in large server warehouses.

Embedded

Embedded operating systems are designed to be used in embedded computer systems. They are designed to operate on small machines like PDAs with less autonomy. They are able to operate with a limited number of resources. They are very compact and extremely efficient by design. Windows CE and Minix 3 are some examples of embedded operating systems.

Real-time

A real-time operating system is an operating system that guarantees to process events or data by a specific moment in time. A real-time operating system may be single- or multi-tasking, but when multitasking, it uses specialized scheduling algorithms so that a deterministic nature of behavior is achieved. An event-driven system switches between tasks based on their priorities or external events while time-sharing operating systems switch tasks based on clock interrupts.

Library

A library operating system is one in which the services that a typical operating system provides, such as networking, are provided in the form of libraries. These libraries are composed with the application and configuration code to construct unikernels – which are specialized, single address space, machine images that can be deployed to cloud or embedded environments.

History

Early computers were built to perform a series of single tasks, like a calculator. Basic operating system features were developed in the 1950s, such as resident monitor functions that could automatically run different programs in succession to speed up processing. Operating systems did not exist in their modern and more complex forms until the early 1960s. Hardware features were added, that enabled use of runtime libraries, interrupts, and parallel processing. When personal computers became popular in the 1980s, operating systems were made for them similar in concept to those used on larger computers.

In the 1940s, the earliest electronic digital systems had no operating systems. Electronic systems of this time were programmed on rows of mechanical switches or by jumper wires on plug boards. These were special-purpose systems that, for example, generated ballistics tables for the military or controlled the printing of payroll checks from data on punched paper cards. After programmable general purpose computers were invented, machine languages (consisting of strings of the binary digits 0 and 1 on punched paper tape) were introduced that speed up the programming process (Stern, 1981).

OS/360 was used on most IBM mainframe computers beginning in 1966,
including computers used by the Apollo program.

In the early 1950s, a computer could execute only one program at a time. Each user had sole use of the computer for a limited period of time and would arrive at a scheduled time with program and data on punched paper cards or punched tape. The program would be loaded into the machine, and the machine would be set to work until the program completed or crashed. Programs could generally be debugged via a front panel using toggle switches and panel lights. It is said that Alan Turing was a master of this on the early Manchester Mark 1 machine, and he was already deriving the primitive conception of an operating system from the principles of the universal Turing machine.

Later machines came with libraries of programs, which would be linked to a user's program to assist in operations such as input and output and generating computer code from human-readable symbolic code. This was the genesis of the modern-day operating system. However, machines still ran a single job at a time. At Cambridge University in England the job queue was at one time a washing line (clothes line) from which tapes were hung with different colored clothes-pegs to indicate job-priority.

An improvement was the Atlas Supervisor introduced with the Manchester Atlas commissioned in 1962, "considered by many to be the first recognisable modern operating system". Brinch Hansen described it as "the most significant breakthrough in the history of operating systems."

Mainframes

Through the 1950s, many major features were pioneered in the field of operating systems, including batch processing, input/output interrupt, buffering, multitasking, spooling, runtime libraries, link-loading, and programs for sorting records in files. These features were included or not included in application software at the option of application programmers, rather than in a separate operating system used by all applications. In 1959, the SHARE Operating System was released as an integrated utility for the IBM 704, and later in the 709 and 7090 mainframes, although it was quickly supplanted by IBSYS/IBJOB on the 709, 7090 and 7094.

During the 1960s, IBM's OS/360 introduced the concept of a single OS spanning an entire product line, which was crucial for the success of the System/360 machines. IBM's current mainframe operating systems are distant descendants of this original system and applications written for OS/360 can still be run on modern machines.

OS/360 also pioneered the concept that the operating system keeps track of all of the system resources that are used, including program and data space allocation in main memory and file space in secondary storage, and file locking during update. When the process is terminated for any reason, all of these resources are re-claimed by the operating system.

The alternative CP-67 system for the S/360-67 started a whole line of IBM operating systems focused on the concept of virtual machines. Other operating systems used on IBM S/360 series mainframes included systems developed by IBM: COS/360 (Compatibility Operating System), DOS/360 (Disk Operating System), TSS/360 (Time Sharing System), TOS/360 (Tape Operating System), BOS/360 (Basic Operating System), and ACP (Airline Control Program), as well as a few non-IBM systems: MTS (Michigan Terminal System), MUSIC (Multi-User System for Interactive Computing), and ORVYL (Stanford Timesharing System).

Control Data Corporation developed the SCOPE operating system in the 1960s, for batch processing. In cooperation with the University of Minnesota, the Kronos and later the NOS operating systems were developed during the 1970s, which supported simultaneous batch and timesharing use. Like many commercial timesharing systems, its interface was an extension of the Dartmouth BASIC operating systems, one of the pioneering efforts in timesharing and programming languages. In the late 1970s, Control Data and the University of Illinois developed the PLATO operating system, which used plasma panel displays and long-distance time sharing networks. Plato was remarkably innovative for its time, featuring real-time chat, and multi-user graphical games.

In 1961, Burroughs Corporation introduced the B5000 with the MCP, (Master Control Program) operating system. The B5000 was a stack machine designed to exclusively support high-level languages with no machine language or assembler, and indeed the MCP was the first OS to be written exclusively in a high-level language – ESPOL, a dialect of ALGOL. MCP also introduced many other ground-breaking innovations, such as being the first commercial implementation of virtual memory.

During development of the AS/400, IBM made an approach to Burroughs to licence MCP to run on the AS/400 hardware. This proposal was declined by Burroughs management to protect its existing hardware production. MCP is still in use today in the Unisys ClearPath/MCP line of computers.

UNIVAC, the first commercial computer manufacturer, produced a series of EXEC operating systems. Like all early main-frame systems, this batch-oriented system managed magnetic drums, disks, card readers and line printers. In the 1970s, UNIVAC produced the Real-Time Basic (RTB) system to support large-scale time sharing, also patterned after the Dartmouth BC system.

General Electric and MIT developed General Electric Comprehensive Operating Supervisor (GE-COS), which introduced the concept of ringed security privilege levels. After acquisition by Honeywell it was renamed General Comprehensive Operating System (GCOS).

Digital Equipment Corporation developed many operating systems for its various computer lines, including TOPS-10 and TOPS-20 time sharing systems for the 36-bit PDP-10 class systems. Before the widespread use of UNIX, TOPS-10 was a particularly popular system in universities, and in the early ARPANET community.

From the late 1960s through the late 1970s, several hardware capabilities evolved that allowed similar or ported software to run on more than one system. Early systems had utilized microprogramming to implement features on their systems in order to permit different underlying computer architectures to appear to be the same as others in a series. In fact, most 360s after the 360/40 (except the 360/165 and 360/168) were microprogrammed implementations.

The enormous investment in software for these systems made since the 1960s caused most of the original computer manufacturers to continue to develop compatible operating systems along with the hardware. Notable supported mainframe operating systems include:

- Burroughs MCP – B5000, 1961 to Unisys Clearpath/MCP, present

- IBM OS/360 – IBM System/360, 1966 to IBM z/OS, present

- IBM CP-67 – IBM System/360, 1967 to IBM z/VM

- UNIVAC EXEC 8 – UNIVAC 1108, 1967, to OS 2200 Unisys Clearpath Dorado, present

Microcomputers

PC DOS was an early personal computer OS that featured a command line interface.

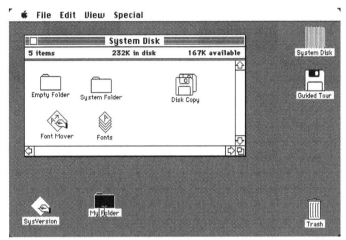

Mac OS by Apple Computer became the first widespread OS to feature a graphical user interface.
Many of its features such as windows and icons would later become commonplace in GUIs.

The first microcomputers did not have the capacity or need for the elaborate operating systems that had been developed for mainframes and minis; minimalistic operating systems were developed, often loaded from ROM and known as monitors. One notable early disk operating system was CP/M, which was supported on many early microcomputers and was closely imitated by Microsoft's MS-DOS, which became widely popular as the operating system chosen for the IBM PC (IBM's version of it was called IBM DOS or PC DOS). In the 1980s, Apple Computer Inc. (now Apple Inc.) abandoned its popular Apple II series of microcomputers to introduce the Apple Macintosh computer with an innovative graphical user interface (GUI) to the Mac OS.

The introduction of the Intel 80386 CPU chip in October 1985, with 32-bit architecture and paging capabilities, provided personal computers with the ability to run multitasking operating systems like those of earlier minicomputers and mainframes. Microsoft responded to this progress by hiring Dave Cutler, who had developed the VMS operating system for Digital Equipment Corporation. He would lead the development of the Windows NT operating system, which continues to serve as the basis for Microsoft's operating systems line. Steve Jobs, a co-founder of Apple Inc., started NeXT Computer Inc., which developed the NEXTSTEP operating system. NEXTSTEP would later be acquired by Apple Inc. and used, along with code from FreeBSD as the core of Mac OS X (macOS after latest name change).

The GNU Project was started by activist and programmer Richard Stallman with the goal of creating a complete free software replacement to the proprietary UNIX operating system. While the project was highly successful in duplicating the functionality of various parts of UNIX, development of the GNU Hurd kernel proved to be unproductive. In 1991, Finnish computer science student Linus Torvalds, with cooperation from volunteers collaborating over the Internet, released the first version of the Linux kernel. It was soon merged with the GNU user space components and system software to form a complete operating system. Since then, the combination of the two major components has usually been referred to as simply "Linux" by the software industry, a naming convention that Stallman and the Free Software Foundation remain opposed to, preferring the name GNU/Linux. The Berkeley Software Distribution, known as BSD, is the UNIX derivative distributed by the University of California, Berkeley, starting in the 1970s. Freely distributed and ported to many minicomputers, it eventually also gained a following for use on PCs, mainly as FreeBSD, NetBSD and OpenBSD.

Examples of Operating Systems

Unix and Unix-like Operating Systems

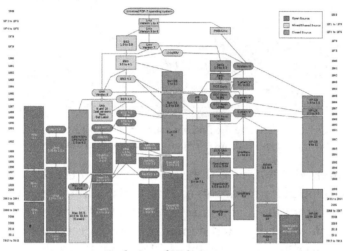

Evolution of Unix systems

Unix was originally written in assembly language. Ken Thompson wrote B, mainly based on BCPL, based on his experience in the MULTICS project. B was replaced by C, and Unix, rewritten in C, developed into a large, complex family of inter-related operating systems which have been influential in every modern operating system.

The Unix-like family is a diverse group of operating systems, with several major sub-categories including System V, BSD, and Linux. The name "UNIX" is a trademark of The Open Group which licenses it for use with any operating system that has been shown to conform to their definitions. "UNIX-like" is commonly used to refer to the large set of operating systems which resemble the original UNIX.

Unix-like systems run on a wide variety of computer architectures. They are used heavily for servers in business, as well as workstations in academic and engineering environments. Free UNIX variants, such as Linux and BSD, are popular in these areas.

Four operating systems are certified by The Open Group (holder of the Unix trademark) as Unix. HP's HP-UX and IBM's AIX are both descendants of the original System V Unix and are designed to run only on their respective vendor's hardware. In contrast, Sun Microsystems's Solaris can run on multiple types of hardware, including x86 and Sparc servers, and PCs. Apple's macOS, a replacement for Apple's earlier (non-Unix) Mac OS, is a hybrid kernel-based BSD variant derived from NeXTSTEP, Mach, and FreeBSD.

Unix interoperability was sought by establishing the POSIX standard. The POSIX standard can be applied to any operating system, although it was originally created for various Unix variants.

BSD and its Descendants

The first server for the World Wide Web ran on NeXTSTEP, based on BSD.

A subgroup of the Unix family is the Berkeley Software Distribution family, which includes FreeBSD, NetBSD, and OpenBSD. These operating systems are most commonly found on webservers, although they can also function as a personal computer OS. The Internet owes much of its existence to BSD, as many of the protocols now commonly used by computers to connect, send and receive data over a network were widely implemented and refined in BSD. The World Wide Web was also first demonstrated on a number of computers running an OS based on BSD called NeXTSTEP.

In 1974, University of California, Berkeley installed its first Unix system. Over time, students and staff in the computer science department there began adding new programs to make things easier, such as text editors. When Berkeley received new VAX computers in 1978 with Unix installed, the school's undergraduates modified Unix even more in order to take advantage of the computer's hardware possibilities. The Defense Advanced Research Projects Agency of the US Department of Defense took interest, and decided to fund the project. Many schools, corporations, and government organizations took notice and started to use Berkeley's version of Unix instead of the official one distributed by AT&T.

Steve Jobs, upon leaving Apple Inc. in 1985, formed NeXT Inc., a company that manufactured high-end computers running on a variation of BSD called NeXTSTEP. One of these computers was used by Tim Berners-Lee as the first webserver to create the World Wide Web.

Developers like Keith Bostic encouraged the project to replace any non-free code that originated with Bell Labs. Once this was done, however, AT&T sued. After two years of legal disputes, the BSD project spawned a number of free derivatives, such as NetBSD and FreeBSD (both in 1993), and OpenBSD (from NetBSD in 1995).

macOS

The standard user interface of macOS

macOS (formerly "Mac OS X" and later "OS X") is a line of open core graphical operating systems developed, marketed, and sold by Apple Inc., the latest of which is pre-loaded on all currently shipping Macintosh computers. macOS is the successor to the original classic Mac OS, which had been Apple's primary operating system since 1984. Unlike its predecessor, macOS is a UNIX operating system built on technology that had been developed at NeXT through the second half of the 1980s and up until Apple purchased the company in early 1997. The operating system was first released in 1999 as Mac OS X Server 1.0, followed in March 2001 by a client version (Mac OS X v10.0 "Cheetah"). Since then, six more distinct "client" and "server" editions of macOS have been released, until the two were merged in OS X 10.7 "Lion".

Prior to its merging with macOS, the server edition – macOS Server – was architecturally identical to its desktop counterpart and usually ran on Apple's line of Macintosh server hardware. macOS Server included work group management and administration software tools that provide simplified access to key network services, including a mail transfer agent, a Samba server, an LDAP server, a domain name server, and others. With Mac OS X v10.7 Lion, all server aspects of Mac OS X Server have been integrated into the client version and the product re-branded as "OS X" (dropping "Mac" from the name). The server tools are now offered as an application.

Linux

The Linux kernel originated in 1991, as a project of Linus Torvalds, while a university student in Finland. He posted information about his project on a newsgroup for computer students and programmers, and received support and assistance from volunteers who succeeded in creating a complete and functional kernel.

Linux is Unix-like, but was developed without any Unix code, unlike BSD and its variants. Because of its open license model, the Linux kernel code is available for study and modification, which resulted in its use on a wide range of computing machinery from supercomputers to smart-watches.

Although estimates suggest that Linux is used on only 1.82% of all "desktop" (or laptop) PCs, it has been widely adopted for use in servers and embedded systems such as cell phones. Linux has superseded Unix on many platforms and is used on most supercomputers including the top 385. Many of the same computers are also on Green500 (but in different order), and Linux runs on the top 10. Linux is also commonly used on other small energy-efficient computers, such as smartphones and smartwatches. The Linux kernel is used in some popular distributions, such as Red Hat, Debian, Ubuntu, Linux Mint and Google's Android.

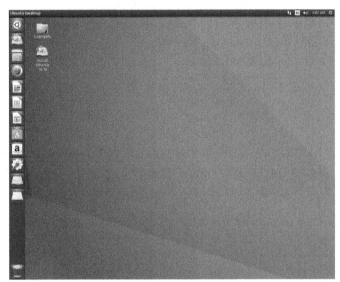

Ubuntu, desktop Linux distribution

Android, a popular mobile operating system based on a modified version of the Linux kernel

Google Chrome OS

Chrome OS is an operating system based on the Linux kernel and designed by Google. It is developed out in the open in the Chromium OS open source variant and Google makes a proprietary variant of it (similar to the split for the Chrome and Chromium browser). Since Chromium OS targets computer users who spend most of their time on the Internet, it is mainly a web browser with limited ability to run local applications, though it has a built-in file manager and media player (in later versions, (modified) Android apps have also been supported, since the browser has been made to support them). Instead, it relies on Internet applications (or Web apps) used in the web browser to accomplish tasks such as word processing. Chromium OS differs from Chrome OS in that Chromium is open-source and used primarily by developers whereas Chrome OS is the operating system shipped out in Chromebooks.

Microsoft Windows

Microsoft Windows is a family of proprietary operating systems designed by Microsoft Corporation and primarily targeted to Intel architecture based computers, with an estimated 88.9 percent total usage share on Web connected computers. The latest version is Windows 10.

In 2011, Windows 7 overtook Windows XP as most common version in use.

Microsoft Windows was first released in 1985, as an operating environment running on top of MS-DOS, which was the standard operating system shipped on most Intel architecture personal computers at the time. In 1995, Windows 95 was released which only used MS-DOS as a bootstrap. For backwards compatibility, Win9x could run real-mode MS-DOS and 16-bit Windows 3.x drivers. Windows ME, released in 2000, was the last version in the Win9x family. Later versions have all been based on the Windows NT kernel. Current client versions of Windows run on IA-32, x86-64 and 32-bit ARM microprocessors. In addition Itanium is still supported in older server version Windows Server 2008 R2. In the past, Windows NT supported additional architectures.

Server editions of Windows are widely used. In recent years, Microsoft has expended significant capital in an effort to promote the use of Windows as a server operating system. However, Windows' usage on servers is not as widespread as on personal computers as Windows competes against Linux and BSD for server market share.

ReactOS is a Windows-alternative operating system, which is being developed on the principles of Windows – without using any of Microsoft's code.

Other

There have been many operating systems that were significant in their day but are no longer so, such as AmigaOS; OS/2 from IBM and Microsoft; classic Mac OS, the non-Unix precursor to Apple's macOS; BeOS; XTS-300; RISC OS; MorphOS; Haiku; BareMetal and FreeMint. Some are still used in niche markets and continue to be developed as minority platforms for enthusiast communities and specialist applications. OpenVMS, formerly from DEC, is still under active development by Hewlett-Packard. Yet other operating systems are used almost exclusively in academia, for operating systems education or to do research on operating system concepts. A typical example of a system that fulfills both roles is MINIX, while for example Singularity is used purely for research.

Other operating systems have failed to win significant market share, but have introduced innovations that have influenced mainstream operating systems, not least Bell Labs' Plan 9.

Components

The components of an operating system all exist in order to make the different parts of a computer work together. All user software needs to go through the operating system in order to use any of the hardware, whether it be as simple as a mouse or keyboard or as complex as an Internet component.

Kernel

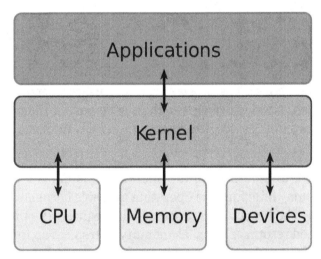

A kernel connects the application software to the hardware of a computer.

With the aid of the firmware and device drivers, the kernel provides the most basic level of control over all of the computer's hardware devices. It manages memory access for programs in the RAM, it determines which programs get access to which hardware resources, it sets up or resets the CPU's operating states for optimal operation at all times, and it organizes the data for long-term non-volatile storage with file systems on such media as disks, tapes, flash memory, etc.

Program Execution

The operating system provides an interface between an application program and the computer hardware, so that an application program can interact with the hardware only by obeying rules and procedures programmed into the operating system. The operating system is also a set of services which simplify development and execution of application programs. Executing an application program involves the creation of a process by the operating system kernel which assigns memory space and other resources, establishes a priority for the process in multi-tasking systems, loads program binary code into memory, and initiates execution of the application program which then interacts with the user and with hardware devices.

Interrupts

Interrupts are central to operating systems, as they provide an efficient way for the operating system to interact with and react to its environment. The alternative – having the operating system "watch" the various sources of input for events (polling) that require action – can be found in older systems with very small stacks (50 or 60 bytes) but is unusual in modern systems with large stacks. Interrupt-based programming is directly supported by most modern CPUs. Interrupts provide a computer with a way of automatically saving local register contexts, and running specific code in response to events. Even very basic computers support hardware interrupts, and allow the programmer to specify code which may be run when that event takes place.

When an interrupt is received, the computer's hardware automatically suspends whatever program is currently running, saves its status, and runs computer code previously associated with the interrupt; this is analogous to placing a bookmark in a book in response to a phone call. In modern operating systems, interrupts are handled by the operating system's kernel. Interrupts may come from either the computer's hardware or the running program.

When a hardware device triggers an interrupt, the operating system's kernel decides how to deal with this event, generally by running some processing code. The amount of code being run depends on the priority of the interrupt (for example: a person usually responds to a smoke detector alarm before answering the phone). The processing of hardware interrupts is a task that is usually delegated to software called a device driver, which may be part of the operating system's kernel, part of another program, or both. Device drivers may then relay information to a running program by various means.

A program may also trigger an interrupt to the operating system. If a program wishes to access hardware, for example, it may interrupt the operating system's kernel, which causes control to be passed back to the kernel. The kernel then processes the request. If a program wishes additional resources (or wishes to shed resources) such as memory, it triggers an interrupt to get the kernel's attention.

Modes

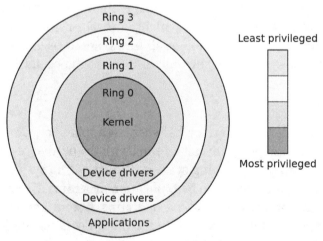

Privilege rings for the x86 microprocessor architecture available in protected mode.
Operating systems determine which processes run in each mode.

Modern microprocessors (CPU or MPU) support multiple modes of operation. CPUs with this capability offer at least two modes: user mode and supervisor mode. In general terms, supervisor mode operation allows unrestricted access to all machine resources, including all MPU instructions. User mode operation sets limits on instruction use and typically disallows direct access to machine resources. CPUs might have other modes similar to user mode as well, such as the virtual modes in order to emulate older processor types, such as 16-bit processors on a 32-bit one, or 32-bit processors on a 64-bit one.

At power-on or reset, the system begins in supervisor mode. Once an operating system kernel has been loaded and started, the boundary between user mode and supervisor mode (also known as kernel mode) can be established.

Supervisor mode is used by the kernel for low level tasks that need unrestricted access to hardware, such as controlling how memory is accessed, and communicating with devices such as disk drives and video display devices. User mode, in contrast, is used for almost everything else. Application programs, such as word processors and database managers, operate within user mode, and can only access machine resources by turning control over to the kernel, a process which causes a switch to supervisor mode. Typically, the transfer of control to the kernel is achieved by executing a software interrupt instruction, such as the Motorola 68000 TRAP instruction. The software interrupt causes the microprocessor to switch from user mode to supervisor mode and begin executing code that allows the kernel to take control.

In user mode, programs usually have access to a restricted set of microprocessor instructions, and generally cannot execute any instructions that could potentially cause disruption to the system's operation. In supervisor mode, instruction execution restrictions are typically removed, allowing the kernel unrestricted access to all machine resources.

The term "user mode resource" generally refers to one or more CPU registers, which contain information that the running program isn't allowed to alter. Attempts to alter these resources generally causes a switch to supervisor mode, where the operating system can deal with the illegal operation the program was attempting, for example, by forceably terminating ("killing") the program).

Memory Management

Among other things, a multiprogramming operating system kernel must be responsible for managing all system memory which is currently in use by programs. This ensures that a program does not interfere with memory already in use by another program. Since programs time share, each program must have independent access to memory.

Cooperative memory management, used by many early operating systems, assumes that all programs make voluntary use of the kernel's memory manager, and do not exceed their allocated memory. This system of memory management is almost never seen any more, since programs often contain bugs which can cause them to exceed their allocated memory. If a program fails, it may cause memory used by one or more other programs to be affected or overwritten. Malicious programs or viruses may purposefully alter another program's memory, or may affect the operation of the operating system itself. With cooperative memory management, it takes only one misbehaved program to crash the system.

Memory protection enables the kernel to limit a process' access to the computer's memory. Various methods of memory protection exist, including memory segmentation and paging. All methods require some level of hardware support (such as the 80286 MMU), which doesn't exist in all computers.

In both segmentation and paging, certain protected mode registers specify to the CPU what memory address it should allow a running program to access. Attempts to access other addresses trigger an interrupt which cause the CPU to re-enter supervisor mode, placing the kernel in charge. This is called a segmentation violation or Seg-V for short, and since it is both difficult to assign a meaningful result to such an operation, and because it is usually a sign of a misbehaving program, the kernel generally resorts to terminating the offending program, and reports the error.

Windows versions 3.1 through ME had some level of memory protection, but programs could easily circumvent the need to use it. A general protection fault would be produced, indicating a segmentation violation had occurred; however, the system would often crash anyway.

Virtual Memory

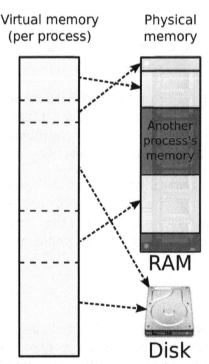

Many operating systems can "trick" programs into using memory scattered around the hard disk and RAM as if it is one continuous chunk of memory, called virtual memory.

The use of virtual memory addressing (such as paging or segmentation) means that the kernel can choose what memory each program may use at any given time, allowing the operating system to use the same memory locations for multiple tasks.

If a program tries to access memory that isn't in its current range of accessible memory, but nonetheless has been allocated to it, the kernel is interrupted in the same way as it would if the program were to exceed its allocated memory. Under UNIX this kind of interrupt is referred to as a page fault.

When the kernel detects a page fault it generally adjusts the virtual memory range of the program which triggered it, granting it access to the memory requested. This gives the kernel discretionary power over where a particular application's memory is stored, or even whether or not it has actually been allocated yet.

In modern operating systems, memory which is accessed less frequently can be temporarily stored on disk or other media to make that space available for use by other programs. This is called swapping, as an area of memory can be used by multiple programs, and what that memory area contains can be swapped or exchanged on demand.

"Virtual memory" provides the programmer or the user with the perception that there is a much larger amount of RAM in the computer than is really there.

Multitasking

Multitasking refers to the running of multiple independent computer programs on the same computer; giving the appearance that it is performing the tasks at the same time. Since most computers can do at most one or two things at one time, this is generally done via time-sharing, which means that each program uses a share of the computer's time to execute.

An operating system kernel contains a scheduling program which determines how much time each process spends executing, and in which order execution control should be passed to programs. Control is passed to a process by the kernel, which allows the program access to the CPU and memory. Later, control is returned to the kernel through some mechanism, so that another program may be allowed to use the CPU. This so-called passing of control between the kernel and applications is called a context switch.

An early model which governed the allocation of time to programs was called cooperative multitasking. In this model, when control is passed to a program by the kernel, it may execute for as long as it wants before explicitly returning control to the kernel. This means that a malicious or malfunctioning program may not only prevent any other programs from using the CPU, but it can hang the entire system if it enters an infinite loop.

Modern operating systems extend the concepts of application preemption to device drivers and kernel code, so that the operating system has preemptive control over internal run-times as well.

The philosophy governing preemptive multitasking is that of ensuring that all programs are given regular time on the CPU. This implies that all programs must be limited in how much time they are allowed to spend on the CPU without being interrupted. To accomplish this, modern operating system kernels make use of a timed interrupt. A protected mode timer is set by the kernel which triggers a return to supervisor mode after the specified time has elapsed.

On many single user operating systems cooperative multitasking is perfectly adequate, as home computers generally run a small number of well tested programs. The AmigaOS is an exception, having preemptive multitasking from its very first version. Windows NT was the first version of Microsoft Windows which enforced preemptive multitasking, but it didn't reach the home user market until Windows XP (since Windows NT was targeted at professionals).

Disk Access and File Systems

File systems allow users and programs to organize and sort files on a computer,
often through the use of directories (or "folders").

Access to data stored on disks is a central feature of all operating systems. Computers store data
on disks using files, which are structured in specific ways in order to allow for faster access, higher
reliability, and to make better use of the drive's available space. The specific way in which files are
stored on a disk is called a file system, and enables files to have names and attributes. It also allows
them to be stored in a hierarchy of directories or folders arranged in a directory tree.

Early operating systems generally supported a single type of disk drive and only one kind of file
system. Early file systems were limited in their capacity, speed, and in the kinds of file names and
directory structures they could use. These limitations often reflected limitations in the operating
systems they were designed for, making it very difficult for an operating system to support more
than one file system.

While many simpler operating systems support a limited range of options for accessing storage
systems, operating systems like UNIX and Linux support a technology known as a virtual file system or VFS. An operating system such as UNIX supports a wide array of storage devices, regardless of their design or file systems, allowing them to be accessed through a common application
programming interface (API). This makes it unnecessary for programs to have any knowledge
about the device they are accessing. A VFS allows the operating system to provide programs with
access to an unlimited number of devices with an infinite variety of file systems installed on them,
through the use of specific device drivers and file system drivers.

A connected storage device, such as a hard drive, is accessed through a device driver. The device
driver understands the specific language of the drive and is able to translate that language into
a standard language used by the operating system to access all disk drives. On UNIX, this is the
language of block devices.

When the kernel has an appropriate device driver in place, it can then access the contents of the
disk drive in raw format, which may contain one or more file systems. A file system driver is used
to translate the commands used to access each specific file system into a standard set of commands
that the operating system can use to talk to all file systems. Programs can then deal with these file

systems on the basis of filenames, and directories/folders, contained within a hierarchical structure. They can create, delete, open, and close files, as well as gather various information about them, including access permissions, size, free space, and creation and modification dates.

Various differences between file systems make supporting all file systems difficult. Allowed characters in file names, case sensitivity, and the presence of various kinds of file attributes makes the implementation of a single interface for every file system a daunting task. Operating systems tend to recommend using (and so support natively) file systems specifically designed for them; for example, NTFS in Windows and ext3 and ReiserFS in Linux. However, in practice, third party drivers are usually available to give support for the most widely used file systems in most general-purpose operating systems (for example, NTFS is available in Linux through NTFS-3g, and ext2/3 and ReiserFS are available in Windows through third-party software).

Support for file systems is highly varied among modern operating systems, although there are several common file systems which almost all operating systems include support and drivers for. Operating systems vary on file system support and on the disk formats they may be installed on. Under Windows, each file system is usually limited in application to certain media; for example, CDs must use ISO 9660 or UDF, and as of Windows Vista, NTFS is the only file system which the operating system can be installed on. It is possible to install Linux onto many types of file systems. Unlike other operating systems, Linux and UNIX allow any file system to be used regardless of the media it is stored in, whether it is a hard drive, a disc (CD, DVD...), a USB flash drive, or even contained within a file located on another file system.

Device Drivers

A device driver is a specific type of computer software developed to allow interaction with hardware devices. Typically this constitutes an interface for communicating with the device, through the specific computer bus or communications subsystem that the hardware is connected to, providing commands to and/or receiving data from the device, and on the other end, the requisite interfaces to the operating system and software applications. It is a specialized hardware-dependent computer program which is also operating system specific that enables another program, typically an operating system or applications software package or computer program running under the operating system kernel, to interact transparently with a hardware device, and usually provides the requisite interrupt handling necessary for any necessary asynchronous time-dependent hardware interfacing needs.

The key design goal of device drivers is abstraction. Every model of hardware (even within the same class of device) is different. Newer models also are released by manufacturers that provide more reliable or better performance and these newer models are often controlled differently. Computers and their operating systems cannot be expected to know how to control every device, both now and in the future. To solve this problem, operating systems essentially dictate how every type of device should be controlled. The function of the device driver is then to translate these operating system mandated function calls into device specific calls. In theory a new device, which is controlled in a new manner, should function correctly if a suitable driver is available. This new driver ensures that the device appears to operate as usual from the operating system's point of view.

Under versions of Windows before Vista and versions of Linux before 2.6, all driver execution was co-operative, meaning that if a driver entered an infinite loop it would freeze the system.

More recent revisions of these operating systems incorporate kernel preemption, where the kernel interrupts the driver to give it tasks, and then separates itself from the process until it receives a response from the device driver, or gives it more tasks to do.

Networking

Currently most operating systems support a variety of networking protocols, hardware, and applications for using them. This means that computers running dissimilar operating systems can participate in a common network for sharing resources such as computing, files, printers, and scanners using either wired or wireless connections. Networks can essentially allow a computer's operating system to access the resources of a remote computer to support the same functions as it could if those resources were connected directly to the local computer. This includes everything from simple communication, to using networked file systems or even sharing another computer's graphics or sound hardware. Some network services allow the resources of a computer to be accessed transparently, such as SSH which allows networked users direct access to a computer's command line interface.

Client/server networking allows a program on a computer, called a client, to connect via a network to another computer, called a server. Servers offer (or host) various services to other network computers and users. These services are usually provided through ports or numbered access points beyond the server's network address. Each port number is usually associated with a maximum of one running program, which is responsible for handling requests to that port. A daemon, being a user program, can in turn access the local hardware resources of that computer by passing requests to the operating system kernel.

Many operating systems support one or more vendor-specific or open networking protocols as well, for example, SNA on IBM systems, DECnet on systems from Digital Equipment Corporation, and Microsoft-specific protocols (SMB) on Windows. Specific protocols for specific tasks may also be supported such as NFS for file access. Protocols like ESound, or esd can be easily extended over the network to provide sound from local applications, on a remote system's sound hardware.

Security

A computer being secure depends on a number of technologies working properly. A modern operating system provides access to a number of resources, which are available to software running on the system, and to external devices like networks via the kernel.

The operating system must be capable of distinguishing between requests which should be allowed to be processed, and others which should not be processed. While some systems may simply distinguish between "privileged" and "non-privileged", systems commonly have a form of requester identity, such as a user name. To establish identity there may be a process of authentication. Often a username must be quoted, and each username may have a password. Other methods of authentication, such as magnetic cards or biometric data, might be used instead. In some cases, especially connections from the network, resources may be accessed with no authentication at all (such as reading files over a network share). Also covered by the concept of requester identity is authorization; the particular services and resources accessible by the requester once logged into a system are tied to either the requester's user account or to the variously configured groups of users to which the requester belongs.

In addition to the allow or disallow model of security, a system with a high level of security also offers auditing options. These would allow tracking of requests for access to resources (such as, "who has been reading this file?"). Internal security, or security from an already running program is only possible if all possibly harmful requests must be carried out through interrupts to the operating system kernel. If programs can directly access hardware and resources, they cannot be secured.

External security involves a request from outside the computer, such as a login at a connected console or some kind of network connection. External requests are often passed through device drivers to the operating system's kernel, where they can be passed onto applications, or carried out directly. Security of operating systems has long been a concern because of highly sensitive data held on computers, both of a commercial and military nature. The United States Government Department of Defense (DoD) created the Trusted Computer System Evaluation Criteria (TCSEC) which is a standard that sets basic requirements for assessing the effectiveness of security. This became of vital importance to operating system makers, because the TCSEC was used to evaluate, classify and select trusted operating systems being considered for the processing, storage and retrieval of sensitive or classified information.

Network services include offerings such as file sharing, print services, email, web sites, and file transfer protocols (FTP), most of which can have compromised security. At the front line of security are hardware devices known as firewalls or intrusion detection/prevention systems. At the operating system level, there are a number of software firewalls available, as well as intrusion detection/prevention systems. Most modern operating systems include a software firewall, which is enabled by default. A software firewall can be configured to allow or deny network traffic to or from a service or application running on the operating system. Therefore, one can install and be running an insecure service, such as Telnet or FTP, and not have to be threatened by a security breach because the firewall would deny all traffic trying to connect to the service on that port.

An alternative strategy, and the only sandbox strategy available in systems that do not meet the Popek and Goldberg virtualization requirements, is where the operating system is not running user programs as native code, but instead either emulates a processor or provides a host for a p-code based system such as Java.

Internal security is especially relevant for multi-user systems; it allows each user of the system to have private files that the other users cannot tamper with or read. Internal security is also vital if auditing is to be of any use, since a program can potentially bypass the operating system, inclusive of bypassing auditing.

User Interface

Every computer that is to be operated by an individual requires a user interface. The user interface is usually referred to as a shell and is essential if human interaction is to be supported. The user interface views the directory structure and requests services from the operating system that will acquire data from input hardware devices, such as a keyboard, mouse or credit card reader, and requests operating system services to display prompts, status messages and such on output hardware devices, such as a video monitor or printer. The two most common forms of a user interface have historically been the command-line interface, where computer commands are typed out line-by-line, and the graphical user interface, where a visual environment (most commonly a WIMP) is present.

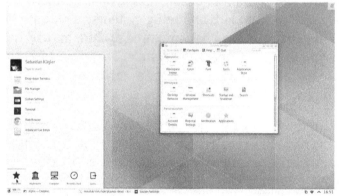

A screenshot of the Bash command line. Each command is typed out after the 'prompt', and then its output appears below, working its way down the screen. The current command prompt is at the bottom.

Graphical User Interfaces

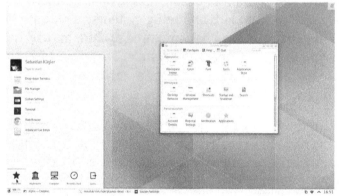

A screenshot of the KDE Plasma 5 graphical user interface. Programs take the form of images on the screen, and the files, folders (directories), and applications take the form of icons and symbols.
A mouse is used to navigate the computer.

Most of the modern computer systems support graphical user interfaces (GUI), and often include them. In some computer systems, such as the original implementation of the classic Mac OS, the GUI is integrated into the kernel.

While technically a graphical user interface is not an operating system service, incorporating support for one into the operating system kernel can allow the GUI to be more responsive by reducing the number of context switches required for the GUI to perform its output functions. Other operating systems are modular, separating the graphics subsystem from the kernel and the Operating System. In the 1980s UNIX, VMS and many others had operating systems that were built this way. Linux and macOS are also built this way. Modern releases of Microsoft

Windows such as Windows Vista implement a graphics subsystem that is mostly in user-space; however the graphics drawing routines of versions between Windows NT 4.0 and Windows Server 2003 exist mostly in kernel space. Windows 9x had very little distinction between the interface and the kernel.

Many computer operating systems allow the user to install or create any user interface they desire. The X Window System in conjunction with GNOME or KDE Plasma 5 is a commonly found setup on most Unix and Unix-like (BSD, Linux, Solaris) systems. A number of Windows shell replacements have been released for Microsoft Windows, which offer alternatives to the included Windows shell, but the shell itself cannot be separated from Windows.

Numerous Unix-based GUIs have existed over time, most derived from X11. Competition among the various vendors of Unix (HP, IBM, Sun) led to much fragmentation, though an effort to standardize in the 1990s to COSE and CDE failed for various reasons, and were eventually eclipsed by the widespread adoption of GNOME and K Desktop Environment. Prior to free software-based toolkits and desktop environments, Motif was the prevalent toolkit/desktop combination (and was the basis upon which CDE was developed).

Graphical user interfaces evolve over time. For example, Windows has modified its user interface almost every time a new major version of Windows is released, and the Mac OS GUI changed dramatically with the introduction of Mac OS X in 1999.

Real-time Operating Systems

A real-time operating system (RTOS) is an operating system intended for applications with fixed deadlines (real-time computing). Such applications include some small embedded systems, automobile engine controllers, industrial robots, spacecraft, industrial control, and some large-scale computing systems.

An early example of a large-scale real-time operating system was Transaction Processing Facility developed by American Airlines and IBM for the Sabre Airline Reservations System.

Embedded systems that have fixed deadlines use a real-time operating system such as VxWorks, PikeOS, eCos, QNX, MontaVista Linux and RTLinux. Windows CE is a real-time operating system that shares similar APIs to desktop Windows but shares none of desktop Windows' codebase.Symbian OS also has an RTOS kernel (EKA2) starting with version 8.0b.

Some embedded systems use operating systems such as Palm OS, BSD, and Linux, although such operating systems do not support real-time computing.

Operating System Development as a Hobby

Operating system development is one of the most complicated activities in which a computing hobbyist may engage. A hobby operating system may be classified as one whose code has not been directly derived from an existing operating system, and has few users and active developers.

In some cases, hobby development is in support of a "homebrew" computing device, for example, a simple single-board computer powered by a 6502 microprocessor. Or, development may be for an architecture already in widespread use. Operating system development may come from entirely new concepts, or may commence by modeling an existing operating system. In either case, the hobbyist is his/her own developer, or may interact with a small and sometimes unstructured group of individuals who have like interests.

Examples of a hobby operating system include Syllable.

Diversity of Operating Systems and Portability

Application software is generally written for use on a specific operating system, and sometimes even for specific hardware. When porting the application to run on another OS, the functionality required by that application may be implemented differently by that OS (the names of functions, meaning of arguments, etc.) requiring the application to be adapted, changed, or otherwise maintained.

Unix was the first operating system not written in assembly language, making it very portable to systems different from its native PDP-11.

This cost in supporting operating systems diversity can be avoided by instead writing applications against software platforms like Java or Qt. These abstractions have already borne the cost of adaptation to specific operating systems and their system libraries.

Another approach is for operating system vendors to adopt standards. For example, POSIX and OS abstraction layers provide commonalities that reduce porting costs.

Market Share

2013 worldwide device shipments by operating system		
Operating system	**2012 (millions of units)**	**2013 (million of units)**
Android	504	878
Windows	346	328
iOS/Mac OS	214	267
BlackBerry	35	24
Others	1,117	803
Total	2,216	2,300

Source: Gartner

In 2014, Android was first (currently not replicated by others, in a single year) operating system ever to ship on a billion devices, becoming the most popular operating system by installed base.

Various Operating System

macOS

macOS is the current series of Unix-based graphical operating systems developed and marketed by Apple Inc. designed to run on Apple's Macintosh computers ("Macs"), having been preinstalled on all Macs since 2002. Within the market of desktop, laptop and home computers, and by web usage, it is the second most widely used desktop OS after Microsoft Windows.

Launched in 2001 as Mac OS X, the series is the latest in the family of Macintosh operating systems. Mac OS X succeeded "classic" Mac OS, which was introduced in 1984, and the final release of which was Mac OS 9 in 1999. An initial, early version of the system, Mac OS X Server 1.0, was released in 1999. The first desktop version, Mac OS X 10.0, followed in March 2001. In 2012, Apple rebranded Mac OS X to OS X. Releases were code named after big cats from the original release up until OS X 10.8 Mountain Lion. Beginning in 2013 with OS X 10.9 Mavericks, releases have been named after landmarks in California. In 2016, Apple rebranded OS X to macOS, adopting the nomenclature that it uses for their other operating systems, iOS, watchOS, and tvOS. The latest version of macOS is macOS 10.12 Sierra, which was publicly released in September 2016.

macOS is based on technologies developed at NeXT between 1985 and 1997, when Apple acquired the company. The "X" in Mac OS X and OS X is pronounced "ten", as it is the Roman numeral for the number 10. The X was a prominent part of the operating system's brand identity, and was used to showcase its Unix compatibility; UNIX 03 certification was achieved for the Intel version of Mac OS X 10.5 Leopard and all releases from Mac OS X 10.6 Snow Leopard up to the current version also have UNIX 03 certification. macOS shares its Unix-based core, named Darwin, and many of its frameworks with iOS, tvOS and watchOS. A heavily modified version of Mac OS X 10.4 Tiger was used for the first-generation Apple TV.

Apple also used to have a separate line of releases of Mac OS X designed for servers. Beginning with Mac OS X 10.7 Lion, the server functions were made available as a separate package on the Mac App Store.

Releases of Mac OS X from 1999 to 2005 can run only on the PowerPC-based Macs from the time period. After Apple announced that they were switching to Intel CPUs from 2006 onwards, a separate version of Mac OS X 10.4 Tiger was made and distributed exclusively with early Intel-based Macs; it included an emulator known as Rosetta, which allowed users to run most PowerPC applications on Intel-based Macs. Mac OS X 10.5 Leopard was released as a Universal binary, meaning the installer disc supported both Intel and PowerPC processors. In 2009, Apple released Mac OS X 10.6 Snow Leopard, which ran exclusively on Intel-based Macs. In 2011, Apple released Mac OS X 10.7 Lion, which no longer supported 32-bit Intel processors and also did not include Rosetta. All versions of the system released since then run exclusively on 64-bit Intel CPUs and do not support PowerPC applications.

History

Development

The heritage of what would become macOS had originated at NeXT, a company founded by Steve Jobs following his departure from Apple in 1985. There, the Unix-like NeXTSTEP operating system was developed, and then launched in 1989. The kernel of NeXTSTEP is based upon the Mach kernel, which was originally developed at Carnegie Mellon University, with additional kernel layers and low-level user space code derived from parts of BSD. Its graphical user interface was built on top of an object-oriented GUI toolkit using the Objective-C programming language.

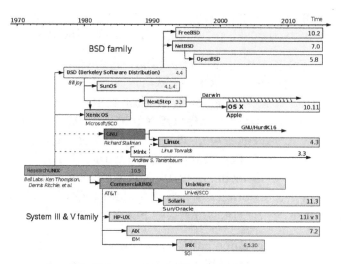

Simplified history of Unix-like operating systems

Throughout the early 1990s, Apple had tried to create a "next-generation" OS to succeed its classic Mac OS through the Taligent, Copland and Gershwin projects, but all of them were eventually abandoned. This led Apple to purchase NeXT in 1996, allowing NeXTSTEP, then called OPEN-STEP, to serve as the basis for Apple's next generation operating system. This purchase also led to Steve Jobs returning to Apple as an interim, and then the permanent CEO, shepherding the transformation of the programmer-friendly OPENSTEP into a system that would be adopted by Apple's primary market of home users and creative professionals. The project was first code named "Rhapsody" and then officially named Mac OS X.

Mac OS X

Launch of Mac OS X

Mac OS X was originally presented as the tenth major version of Apple's operating system for Macintosh computers; current versions of macOS retain the major version number "10". Previous Macintosh operating systems (versions of the classic Mac OS) were named using Arabic numerals, e.g. Mac OS 8 and Mac OS 9. The letter "X" in Mac OS X's name refers to the number 10, a Roman numeral. It is therefore correctly pronounced "ten" in this context. However, a common mispronunciation is "X" .

The first version of Mac OS X, Mac OS X Server 1.0, was a transitional product, featuring an interface resembling the classic Mac OS, though it was not compatible with software designed for the older system. Consumer releases of Mac OS X included more backward compatibility. Mac OS applications could be rewritten to run natively via the Carbon API; many could also be run directly through the Classic Environment with a reduction in performance.

The consumer version of Mac OS X was launched in 2001 with Mac OS X 10.0. Reviews were variable, with extensive praise for its sophisticated, glossy Aqua interface but criticizing it for sluggish performance. With Apple's popularity at a low, the makers of several classic Mac applications such as FrameMaker and PageMaker declined to develop new versions of their software for Mac OS X. *Ars Technica* columnist John Siracusa, who reviewed every major OS

X release up to 10.10, described the early releases in retrospect as 'dog-slow, feature poor' and Aqua as 'unbearably slow and a huge resource hog'.

Following Releases

Apple rapidly developed several new releases of Mac OS X. Siracusa's review of version 10.3, Panther, noted "It's strange to have gone from years of uncertainty and vaporware to a steady annual supply of major new operating system releases." Version 10.4, Tiger, reportedly shocked executives at Microsoft by offering a number of features, such as fast file searching and improved graphics processing, that Microsoft had spent several years struggling to add to Windows with acceptable performance.

In 2006, the first Intel Macs released used a specialized version of Mac OS X 10.4 Tiger. In 2007, Mac OS X 10.5 Leopard was the first to run on both PowerPC and Intel Macs with the use of universal binaries. Mac OS X 10.6 Snow Leopard was the first version of OS X to drop support for PowerPC Macs.

As the operating system evolved, it moved away from the classic Mac OS, with applications being added and removed. Targeting the consumer and media markets, Apple emphasized its new "digital lifestyle" applications such as the iLife suite, integrated home entertainment through the Front Row media center and the Safari web browser. With increasing popularity of the internet, Apple offered additional online services, including the .Mac, MobileMe and most recently iCloud products. It also began selling third-party applications through the Mac App Store.

Newer versions of Mac OS X also included modifications to the general interface, moving away from the striped gloss and transparency of the initial versions. Some applications began to use a brushed metal appearance, or non-pinstriped titlebar appearance in version 10.4. In Leopard, Apple announced a unification of the interface, with a standardized gray-gradient window style.

A key development for the system was the announcement and release of the iPhone from 2007 onwards. While Apple's previous iPod media players used a minimal operating system, the iPhone used an operating system based on Mac OS X, which would later be called "iPhone OS" and then iOS. The simultaneous release of two operating systems based on the same frameworks placed tension on Apple, which cited the iPhone as forcing it to delay Mac OS X 10.5 Leopard. However, after Apple opened the iPhone to third-party developers its commercial success drew attention to Mac OS X, with many iPhone software developers showing interest in Mac development.

In two succeeding versions, Lion and Mountain Lion, Apple moved some applications to a highly skeumorphic style of design inspired by contemporary versions of iOS, at the same time simplifying some elements by making controls such as scroll bars fade out when not in use. This direction was, like brushed metal interfaces, unpopular with some users, although it continued a trend of greater animation and variety in the interface previously seen in design aspects such as the Time Machine backup utility, which presented past file versions against a swirling nebula, and the glossy translucent dock of Leopard and Snow Leopard. In addition, with Mac OS X 10.7 Lion, Apple ceased to release separate server versions of Mac OS X, selling server tools as a separate downloadable application through the Mac App Store. A review described the trend in the server products as becoming "cheaper and simpler... shifting its focus from large businesses to small ones."

OS X

OS X logo from 2012-2013

In 2012, with the release of OS X 10.8 Mountain Lion, the name of the system was shortened from Mac OS X to OS X. That year, Apple removed the head of OS X development, Scott Forstall, and design was changed towards a more minimal direction. Apple's new user interface design, using deep color saturation, text-only buttons and a minimal, 'flat' interface, was debuted with iOS 7 in 2013. With OS X engineers reportedly working on iOS 7, the version released in 2013, OS X 10.9 Mavericks, was something of a transitional release, with some of the skeuomorphic design removed, while most of the general interface of Mavericks remained unchanged. The next version, OS X 10.10 Yosemite, adopted a design similar to iOS 7 but with greater complexity suitable for an interface controlled with a mouse.

From 2012 onwards, the system has shifted to an annual release schedule similar to that of iOS. It also steadily cut the cost of updates from Snow Leopard onwards, before removing upgrade fees altogether from 2013 onwards. Some journalists and third-party software developers have suggested that this decision, while allowing more rapid feature release, meant less opportunity to focus on stability, with no version of OS X recommendable for users requiring stability and performance above new features. Apple's 2015 update, OS X 10.11 El Capitan, was announced to focus specifically on stability and performance improvements.

macOS

In 2016, with the release of macOS 10.12 Sierra, the name was changed from OS X to macOS. macOS 10.12 Sierra's main features are the introduction of Siri to macOS, Optimized Storage, improvements to included applications, and greater integration with Apple's iPhone and Apple Watch. The Apple File System was announced at the Apple Worldwide Developers Conference in 2016 as a replacement for HFS Plus, a highly-criticized file system. This new file system will be implemented at a later date.

Architecture

At macOS's core is a POSIX compliant operating system built on top of the XNU kernel, with standard Unix facilities available from the command line interface. Apple has released this family of software as a free and open source operating system named Darwin. On top of Darwin, Apple layered a number of components, including the Aqua interface and the Finder, to complete the GUI-based operating system which is macOS.

With its original introduction as Mac OS X, the system brought a number of new capabilities to provide a more stable and reliable platform than its predecessor, the classic Mac OS. For example, pre-emptive multitasking and memory protection improved the system's ability to run multiple applications simultaneously without them interrupting or corrupting each other. Many aspects of macOS's architecture are derived from OPENSTEP, which was designed to be portable, to ease the transition from one platform to another. For example, NeXTSTEP was ported from the original 68k-based NeXT workstations to x86 and other architectures before NeXT was purchased by Apple, and OPENSTEP was later ported to the PowerPC architecture as part of the Rhapsody project.

The default macOS file system is HFS+, which it inherited from the classic Mac OS. Operating system designer Linus Torvalds has criticized HFS+, saying it is "probably the worst file system ever", whose design is "actively corrupting user data". He criticized the case insensitivity of file names, a design made worse when Apple extended the file system to support Unicode. Initially, HFS+ was designed for classic Mac OS, which runs on big-endian 68K and PowerPC systems. When Apple switched Macintosh to little-endian Intel processors, it continued to use big-endian byte order on HFS+ file systems. As a result, macOS on current Macs must do byte swap when it reads file system data. These concerns are being addressed with the new Apple File System, which will be included in a later update.

The Darwin subsystem in macOS is in charge of managing the file system, which includes the Unix permissions layer. In 2003 and 2005, two Macworld editors expressed criticism of the permission scheme; Ted Landau called misconfigured permissions "the most common frustration" in macOS, while Rob Griffiths suggested that some users may even have to reset permissions every day, a process which can take up to 15 minutes. More recently, another Macworld editor, Dan Frakes, called the procedure of repairing permissions vastly overused. He argues that macOS typically handles permissions properly without user interference, and resetting permissions should just be tried when problems emerge.

The architecture of macOS incorporates a layered design: the layered frameworks aid rapid development of applications by providing existing code for common tasks. Apple provides its own software development tools, most prominently an integrated development environment called Xcode. Xcode provides interfaces to compilers that support several programming languages including C, C++, Objective-C, and Swift. For the Apple–Intel transition, it was modified so that developers could build their applications as a universal binary, which provides compatibility with both the Intel-based and PowerPC-based Macintosh lines. First and third-party applications can be controlled programatically using the AppleScript framework, retained from the classic Mac OS, or using the newer Automator application that offers pre-written tasks that do not require programming knowledge.

Software Compatibility

List of macOS versions and the software they run						
Operating system	**Safari**	**Mail**	**QuickTime**	**iTunes**	**Messages/iChat**	**iWork**
10.12 "Sierra"	10.1	10.3	10.4	12.6	10.0	2016
10.11 "El Capitan"						
10.10 "Yosemite"	9.1.3				?	2014
10.9 "Mavericks"		7.3	10.3		8.0	2013

10.8 "Mountain Lion"	6.1	?	10.2	12.4	?	'09
10.7 "Lion"		?	10.1	12.2.2	Beta or 6.0.1	
10.6 "Snow Leopard"	5.1.10	4.5		11.4	5.0	
10.5 "Leopard"	5.0.6	3.6	7.7	10.6.3	4.0	
10.4 "Tiger"	4.1.3	2.1.3	7.6.4	9.2.1	3.0	
10.3 "Panther"	1.3.2	1.x	7.5	7.7.1	2.1	'05
10.2 "Jaguar"	1.0.3		6.5.3	6.0.5	2.0	Keynote
10.1 "Puma"	N/A		6.3.1	4.7.1	N/A	N/A
10.0 "Cheetah"			5.0	2.0.4		

1. Keynote 1.0 is the only iLife program that is compatible with Mac OS X 10.2 "Jaguar". Two minor updates, 1.1 and 1.1.1, can be applied to this version.

2. iTunes 2.0.4 can only run if Classic is installed. Otherwise, Mac OS X 10.0 can only run iTunes 1.1.1 natively.

Apple offered two main APIs to develop software natively for macOS: Cocoa and Carbon. Cocoa was a descendant of APIs inherited from OPENSTEP with no ancestry from the classic Mac OS, while Carbon was an adaptation of classic Mac OS APIs, allowing Mac software to be minimally rewritten in order to run natively on Mac OS X.

The Cocoa API was created as the result of a 1993 collaboration between NeXT Computer and Sun Microsystems. This heritage is highly visible for Cocoa developers, since the "NS" prefix is ubiquitous in the framework, standing variously for NeXTSTEP or NeXT/Sun. The official OPENSTEP API, published in September 1994, was the first to split the API between Foundation and ApplicationKit and the first to use the "NS" prefix. Traditionally, Cocoa programs have been mostly written in Objective-C, with Java as an alternative. However, on July 11, 2005, Apple announced that "features added to Cocoa in Mac OS X versions later than 10.4 will not be added to the Cocoa-Java programming interface." macOS also used to support the Java Platform as a "preferred software package"—in practice this means that applications written in Java fit as neatly into the operating system as possible while still being cross-platform compatible, and that graphical user interfaces written in Swing look almost exactly like native Cocoa interfaces. Since 2014, Apple has promoted its new programming language Swift as the preferred language for software development on Apple platforms.

Apple's original plan with macOS was to require all developers to rewrite their software into the Cocoa APIs. This caused much outcry among existing Mac developers, who threatened to abandon the platform rather than invest in a costly rewrite, and the idea was shelved. To permit a smooth transition from Mac OS 9 to Mac OS X, the Carbon Application Programming Interface (API) was created. Applications written with Carbon were initially able to run natively on both classic Mac OS and Mac OS X, although this ability was later dropped as Mac OS X developed. Carbon was not included in the first product sold as Mac OS X: the little-used original release of Mac OS X Server 1.0, which also did not include the Aqua interface. Apple limited further development of Carbon from the release of Leopard onwards, announcing Carbon applications would not receive the ability to run at 64-bit. As of 2015, a small number of older Mac OS X apps with heritage dating back to the classic Mac OS still used Carbon, including Microsoft Office. Early versions of macOS could also run some classic Mac OS applications through the Classic Environment with performance limitations; this feature was removed from 10.5 onwards and all Macs using Intel processors.

Because macOS is POSIX compliant, many software packages written for the other Unix-like systems such as Linux can be recompiled to run on it, including much scientific and technical software. Third-party projects such as Homebrew, Fink, MacPorts and pkgsrc provide pre-compiled or pre-formatted packages. Apple and others have provided versions of the X Window System graphical interface which can allow these applications to run with an approximation of the macOS look-and-feel. The current Apple-endorsed method is the open-source XQuartz project; earlier versions could use the X11 application provided by Apple, or before that the XDarwin project.

Applications can be distributed to Macs and installed by the user from any source and by any method such as downloading (with or without code signing, available via an Apple developer account) or through the Mac App Store, a marketplace of software maintained by Apple by way of a process requiring the company's approval. Apps installed through the Mac App Store run within a sandbox, restricting their ability to exchange information with other applications or modify the core operating system and its features. This has been cited as an advantage, by allowing users to install apps with confidence that they should not be able to damage their system, but also as a disadvantage, by blocking the Mac App Store's use by professional applications that require elevated privileges. Applications without any code signature cannot be run by default except from a computer's administrator account.

Apple produces macOS applications, some of which are included and some sold separately. This includes iWork, Final Cut Pro, Logic Pro, iLife, and the database application FileMaker. Numerous other developers also offer software for macOS.

Hardware Compatibility

List of macOS versions, the supported systems on which they run, and their RAM requirements		
Operating system	**Supported systems**	**RAM requirement**
10.12	Intel Macs (64-bit) released in: 2009 (iMac and main MacBook line), 2010 (other) or later	2 GB
10.8 – 10.11	Intel Macs (64-bit) released in: 2007 (prosumer and iMac), 2008 (other consumer), 2009 (Xserve) or later	
10.7	Intel Macs (64-bit) Rosetta support dropped from 10.7 and newer.	
10.6	Intel Macs (32-bit or 64-bit)	1 GB
10.5	G4, G5 and Intel Macs (32-bit or 64-bit) at 867 MHz or faster Classic support dropped from 10.5 and newer.	512 MB
10.4	Macs with built-in FireWire and either a New World ROM or Intel processor	256 MB
10.3	Macs with a New World ROM	128 MB
10.0 – 10.2	G3, G4 and G5 iBook and PowerBook, Power Mac and iMac (except PowerBook G3 "Kanga")	

Tools such as XPostFacto and patches applied to the installation media have been developed by third parties to enable installation of newer versions of macOS on systems not officially supported by Apple. This includes a number of pre-G3 Power Macintosh systems that can be made to run up to and including Mac OS X 10.2 Jaguar, all G3-based Macs which can run up to and including Tiger, and sub-867 MHz G4 Macs can run Leopard by removing the restriction from the installation DVD or entering a command in the Mac's Open Firmware interface to tell the Leopard Installer that it has a clock rate of 867 MHz or greater. Except for features requiring specific hardware (e.g. graphics acceleration or DVD writing), the operating system offers the same functionality on all supported hardware.

As most Mac hardware components, or components similar to those, since the Intel transition are available for purchase, some technology-capable groups have developed software to install macOS on non-Apple computers. These are referred to as Hackintoshes, a portmanteau of the words "hack" and "Macintosh". This violates Apple's EULA (and is therefore unsupported by Apple technical support, warranties etc.), but communities that cater to personal users, who do not install for resale and profit, have generally been ignored by Apple. These self-made computers allow more flexibility and customization of hardware, but at a cost of leaving the user more responsible for their own machine, such as on matter of data integrity or security. Psystar, a business that attempted to profit from selling macOS on non-Apple certified hardware, was sued by Apple in 2008.

PowerPC–Intel Transition

In April 2002, eWeek announced a rumor that Apple had a version of Mac OS X code-named Marklar, which ran on Intel x86 processors. The idea behind Marklar was to keep Mac OS X running on an alternative platform should Apple become dissatisfied with the progress of the PowerPC platform. These rumors subsided until late in May 2005, when various media outlets, such as *The Wall Street Journal* and CNET, announced that Apple would unveil Marklar in the coming months.

Steve Jobs talks about the transition to Intel processors

On June 6, 2005, Steve Jobs announced in his keynote address at the annual Apple Worldwide Developers Conference that Apple would be making the transition from PowerPC to Intel processors over the following two years, and that Mac OS X would support both platforms during the transition. Jobs also confirmed rumors that Apple had versions of Mac OS X running on Intel processors for most of its developmental life. Intel-based Macs would run a new recompiled version of OS X along with Rosetta, a binary translation layer which enables software compiled for PowerPC Mac OS X to run on Intel Mac OS X machines. The system was included with Mac OS X versions up to version 10.6.8. Apple dropped support for Classic mode on the new Intel Macs. Third party emulation software such as Mini vMac, Basilisk II and Sheep-Shaver provided support for some early versions of Mac OS. A new version of Xcode and the underlying command-line compilers supported building universal binaries that would run on either architecture.

PowerPC-only software is supported with Apple's official emulation software, Rosetta, though applications eventually had to be rewritten to run properly on the newer versions released for Intel processors. Apple initially encouraged developers to produce universal binaries with support for both PowerPC and Intel. There is a performance penalty when PowerPC binaries run on Intel Macs through Rosetta. Moreover, some PowerPC software, such as kernel extensions and System Preferences plugins, are not supported on Intel Macs at all. Some PowerPC applications would not run on macOS at all. Plugins for Safari need to be compiled for the same platform as Safari, so when Safari is running on Intel, it requires plug-ins that have been compiled as Intel-only or universal binaries, so PowerPC-only plug-ins will not work. While Intel Macs are able to run PowerPC, Intel, and universal binaries; PowerPC Macs support only universal and PowerPC builds.

Support for the PowerPC platform was dropped following the transition. In 2009, Apple announced at its Worldwide Developers Conference that Mac OS X 10.6 Snow Leopard would drop support for PowerPC processors and be Intel-only. Rosetta continued to be offered as an optional download or installation choice in Snow Leopard before it was discontinued with Mac OS X 10.7 Lion. In addition, new versions of Mac OS X first- and third-party software increasingly required Intel processors, including new versions of iLife, iWork, Aperture and Logic Pro.

Features

Aqua User Interface

One of the major differences between the classic Mac OS and the current macOS was the addition of Aqua, a graphical user interface with water-like elements, in the first major release of Mac OS X. Every window element, text, graphic, or widget is drawn on-screen using spatial anti-aliasing technology. ColorSync, a technology introduced many years before, was improved and built into the core drawing engine, to provide color matching for printing and multimedia professionals. Also, drop shadows were added around windows and isolated text elements to provide a sense of depth. New interface elements were integrated, including sheets (dialog boxes attached to specific windows) and drawers, which would slide out and provide options.

The original Aqua user interface as seen in the Mac OS X Public Beta from 2000

The use of soft edges, translucent colors, and pinstripes, similar to the hardware design of the first iMacs, brought more texture and color to the user interface when compared to what Mac OS 9 and Mac OS X Server 1.0's "Platinum" appearance had offered. According to John Siracusa, an editor of Ars Technica, the introduction of Aqua and its departure from the then conventional look "hit like a ton of bricks." Bruce Tognazzini (who founded the original Apple Human Interface Group) said that the Aqua interface in Mac OS X 10.0 represented a step backwards in usability compared with the original Mac OS interface. Third-party developers started producing skins for customizable applications and other operating systems which mimicked the Aqua appearance. To some extent, Apple has used the successful transition to this new design as leverage, at various times threatening legal action against people who make or distribute software with an interface the company says is derived from its copyrighted design.

Apple has continued to change aspects of the macOS appearance and design, particularly with tweaks to the appearance of windows and the menu bar. Since 2012, Apple has sold many of its Mac models with high-resolution Retina displays, and macOS and its APIs have extensive support for resolution-independent development on supporting high-resolution displays. Reviewers have described Apple's support for the technology as superior to that on Windows.

The human interface guidelines published by Apple for macOS are followed by many applications, giving them consistent user interface and keyboard shortcuts. In addition, new services for applications are included, which include spelling and grammar checkers, special characters palette, color picker, font chooser and dictionary; these global features are present in every Cocoa application, adding consistency. The graphics system OpenGL composites windows onto the screen to allow hardware-accelerated drawing. This technology, introduced in version 10.2, is called Quartz Extreme, a component of Quartz. Quartz's internal imaging model correlates well with the Portable Document Format (PDF) imaging model, making it easy to output PDF to multiple devices. As a side result, PDF viewing and creating PDF documents from any application are built-in features. Reflecting its popularity with design users, macOS also has system support for a variety of professional video and image formats and includes an extensive pre-installed font library, featuring many prominent brand-name designs.

Components

The Finder is a file browser allowing quick access to all areas of the computer, which has been modified throughout subsequent releases of macOS. Quick Look is part of the Finder since version 10.5. It allows for dynamic previews of files, including videos and multi-page documents without opening any other applications. Spotlight, a file searching technology which has been integrated into the Finder since version 10.4, allows rapid real-time searches of data files; mail messages; photos; and other information based on item properties (metadata) and/or content. macOS makes use of a Dock, which holds file and folder shortcuts as well as minimized windows.

Apple added "Exposé" in version 10.3 (called Mission Control since version 10.7), a feature which includes three functions to help accessibility between windows and desktop. Its functions are to instantly display all open windows as thumbnails for easy navigation to different tasks, display all open windows as thumbnails from the current application, and hide all windows to access the desktop. Also, FileVault was introduced, which is an optional encryption of the user's files with the 128-bit Advanced Encryption Standard (AES-128).

Features introduced in version 10.4 include Automator, an application designed to create an automatic workflow for different tasks; Dashboard, a full-screen group of small applications called desktop widgets that can be called up and dismissed in one keystroke; and Front Row, a media viewer interface accessed by the Apple Remote. Moreover, the Sync Services were included, which is a system that allows applications to access a centralized extensible database for various elements of user data, including calendar and contact items. The operating system then managed conflicting edits and data consistency.

All system icons are scalable up to 512×512 pixels as of version 10.5 to accommodate various places where they appear in larger size, including for example the Cover Flow view, a three-dimensional graphical user interface included with iTunes, the Finder, and other Apple products for visually skimming through files and digital media libraries via cover artwork. That version also introduced Spaces, a virtual desktop implementation which enables the user to have more than one desktop and display them in an Exposé-like interface; an automatic backup technology called Time Machine, which provides the ability to view and restore previous versions of files and application data; and Screen Sharing was built in for the first time.

In more recent releases, Apple has developed support for emoji characters by including the proprietary Apple Color Emoji font. Apple has also connected macOS with social networks such as Twitter and Facebook through the addition of share buttons for content such as pictures and text. Apple has brought several applications and features that originally debuted in iOS, its mobile operating system, to macOS in recent releases, notably the intelligent personal assistant Siri, which was introduced in version 10.12 of macOS.

Multilingual Support

There are 34 system languages available in macOS for the user at the moment of installation; the system language is used throughout the entire operating system environment. Input methods for typing in dozens of scripts can be chosen independently of the system language. Recent updates have added increasing support for Chinese characters and interconnections with popular social networks in China.

Updating Methods

macOS can be updated using the Mac App Store application or the softwareupdate command line utility. Until OS X 10.8 Mountain Lion, a separate Software Update application performed this functionality. In Mountain Lion and later, this was merged into the Mac App Store application, although the underlying update mechanism remains unchanged and is fundamentally different than the download mechanism used when purchasing an App Store application.

Release History

Box/Mac App Store artwork for every version of macOS. Left to right: Cheetah/Puma (1), Jaguar (2), Panther (3), Tiger (4), Leopard (5), Snow Leopard (6), Lion (7), Mountain Lion (8), Mavericks (9), Yosemite (10), El Capitan (11), Sierra (12).

Mac OS X, OS X, and macOS version information								
Version	**Codename**	**Darwin version**	**Processor support**	**Application support**	**Kernel**	**Date announced**	**Release date**	**Most recent version**
Rhapsody Developer Release	Grail1Z4 / Titan1U					Unknown	August 31, 1997	DR2 (May 14, 1998)
Mac OS X Server 1.0	Hera					Unknown	March 16, 1999	1.2v3 (October 27, 2000)
Mac OS X Developer Preview	Unknown		32-bit PowerPC			May 11, 1998	March 16, 1999	DP4 (April 5, 2000)
Mac OS X Public Beta	Kodiak	1.2.1		32-bit PowerPC		Unknown	September 13, 2000	N/A
Mac OS X 10.0	Cheetah	1.3.1			32-bit	Unknown	March 24, 2001	10.0.4 (June 22, 2001)
Mac OS X 10.1	Puma	1.4.1 / 5				July 18, 2001	September 25, 2001	10.1.5 (June 6, 2002)
Mac OS X 10.2	Jaguar	6	32/64-bit PowerPC			May 6, 2002	August 24, 2002	10.2.8 (October 3, 2003)
Mac OS X 10.3	Panther	7	32/64-bit PowerPC			June 23, 2003	October 24, 2003	10.3.9 (April 15, 2005)
Mac OS X 10.4	Tiger	8	32/64-bit PowerPC and Intel	32/64-bit Power PC and Intel		May 4, 2004	April 29, 2005	10.4.11 (November 14, 2007)
Mac OS X 10.5	Leopard	9		32/64-bit PowerPC and Intel		June 26, 2006	October 26, 2007	10.5.8 (August 5, 2009)

Mac OS X 10.6	Snow Leopard	10	32/64-bit Intel	32/64-bit Intel 32-bit PowerPC	32/64-bit	June 9, 2008	August 28, 2009	10.6.8 v1.1 (July 25, 2011)
Mac OS X 10.7	Lion	11	64-bit Intel	32/64-bit Intel		October 20, 2010	July 20, 2011	10.7.5 (September 19, 2012)
OS X 10.8	Mountain Lion	12			64-bit	February 16, 2012	July 25, 2012	10.8.5 (12F45) (October 3, 2013)
OS X 10.9	Mavericks	13				June 10, 2013	October 22, 2013	10.9.5 (13F1112) (September 18, 2014)
OS X 10.10	Yosemite	14				June 2, 2014	October 16, 2014	10.10.5 (14F27) (August 13, 2015)
OS X 10.11	El Capitan	15				June 8, 2015	September 30, 2015	10.11.6 (15G31) (July 18, 2016)
macOS 10.12	Sierra	16				June 13, 2016	September 20, 2016	10.12.4 (16E195) (March 27, 2017)

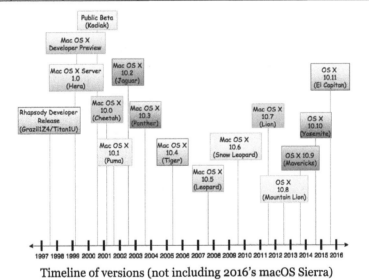

Timeline of versions (not including 2016's macOS Sierra)

The PowerMac G5 had special Jaguar builds.

Tiger did not support 64-bit GUI applications, only 64-bit CLI applications.

32-bit PowerPC applications were supported on Intel processors with Rosetta.

With the exception of Mac OS X Server 1.0 and the original public beta, OS X versions were named after big cats until OS X 10.9 Mavericks, when Apple switched to using California locations. Prior to its release, Mac OS X 10.0 was code named "Cheetah" internally at Apple, and Mac OS X 10.1 was code named internally as "Puma". After the immense buzz surrounding Mac OS X 10.2, code-named "Jaguar", Apple's product marketing began openly using the code names to promote the operating system. Mac OS X 10.3 was marketed as "Panther", Mac OS X 10.4 as "Tiger", Mac OS X 10.5 as "Leopard", Mac OS X 10.6 as "Snow Leopard", Mac OS X 10.7 as "Lion", OS X 10.8 as "Mountain Lion", and OS X 10.9 as "Mavericks".

"Panther", "Tiger" and "Leopard" are registered as trademarks of Apple, but "Cheetah", "Puma" and "Jaguar" have never been registered. Apple has also registered "Lynx" and "Cougar" as trademarks, though these were allowed to lapse. Computer retailer Tiger Direct sued Apple for its use of the name "Tiger". On May 16, 2005 a US federal court in the Southern District of Florida ruled that Apple's use did not infringe on Tiger Direct's trademark.

Mac OS X Public Beta

On September 13, 2000, Apple released a $29.95 "preview" version of Mac OS X internally codenamed Kodiak in order to gain feedback from users.

The "PB" as it was known marked the first public availability of the Aqua interface and Apple made many changes to the UI based on customer feedback. Mac OS X Public Beta expired and ceased to function in Spring 2001.

Mac OS X 10.0 Cheetah

On March 24, 2001, Apple released Mac OS X 10.0 (internally codenamed Cheetah). The initial version was slow, incomplete, and had very few applications available at the time of its launch, mostly from independent developers. While many critics suggested that the operating system was not ready for mainstream adoption, they recognized the importance of its initial launch as a base on which to improve. Simply releasing Mac OS X was received by the Macintosh community as a great accomplishment, for attempts to completely overhaul the Mac OS had been underway since 1996, and delayed by countless setbacks. Following some bug fixes, kernel panics became much less frequent.

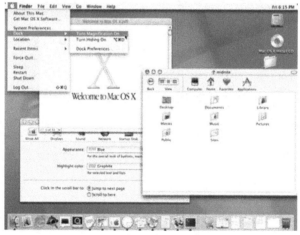

Screenshot of OS X 10.0

Mac OS X 10.1 Puma

Later that year on September 25, 2001, Mac OS X 10.1 (internally codenamed Puma) was released. It featured increased performance and provided missing features, such as DVD playback. Apple released 10.1 as a free upgrade CD for 10.0 users, in addition to the US$129 boxed version for people running Mac OS 9. It was discovered that the upgrade CDs were full install CDs that could be used with Mac OS 9 systems by removing a specific file; Apple later re-released the CDs in an actual stripped-down format that did not facilitate installation on such systems. On January 7, 2002, Apple announced that Mac OS X was to be the default operating system for all Macintosh products by the end of that month.

Mac OS X 10.2 Jaguar

On August 23, 2002, Apple followed up with Mac OS X 10.2 Jaguar, the first release to use its code name as part of the branding. It brought great raw performance improvements, a sleeker look, and many powerful user-interface enhancements (over 150, according to Apple), including Quartz Extreme for compositing graphics directly on an ATI Radeon or Nvidia GeForce2 MX AGP-based video card with at least 16 MB of VRAM, a system-wide repository for contact information in the new Address Book, and an instant messaging client named iChat. The Happy Mac which had appeared during the Mac OS startup sequence for almost 18 years was replaced with a large grey Apple logo with the introduction of Mac OS X v10.2.

Mac OS X 10.3 Panther

Mac OS X v10.3 Panther was released on October 24, 2003. In addition to providing much improved performance, it also incorporated the most extensive update yet to the user interface. Panther included as many or more new features as Jaguar had the year before, including an updated Finder, incorporating a brushed-metal interface, Fast user switching, Exposé (Window manager), FileVault, Safari, iChat AV (which added videoconferencing features to iChat), improved Portable Document Format (PDF) rendering and much greater Microsoft Windows interoperability. Support for some early G3 computers such as "beige" Power Macs and "WallStreet" PowerBooks was discontinued.

Mac OS X 10.4 Tiger

Screenshot of Tiger

Mac OS X 10.4 Tiger was released on April 29, 2005. Apple stated that Tiger contained more than 200 new features. As with Panther, certain older machines were no longer supported; Tiger requires a Mac with 256 MB and a built-in FireWire port. Among the new features, Tiger introduced Spotlight, Dashboard, Smart Folders, updated Mail program with Smart Mailboxes, QuickTime 7, Safari 2, Automator, VoiceOver, Core Image and Core Video. The initial release of the Apple TV used a modified version of Tiger with a different graphical interface and fewer applications and services. On January 10, 2006, Apple released the first Intel-based Macs along with the 10.4.4 update to Tiger.

This operating system functioned identically on the PowerPC-based Macs and the new Intel-based machines, with the exception of the Intel release dropping support for the Classic environment.

Mac OS X 10.5 Leopard

Mac OS X 10.5 Leopard was released on October 26, 2007. It was called by Apple "the largest update of Mac OS X". It brought more than 300 new features. Leopard supports both PowerPC- and Intel x86-based Macintosh computers; support for the G3 processor was dropped and the G4 processor required a minimum clock rate of 867 MHz, and at least 512 MB of RAM to be installed. The single DVD works for all supported Macs (including 64-bit machines). New features include a new look, an updated Finder, Time Machine, Spaces, Boot Camp pre-installed, full support for 64-bit applications (including graphical applications), new features in Mail and iChat, and a number of new security features. Leopard is an Open Brand UNIX 03 registered product on the Intel platform. It was also the first BSD-based OS to receive UNIX 03 certification. Leopard dropped support for the Classic Environment and all Classic applications. It was the final version of Mac OS X to support the PowerPC architecture.

Mac OS X 10.6 Snow Leopard

Mac OS X 10.6 Snow Leopard was released on August 28, 2009. Rather than delivering big changes to the appearance and end user functionality like the previous releases of Mac OS X, Snow Leopard focused on "under the hood" changes, increasing the performance, efficiency, and stability of the operating system. For most users, the most noticeable changes were: the disk space that the operating system frees up after a clean install compared to Mac OS X 10.5 Leopard, a more responsive Finder rewritten in Cocoa, faster Time Machine backups, more reliable and user friendly disk ejects, a more powerful version of the Preview application, as well as a faster Safari web browser. Snow Leopard only supported machines with Intel CPUs, required at least 1 GB of RAM, and dropped default support for applications built for the PowerPC architecture (Rosetta could be installed as an additional component to retain support for PowerPC-only applications).

Snow Leopard also featured new 64-bit technology capable of supporting greater amounts of RAM, improved support for multi-core processors through Grand Central Dispatch, and advanced GPU performance with OpenCL.

An update introduced support for the Mac App Store, Apple's digital distribution platform for macOS applications.

Mac OS X Lion was announced at WWDC 2011 at Moscone West

Mac OS X 10.7 Lion

Mac OS X 10.7 Lion was released on July 20, 2011. It brought developments made in Apple's iOS, such as an easily navigable display of installed applications called Launchpad and a greater use of multi-touch gestures, to the Mac. This release removed Rosetta, making it incompatible with PowerPC applications.

Changes made to the GUI include auto-hiding scrollbars that only appear when they are being used, and Mission Control which unifies Exposé, Spaces, Dashboard, and full-screen applications within a single interface. Apple also made changes to applications: they resume in the same state as they were before they were closed, similar to iOS. Documents auto-save by default.

OS X 10.8 Mountain Lion

OS X 10.8 Mountain Lion was released on July 25, 2012. It incorporates some features seen in iOS 5, which include Game Center, support for iMessage in the new Messages messaging application, and Reminders as a to-do list app separate from iCal (which is renamed as Calendar, like the iOS app). It also includes support for storing iWork documents in iCloud. Notification Center, which makes its debut in Mountain Lion, is a desktop version similar to the one in iOS 5.0 and higher. Application pop-ups are now concentrated on the corner of the screen, and the Center itself is pulled from the right side of the screen. Mountain Lion also includes more Chinese features including support for Baidu as an option for Safari search engine, QQ, 163.com and 126.com services for Mail, Contacts and Calendar, Youku, Tudou and Sina Weibo are integrated into share sheets.

Starting with Mountain Lion, Apple software updates (including the OS) are distributed via the App Store. This updating mechanism replaced the Apple Software Update utility.

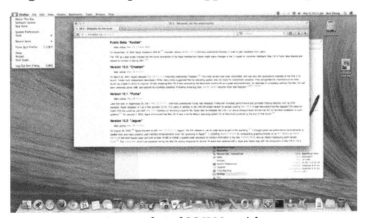
A screenshot of OS X Mavericks

OS X 10.9 Mavericks

OS X 10.9 Mavericks was released on October 22, 2013. It was a free upgrade to all users running Snow Leopard or later with a 64-bit Intel processor. Its changes include the addition of the previously iOS-only Maps and iBooks applications, improvements to the Notification Center, enhancements to several applications, and many under-the-hood improvements.

OS X 10.10 Yosemite

OS X 10.10 Yosemite was released on October 16, 2014. It features a redesigned user interface similar to that of iOS 7, intended to feature a more minimal, text-based 'flat' design, with use of translucency effects and intensely saturated colors. Apple's showcase new feature in Yosemite is Handoff, which enables users with iPhones running iOS 8.1 or later to answer phone calls, receive and send SMS messages, and complete unfinished iPhone emails on their Mac.

OS X 10.11 El Capitan

OS X 10.11 El Capitan was released on September 30, 2015. Similar to Mac OS X 10.6 Snow Leopard, Apple described this release as containing "refinements to the Mac experience" and "improvements to system performance" rather than new features. Refinements include public transport built into the Maps application, GUI improvements to the Notes application, adopting San Francisco as the system font for clearer legibility, and the introduction of System Integrity Protection. The Metal API, first introduced in iOS 8, was also included in this operating system for "all Macs since 2012".

Screenshot of El Capitan

macOS 10.12 Sierra

During the keynote at WWDC on June 13, 2016, Apple announced that OS X would be renamed macOS to stylistically match Apple's other operating systems, such as iOS, watchOS, and tvOS.

macOS 10.12 Sierra was released to the public on September 20, 2016. New features include the addition of Siri, Optimized Storage, and updates to Photos, Messages, and iTunes.

Reception

Usage Share

As of July 2016, macOS is the second-most-active general-purpose desktop client operating system in use on the World Wide Web following Microsoft Windows, with a 4.90% usage share according to statistics compiled. It is the most successful Unix-like desktop operating system on the web, estimated at approximately 5 times the usage of Linux (which has 1.01%). Usage share generally continues to shift away from the desktop and toward mobile operating systems such as iOS and Android.

Malware and Spyware

In its earlier years, Mac OS X enjoyed a near-absence of the types of malware and spyware that have affected Microsoft Windows users. macOS has a smaller usage share compared to Windows, but it also has traditionally more secure Unix roots. Worms, as well as potential vulnerabilities, were noted in 2006, which led some industry analysts and anti-virus companies to issue warnings that Apple's Mac OS X is not immune to malware. Increasing market share coincided with additional reports of a variety of attacks. In early 2011, Mac OS X experienced a large increase in malware attacks, and malware such as Mac Defender, MacProtector, and MacGuard were seen as an increasing problem for Mac users. At first, the malware installer required the user to enter the administrative password, but later versions were able to install without user input. Initially, Apple support staff were instructed not to assist in the removal of the malware or admit the existence of the malware issue, but as the malware spread, a support document was issued. Apple announced an OS X update to fix the problem. An estimated 100,000 users were affected. Apple releases security updates for macOS regularly.

Promotion

As a devices company, most large-scale Apple promotion for macOS has been part of the sale of Macs, with promotion of macOS updates generally focused on existing users, promotion at Apple Store and other retail partners, or through events for developers. In larger scale advertising campaigns, Apple specifically promoted macOS as better for handling media and other home-user applications, and comparing Mac OS X (especially versions Tiger and Leopard) with the heavy criticism Microsoft received for the long-awaited Windows Vista operating system.

Linux

Linux is a Unix-like computer operating system assembled under the model of free and open-source software development and distribution. The defining component of Linux is the Linux kernel, an operating system kernel first released on September 17, 1991 by Linus Torvalds. The Free Software Foundation uses the name *GNU/Linux* to describe the operating system, which has led to some controversy.

Linux was originally developed for personal computers based on the Intel x86 architecture, but has since been ported to more platforms than any other operating system. Because of the dominance of Android on smartphones, Linux has the largest installed base of all general-purpose operating systems. Linux is also the leading operating system on servers and other big iron systems such as mainframe computers, and is used on 99.6% of the TOP500 supercomputers. It is used by around 2.3% of desktop computers. The Chromebook, which runs on Chrome OS, dominates the US K–12 education market and represents nearly 20% of the sub-$300 notebook sales in the US. Linux also runs on embedded systems – devices whose operating system is typically built into the firmware and is highly tailored to the system. This includes TiVo and similar DVR devices, network routers, facility automation controls, televisions, video game consoles and smartwatches. Many smartphones and tablet computers run Android and other Linux derivatives.

The development of Linux is one of the most prominent examples of free and open-source software collaboration. The underlying source code may be used, modified and distributed—commercially or non-commercially—by anyone under the terms of its respective licenses, such as the GNU General Public License. Typically, Linux is packaged in a form known as a *Linux distribution* (or *distro* for short) for both desktop and server use. Some of the most popular mainstream Linux distributions are Arch Linux, CentOS, Debian, Fedora, Gentoo Linux, Linux Mint, Mageia, openSUSE and Ubuntu, together with commercial distributions such as Red Hat Enterprise Linux and SUSE Linux Enterprise Server. Distributions include the Linux kernel, supporting utilities and libraries, many of which are provided by the GNU Project, and usually a large amount of application software to fulfil the distribution's intended use.

Desktop Linux distributions include a windowing system, such as X11, Mir or a Wayland implementation, and an accompanying desktop environment such as GNOME or the KDE Software Compilation; some distributions may also include a less resource-intensive desktop, such as LXDE or Xfce. Distributions intended to run on servers may omit all graphical environments from the standard install, and instead include other software to set up and operate a solution stack such as LAMP. Because Linux is freely redistributable, anyone may create a distribution for any intended use.

History

Antecedents

Linus Torvalds, principal author of the Linux kernel

The Unix operating system was conceived and implemented in 1969 at AT&T's Bell Laboratories in the United States by Ken Thompson, Dennis Ritchie, Douglas McIlroy, and Joe Ossanna. First released in 1971, Unix was written entirely in assembly language, as was common practice at the time. Later, in a key pioneering approach in 1973, it was rewritten in the C programming language by Dennis Ritchie (with exceptions to the kernel and I/O). The availability of a high-level language implementation of Unix made its porting to different computer platforms easier.

Due to an earlier antitrust case forbidding it from entering the computer business, AT&T was required to license the operating system's source code to anyone who asked. As a result, Unix grew quickly and became widely adopted by academic institutions and businesses. In 1984, AT&T divested itself of Bell Labs; freed of the legal obligation requiring free licensing, Bell Labs began selling Unix as a proprietary product.

The GNU Project, started in 1983 by Richard Stallman, has the goal of creating a "complete Unix-compatible software system" composed entirely of free software. Work began in 1984. Later, in 1985, Stallman started the Free Software Foundation and wrote the GNU General Public License (GNU GPL) in 1989. By the early 1990s, many of the programs required in an operating system (such as libraries, compilers, text editors, a Unix shell, and a windowing system) were completed, although low-level elements such as device drivers, daemons, and the kernel were stalled and incomplete.

Linus Torvalds has stated that if the GNU kernel had been available at the time (1991), he would not have decided to write his own.

Although not released until 1992 due to legal complications, development of 386BSD, from which NetBSD, OpenBSD and FreeBSD descended, predated that of Linux. Torvalds has also stated that if 386BSD had been available at the time, he probably would not have created Linux.

MINIX was created by Andrew S. Tanenbaum, a computer science professor, and released in 1987 as a minimal Unix-like operating system targeted at students and others who wanted to learn the operating system principles. Although the complete source code of MINIX was freely available, the licensing terms prevented it from being free software until the licensing changed in April 2000.

Creation

In 1991, while attending the University of Helsinki, Torvalds became curious about operating systems and frustrated by the licensing of MINIX, which at the time limited it to educational use only. He began to work on his own operating system kernel, which eventually became the Linux kernel.

Torvalds began the development of the Linux kernel on MINIX and applications written for MINIX were also used on Linux. Later, Linux matured and further Linux kernel development took place on Linux systems. GNU applications also replaced all MINIX components, because it was advantageous to use the freely available code from the GNU Project with the fledgling operating system; code licensed under the GNU GPL can be reused in other computer programs as long as they also are released under the same or a compatible license. Torvalds initiated a switch from his original license, which prohibited commercial redistribution, to the GNU GPL. Developers worked to integrate GNU components with the Linux kernel, making a fully functional and free operating system.

Naming

Linus Torvalds had wanted to call his invention "Freax", a portmanteau of "free", "freak", and "x" (as an allusion to Unix). During the start of his work on the system, some of the project's makefiles included the name "Freax" for about half a year. Torvalds had already considered the name "Linux", but initially dismissed it as too egotistical.

5.25-inch floppy disks holding a very early version of Linux

In order to facilitate development, the files were uploaded to the FTP server (ftp.funet.fi) of FU-NET in September 1991. Ari Lemmke, Torvalds' coworker at the Helsinki University of Technology (HUT), who was one of the volunteer administrators for the FTP server at the time, did not think that "Freax" was a good name. So, he named the project "Linux" on the server without consulting Torvalds. Later, however, Torvalds consented to "Linux".

To demonstrate how the word "Linux" should be pronounced, Torvalds included an audio guide with the kernel source code.

Commercial and Popular Uptake

Ubuntu, a popular Linux distribution

Nexus 5X running Android

Adoption of Linux in production environments, rather than being used only by hobbyists, started to take off first in the mid-1990s in the supercomputing community, where organizations such as NASA started to replace their increasingly expensive machines with clusters of inexpensive commodity computers running Linux. Commercial use followed when Dell and IBM, followed by Hewlett-Packard, started offering Linux support to escape Microsoft's monopoly in the desktop operating system market.

Today, Linux systems are used throughout computing, from embedded systems to supercomputers, and have secured a place in server installations such as the popular LAMP application stack. Use of Linux distributions in home and enterprise desktops has been growing. Linux distributions have also become popular in the netbook market, with many devices shipping with customized Linux distributions installed, and Google releasing their own Chrome OS designed for netbooks.

Linux's greatest success in the consumer market is perhaps the mobile device market, with Android being one of the most dominant operating systems on smartphones and very popular on tablets and, more recently, on wearables. Linux gaming is also on the rise with Valve showing its support for Linux and rolling out its own gaming oriented Linux distribution. Linux distributions have also gained popularity with various local and national governments, such as the federal government of Brazil.

Current Development

Torvalds continues to direct the development of the kernel. Stallman heads the Free Software Foundation, which in turn supports the GNU components. Finally, individuals and corporations develop third-party non-GNU components. These third-party components comprise a vast body of work and may include both kernel modules and user applications and libraries.

Linux vendors and communities combine and distribute the kernel, GNU components, and non-GNU components, with additional package management software in the form of Linux distributions.

Design

A Linux-based system is a modular Unix-like operating system, deriving much of its basic design from principles established in Unix during the 1970s and 1980s. Such a system uses a monolithic kernel, the Linux kernel, which handles process control, networking, access to the peripherals, and file systems. Device drivers are either integrated directly with the kernel, or added as modules that are loaded while the system is running.

Separate projects that interface with the kernel provide much of the system's higher-level functionality. The GNU userland is an important part of most Linux-based systems, providing the most common implementation of the C library, a popular CLI shell, and many of the common Unix tools which carry out many basic operating system tasks. The graphical user interface (or GUI) used by most Linux systems is built on top of an implementation of the X Window System. More recently, the Linux community seeks to advance to Wayland as the new display server protocol in place of X11; Ubuntu, however, develops Mir instead of Wayland.

Various layers within Linux, also showing separation between the userland and kernel space						
User mode	**User applications**	For example, bash, LibreOffice, GIMP, Blender, o A.D., Mozilla Firefox, etc.				
	Low-level system components:	**System daemons**: *systemd, runit, logind, networkd, soundd, ...*	**Windowing system**: *X11, Wayland, Mir, SurfaceFlinger (Android)*	**Other libraries**: *GTK+, Qt, EFL, SDL, SFML, FLTK, GNUstep*, etc.	**Graphics**: *Mesa, AMD Catalyst, ...*	
	C standard library	open(), exec(), sbrk(), socket(), fopen(), calloc(), ... (up to 2000 subroutines) *glibc* aims to be POSIX/SUS-compatible, *uClibc* targets embedded systems, *bionic* written for Android, etc.				
Kernel mode	**Linux kernel**	stat, splice, dup, read, open, ioctl, write, mmap, close, exit, etc. (about 380 system calls) The Linux kernel System Call Interface (SCI, aims to be POSIX/SUS-compatible)				
		Process scheduling subsystem	IPC subsystem	Memory management subsystem	Virtual files subsystem	Network subsystem
		Other components: ALSA, DRI, evdev, LVM, device mapper, Linux Network Scheduler, Netfilter Linux Security Modules: *SELinux, TOMOYO, AppArmor, Smack*				
Hardware (CPU, main memory, data storage devices, etc.)						

Installed components of a Linux system include the following:

- A bootloader, for example GNU GRUB, LILO, SYSLINUX, or Gummiboot. This is a program that loads the Linux kernel into the computer's main memory, by being executed by the computer when it is turned on and after the firmware initialization is performed.

- An init program, such as the traditional sysvinit and the newer systemd, OpenRC and Upstart. This is the first process launched by the Linux kernel, and is at the root of the process tree: in other terms, all processes are launched through init. It starts processes such as system services and login prompts (whether graphical or in terminal mode).

- Software libraries, which contain code that can be used by running processes. On Linux systems using ELF-format executable files, the dynamic linker that manages use of dynamic libraries is known as ld-linux.so. If the system is set up for the user to compile software themselves, header files will also be included to describe the interface of installed libraries. Besides the most commonly used software library on Linux systems, the GNU C Library (glibc), there are numerous other libraries.

- C standard library is the library needed to run standard C programs on a computer system, with the GNU C Library being the most commonly used. Several alternatives are available, such as the EGLIBC (which was used by Debian for some time) and uClibc (which was designed for uClinux).

- Widget toolkits are the libraries used to build graphical user interfaces (GUIs) for software applications. Numerous widget toolkits are available, including GTK+ and Clutter developed by the GNOME project, Qt developed by the Qt Project and led by Digia, and Enlightenment Foundation Libraries (EFL) developed primarily by the Enlightenment team.

- User interface programs such as command shells or windowing environments.

User Interface

The user interface, also known as the shell, is either a command-line interface (CLI), a graphical user interface (GUI), or through controls attached to the associated hardware, which is common for embedded systems. For desktop systems, the default mode is usually a graphical user interface, although the CLI is available through terminal emulator windows or on a separate virtual console.

CLI shells are text-based user interfaces, which use text for both input and output. The dominant shell used in Linux is the Bourne-Again Shell (bash), originally developed for the GNU project. Most low-level Linux components, including various parts of the userland, use the CLI exclusively. The CLI is particularly suited for automation of repetitive or delayed tasks, and provides very simple inter-process communication.

On desktop systems, the most popular user interfaces are the GUI shells, packaged together with extensive desktop environments, such as the K Desktop Environment (KDE), GNOME, MATE, Cinnamon, Unity, LXDE, Pantheon and Xfce, though a variety of additional user interfaces exist. Most popular user interfaces are based on the X Window System, often simply called "X". It provides network transparency and permits a graphical application running on one system to be displayed on another where a user may interact with the application; however, certain extensions of the X Window System are not capable of working over the network. Several X display servers exist, with the reference implementation, X.Org Server, being the most popular.

Several types of window managers exist for X11, including tiling, dynamic, stacking and compositing. Window managers provide means to control the placement and appearance of individual application windows, and interact with the X Window System. Simpler X window managers such as dwm or ratpoison provide a minimalist functionality, while more elaborate window managers such as FVWM, Enlightenment or Window Maker provide more features such as a built-in taskbar and themes, but are still lightweight when compared to desktop environments. Desktop environments include window managers as part of their standard installations, such as Mutter (GNOME), KWin (KDE) or Xfwm (xfce), although users may choose to use a different window manager if preferred.

Wayland is a display server protocol intended as a replacement for the X11 protocol; as of 2014, it has not received wider adoption. Unlike X11, Wayland does not need an external window manager and compositing manager. Therefore, a Wayland compositor takes the role of the display server, window manager and compositing manager. Weston is the reference implementation of Wayland, while GNOME's Mutter and KDE's KWin are being ported to Wayland as standalone display servers. Enlightenment has already been successfully ported since version 19.

Video Input Infrastructure

Linux currently has two modern kernel-userspace APIs for handing video input devices: V4L2 API for video streams and radio, and DVB API for digital TV reception.

Due to the complexity and diversity of different devices, and due to the large amount of formats and standards handled by those APIs, this infrastructure needs to evolve to better fit other devices. Also, a good userspace device library is the key of the success for having userspace applications to be able to work with all formats supported by those devices.

Development

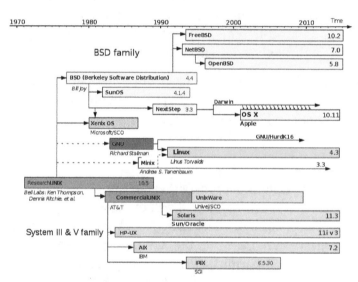

Simplified history of Unix-like operating systems. Linux shares similar architecture and concepts (as part of the POSIX standard) but does not share non-free source code with the original Unix or MINIX.

The primary difference between Linux and many other popular contemporary operating systems is that the Linux kernel and other components are free and open-source software. Linux is not the only such operating system, although it is by far the most widely used. Some free and open-source software licenses are based on the principle of copyleft, a kind of reciprocity: any work derived from a copyleft piece of software must also be copyleft itself. The most common free software license, the GNU General Public License (GPL), is a form of copyleft, and is used for the Linux kernel and many of the components from the GNU Project.

Linux based distributions are intended by developers for interoperability with other operating systems and established computing standards. Linux systems adhere to POSIX, SUS, LSB, ISO, and ANSI standards where possible, although to date only one Linux distribution has been POSIX.1 certified, Linux-FT.

Free software projects, although developed through collaboration, are often produced independently of each other. The fact that the software licenses explicitly permit redistribution, however, provides a basis for larger scale projects that collect the software produced by stand-alone projects and make it available all at once in the form of a Linux distribution.

Many Linux distributions, or "distros", manage a remote collection of system software and application software packages available for download and installation through a network connection. This allows users to adapt the operating system to their specific needs. Distributions are maintained by individuals, loose-knit teams, volunteer organizations, and commercial entities. A distribution is responsible for the default configuration of the installed Linux kernel, general system security, and more generally integration of the different software packages into a coherent whole. Distributions typically use a package manager such as apt, yum, zypper, pacman or portage to install, remove, and update all of a system's software from one central location.

Community

A distribution is largely driven by its developer and user communities. Some vendors develop and fund their distributions on a volunteer basis, Debian being a well-known example. Others maintain a community version of their commercial distributions, as Red Hat does with Fedora, and SUSE does with openSUSE.

In many cities and regions, local associations known as Linux User Groups (LUGs) seek to promote their preferred distribution and by extension free software. They hold meetings and provide free demonstrations, training, technical support, and operating system installation to new users. Many Internet communities also provide support to Linux users and developers. Most distributions and free software / open-source projects have IRC chatrooms or newsgroups. Online forums are another means for support, with notable examples being LinuxQuestions.org and the various distribution specific support and community forums, such as ones for Ubuntu, Fedora, and Gentoo. Linux distributions host mailing lists; commonly there will be a specific topic such as usage or development for a given list.

There are several technology websites with a Linux focus. Print magazines on Linux often bundle cover disks that carry software or even complete Linux distributions.

Although Linux distributions are generally available without charge, several large corporations sell, support, and contribute to the development of the components of the system and of free software. An analysis of the Linux kernel showed 75 percent of the code from December 2008 to January 2010 was developed by programmers working for corporations, leaving about 18 percent to volunteers and 7% unclassified. Major corporations that provide contributions include Dell, IBM, HP, Oracle, Sun Microsystems (now part of Oracle) and Nokia. A number of corporations, notably Red Hat, Canonical and SUSE, have built a significant business around Linux distributions.

The free software licenses, on which the various software packages of a distribution built on the Linux kernel are based, explicitly accommodate and encourage commercialization; the relationship between a Linux distribution as a whole and individual vendors may be seen as symbiotic. One common business model of commercial suppliers is charging for support, especially for business users. A number of companies also offer a specialized business version of their distribution, which adds proprietary support packages and tools to administer higher numbers of installations or to simplify administrative tasks.

Another business model is to give away the software in order to sell hardware. This used to be the norm in the computer industry, with operating systems such as CP/M, Apple DOS and versions of Mac OS prior to 7.6 freely copyable (but not modifiable). As computer hardware standardized throughout the 1980s, it became more difficult for hardware manufacturers to profit from this tactic, as the OS would run on any manufacturer's computer that shared the same architecture.

Programming on Linux

Linux distributions support dozens of programming languages. The original development tools used for building both Linux applications and operating system programs are found within the GNU toolchain, which includes the GNU Compiler Collection (GCC) and the GNU Build System. Amongst others, GCC provides compilers for Ada, C, C++, Go and Fortran. Many programming languages have a cross-platform reference implementation that supports Linux, for example PHP, Perl, Ruby, Python, Java, Go, Rust and Haskell. First released in 2003, the LLVM project provides an alternative cross-platform open-source compiler for many languages. Proprietary compilers for Linux include the Intel C++ Compiler, Sun Studio, and IBM XL C/C++ Compiler. BASIC in the form of Visual Basic is supported in such forms as Gambas, FreeBASIC, and XBasic, and in terms of terminal programming or QuickBASIC or Turbo BASIC programming in the form of QB64.

A common feature of Unix-like systems, Linux includes traditional specific-purpose programming languages targeted at scripting, text processing and system configuration and management in general. Linux distributions support shell scripts, awk, sed and make. Many programs also have an embedded programming language to support configuring or programming themselves. For example, regular expressions are supported in programs like grep and locate, the traditional Unix MTA Sendmail contains its own Turing complete scripting system, and the advanced text editor GNU Emacs is built around a general purpose Lisp interpreter.

Most distributions also include support for PHP, Perl, Ruby, Python and other dynamic languages. While not as common, Linux also supports C# (via Mono), Vala, and Scheme. Guile Scheme acts as an extension language targeting the GNU system utilities, seeking to make the conventionally small, static, compiled C programs of Unix design rapidly and dynamically extensible via an elegant, functional high-level scripting system; many GNU programs can be compiled with optional Guile bindings to this end. A number of Java Virtual Machines and development kits run on Linux, including the original Sun Microsystems JVM (HotSpot), and IBM's J2SE RE, as well as many open-source projects like Kaffe and JikesRVM.

GNOME and KDE are popular desktop environments and provide a framework for developing applications. These projects are based on the GTK+ and Qt widget toolkits, respectively, which can also be used independently of the larger framework. Both support a wide variety of languages. There are a number of Integrated development environments available including Anjuta, Code:-Blocks, Code Lite, Eclipse, Geany, Active State Komodo, KDevelop, Lazarus, MonoDevelop, Net-Beans, and Qt Creator, while the long-established editors Vim, nano and Emacs remain popular.

Hardware Support

The Linux kernel is a widely ported operating system kernel, available for devices ranging from mobile phones to supercomputers; it runs on a highly diverse range of computer architectures, including the hand-held ARM-based iPAQ and the IBM mainframes System z9 or System z10. Specialized distributions and kernel forks exist for less mainstream architectures; for example, the ELKS kernel fork can run on Intel 8086 or Intel 80286 16-bit microprocessors, while the μClinux kernel fork may run on systems without a memory management unit. The kernel also runs on architectures that were only ever intended to use a manufacturer-created operating system, such as Macintosh computers (with both PowerPC and Intel processors), PDAs, video game consoles, portable music players, and mobile phones.

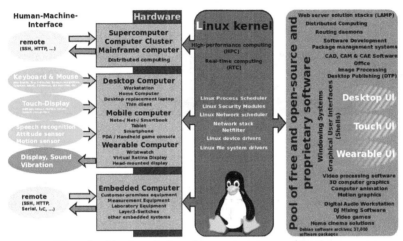

Linux is ubiquitously found on various types of hardware.

There are several industry associations and hardware conferences devoted to maintaining and improving support for diverse hardware under Linux, such as FreedomHEC. Over time, support for different hardware has improved in Linux, resulting in any off-the-shelf purchase having a "good chance" of being compatible.

Uses

Beside the Linux distributions designed for general-purpose use on desktops and servers, distributions may be specialized for different purposes including: computer architecture support, embedded systems, stability, security, localization to a specific region or language, targeting of specific user groups, support for real-time applications, or commitment to a given desktop environment. Furthermore, some distributions deliberately include only free software. As of 2015, over four hundred Linux distributions are actively developed, with about a dozen distributions being most popular for general-purpose use.

Desktop

The popularity of Linux on standard desktop computers and laptops has been increasing over the years. Most modern distributions include a graphical user environment, with, as of February 2015, the two most popular environments being the KDE Plasma Desktop and Xfce.

No single official Linux desktop exists: rather desktop environments and Linux distributions select components from a pool of free and open-source software with which they construct a GUI implementing some more or less strict design guide. GNOME, for example, has its human interface guidelines as a design guide, which gives the human–machine interface an important role, not just when doing the graphical design, but also when considering people with disabilities, and even when focusing on security.

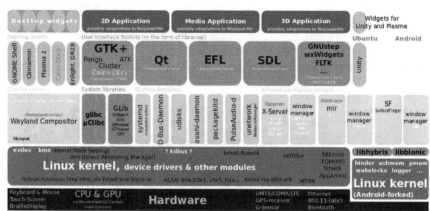

Visible software components of the Linux desktop stack include the display server, widget engines, and some of the more widespread widget toolkits. There are also components not directly visible to end users, including D-Bus and PulseAudio.

The collaborative nature of free software development allows distributed teams to perform language localization of some Linux distributions for use in locales where localizing proprietary systems would not be cost-effective. For example, the Sinhalese language version of the Knoppix distribution became available significantly before Microsoft translated Windows XP into Sinhalese. In this case the Lanka Linux User Group played a major part in developing the localized system by combining the knowledge of university professors, linguists, and local developers.

Performance and Applications

The performance of Linux on the desktop has been a controversial topic; for example in 2007 Con Kolivas accused the Linux community of favoring performance on servers. He quit Linux kernel development out of frustration with this lack of focus on the desktop, and then gave a "tell all" interview on the topic. Since then a significant amount of development has focused on improving the desktop experience. Projects such as Upstart and systemd aim for a faster boot time; the Wayland and Mir projects aim at replacing X11 while enhancing desktop performance, security and appearance.

Many popular applications are available for a wide variety of operating systems. For example, Mozilla Firefox, OpenOffice.org/LibreOffice and Blender have downloadable versions for all major operating systems. Furthermore, some applications initially developed for Linux, such as Pidgin, and GIMP, were ported to other operating systems (including Windows and Mac OS X) due to their popularity. In addition, a growing number of proprietary desktop applications are also supported on Linux, such as Autodesk Maya, Softimage XSI and Apple Shake in the high-end field of animation and visual effects. There are also several companies that have ported their own or other companies' games to Linux, with Linux also being a supported platform on both the popular Steam and Desura digital-distribution services.

Many other types of applications available for Microsoft Windows and Mac OS X also run on Linux. Commonly, either a free software application will exist which does the functions of an application found on another operating system, or that application will have a version that works on Linux, such as with Skype and some video games like *Dota 2* and *Team Fortress 2*. Furthermore, the Wine project provides a Windows compatibility layer to run unmodified Windows applications on Linux. It is sponsored by commercial interests including CodeWeavers, which produces a commercial version of the software. Since 2009, Google has also provided funding to the Wine project. CrossOver, a proprietary solution based on the open-source Wine project, supports running Windows versions of Microsoft Office, Intuit applications such as Quicken and QuickBooks, Adobe Photoshop versions through CS2, and many popular games such as *World of Warcraft*. In other cases, where there is no Linux port of some software in areas such as desktop publishing and professional audio, there is equivalent software available on Linux.

Components and Installation

Besides externally visible components, such as X window managers, a non-obvious but quite central role is played by the programs hosted by freedesktop.org, such as D-Bus or PulseAudio; both major desktop environments (GNOME and KDE) include them, each offering graphical front-ends written using the corresponding toolkit (GTK+ or Qt). A display server is another component, which for the longest time has been communicating in the X11 display server protocol with its clients; prominent software talking X11 includes the X.Org Server and Xlib. Frustration over the cumbersome X11 core protocol, and especially over its numerous extensions, has led to the creation of a new display server protocol, Wayland.

Installing, updating and removing software in Linux is typically done through the use of package managers such as the Synaptic Package Manager, PackageKit, and Yum Extender. While most major Linux distributions have extensive repositories, often containing tens of thousands of packages, not all the software that can run on Linux is available from the official repositories. Alternatively, users can install packages from unofficial repositories, download pre-compiled packages directly from websites, or compile the source code by themselves. All these methods come with different degrees of difficulty; compiling the source code is in general considered a challenging process for new Linux users, but it is hardly needed in modern distributions and is not a method specific to Linux.

- Samples of graphical desktop interfaces

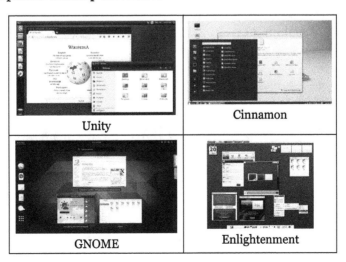

Unity	Cinnamon
GNOME	Enlightenment

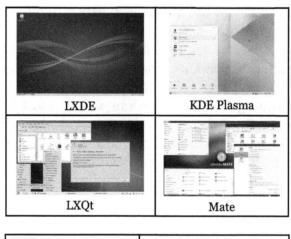

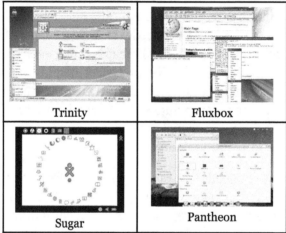

Netbooks

Linux distributions have also become popular in the netbook market, with many devices such as the Asus Eee PC and Acer Aspire One shipping with customized Linux distributions installed.

In 2009, Google announced its Chrome OS as a minimal Linux-based operating system, using the Chrome browser as the main user interface. Chrome OS does not run any non-web applications, except for the bundled file manager and media player (a certain level of support for Android applications was added in later versions). The netbooks that shipped with the operating system, termed Chromebooks, started appearing on the market in June 2011.

Servers, Mainframes and Supercomputers

Linux distributions have long been used as server operating systems, and have risen to prominence in that area; Netcraft reported in September 2006, that eight of the ten most reliable internet hosting companies ran Linux distributions on their web servers. In June 2008, Linux distributions represented five of the top ten, FreeBSD three of ten, and Microsoft two of ten; since February 2010, Linux distributions represented six of the top ten, FreeBSD two of ten, and Microsoft one of ten.

Linux distributions are the cornerstone of the LAMP server-software combination (Linux, Apache,

MariaDB/MySQL, Perl/PHP/Python) which has achieved popularity among developers, and which is one of the more common platforms for website hosting.

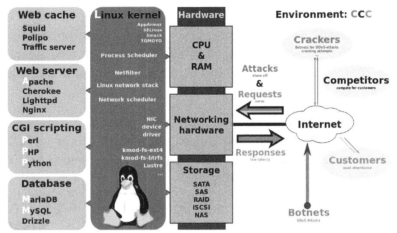

Broad overview of the LAMP software bundle, displayed here together with Squid. A high-performance and high-availability web server solution providing security in a hostile environment.

Linux distributions have become increasingly popular on mainframes, partly due to pricing and the open-source model. In December 2009, computer giant IBM reported that it would predominantly market and sell mainframe-based Enterprise Linux Server. At LinuxCon North America 2015, IBM announced LinuxONE, a series of mainframes specifically designed to run Linux and open-source software.

Linux distributions are also most commonly used as operating systems for supercomputers; in the decade since the Earth Simulator supercomputer, all the fastest supercomputers have used Linux. As of November 2016, 99.6% of the world's 500 fastest supercomputers run some variant of Linux, (the only exceptions, are ranked 386th and 387th and they run AIX Unix). Linux is also dominant on the Green500 list.

Smart Devices

Android smartphones

Several operating systems for smart devices, such as smartphones, tablet computers, smart TVs, and in-vehicle infotainment (IVI) systems, are based on Linux. Major platforms for such systems include Android, Firefox OS, Mer and Tizen.

Android has become the dominant mobile operating system for smartphones, running on 79.3% of units sold worldwide during the second quarter of 2013. Android is also a popular operating system for tablets, and Android smart TVs and in-vehicle infotainment systems have also appeared in the market.

Cellphones and PDAs running Linux on open-source platforms became more common from 2007; examples include the Nokia N810, Openmoko's Neo1973, and the Motorola ROKR E8. Continuing the trend, Palm (later acquired by HP) produced a new Linux-derived operating system, webOS, which is built into its line of Palm Pre smartphones.

Nokia's Maemo, one of the earliest mobile operating systems, was based on Debian. It was later merged with Intel's Moblin, another Linux-based operating system, to form MeeGo. The project was later terminated in favor of Tizen, an operating system targeted at mobile devices as well as IVI. Tizen is a project within The Linux Foundation. Several Samsung products are already running Tizen, Samsung Gear 2 being the most significant example. Samsung Z smartphones will use Tizen instead of Android.

As a result of MeeGo's termination, the Mer project forked the MeeGo codebase to create a basis for mobile-oriented operating systems. In July 2012, Jolla announced Sailfish OS, their own mobile operating system built upon Mer technology.

Mozilla's Firefox OS consists of the Linux kernel, a hardware abstraction layer, a web-standards-based runtime environment and user interface, and an integrated web browser.

Canonical has released Ubuntu Touch, aiming to bring convergence to the user experience on this mobile operating system and its desktop counterpart, Ubuntu. The operating system also provides a full Ubuntu desktop when connected to an external monitor.

Embedded Devices

| The Jolla Phone has the Linux-based Sailfish OS | In-car entertainment system of the Tesla Model S is based on Ubuntu |

Due to its low cost and ease of customization, Linux is often used in embedded systems. In the non-mobile telecommunications equipment sector, the majority of customer-premises equipment (CPE) hardware runs some Linux-based operating system. OpenWrt is a community driven example upon which many of the OEM firmwares are based.

Nokia X, a smartphone that runs Linux kernel

For example, the popular TiVo digital video recorder also uses a customized Linux, as do several network firewalls and routers from such makers as Cisco/Linksys. The Korg OASYS, the Korg KRONOS, the Yamaha Motif XS/Motif XF music workstations, Yamaha S90XS/S70XS, Yamaha MOX6/MOX8 synthesizers, Yamaha Motif-Rack XS tone generator module, and Roland RD-700GX digital piano also run Linux. Linux is also used in stage lighting control systems, such as the WholeHogIII console.

Gaming

In the past, not many games were available for Linux, but in the recent years, more games have been released with support for Linux. Nowadays, many games support Linux (especially Indie games), except for a few AAA title games. On the other hand, as a popular mobile platform, Android (which uses the Linux kernel) has gained much developer interest and is one of the main platforms for mobile game development along with iOS operating system by Apple for iPhone and iPad devices.

On February 14, 2013, Valve released a Linux version of Steam, a popular game distribution platform on PC. Many Steam games were ported to Linux. On December 13, 2013, Valve released SteamOS, a gaming oriented OS based on Debian, for beta testing, and has plans to ship Steam Machines as a gaming and entertainment platform. Valve has also developed VOGL, an OpenGL debugger intended to aid video game development, as well as porting its Source game engine to desktop Linux. As a result of Valve's effort, several prominent games such as *DotA 2*, *Team Fortress 2*, *Portal*, *Portal 2* and *Left 4 Dead 2* are now natively available on desktop Linux.

On July 31, 2013, Nvidia released Shield as an attempt to use Android as a specialized gaming platform.

Some Linux users play Windows games through Wine or CrossOver Linux.

Specialized Uses

Due to the flexibility, customizability and free and open-source nature of Linux, it becomes possible to highly tune Linux for a specific purpose. There are two main methods for creating a specialized Linux distribution: building from scratch or from a general-purpose distribution as a base. The distributions often used for this purpose include Debian, Fedora, Ubuntu (which is itself based on Debian), Arch Linux, Gentoo, and Slackware. In contrast, Linux distributions built from scratch do not have general-purpose bases; instead, they focus on the JeOS philosophy by including only necessary components and avoiding resource overhead caused by components considered redundant in the distribution's use cases.

Home Theater PC

A home theater PC (HTPC) is a PC that is mainly used as an entertainment system, especially a Home theater system. It is normally connected to a television, and often an additional audio system.

OpenELEC, a Linux distribution that incorporates the media center software Kodi, is an OS tuned specifically for an HTPC. Having been built from the ground up adhering to the JeOS principle, the OS is very lightweight and very suitable for the confined usage range of an HTPC.

There are also special editions of Linux distributions that include the MythTV media center software, such as Mythbuntu, a special edition of Ubuntu.

Digital Security

Kali Linux is a Debian-based Linux distribution designed for digital forensics and penetration testing. It comes preinstalled with several software applications for penetration testing and identifying security exploits. The Ubuntu derivative BackBox provides pre-installed security and network analysis tools for ethical hacking.

There are many Linux distributions created with privacy, secrecy, network anonymity and information security in mind, including Tails, Tin Hat Linux and Tinfoil Hat Linux. Lightweight Portable Security is a distribution based on Arch Linux and developed by the United States Department of Defense. Tor-ramdisk is a minimal distribution created solely to host the network anonymity software Tor.

System Rescue

Linux Live CD sessions have long been used as a tool for recovering data from a broken computer system and for repairing the system. Building upon that idea, several Linux distributions tailored for this purpose have emerged, most of which use GParted as a partition editor, with additional data recovery and system repair software:

- GParted Live – a Debian-based distribution developed by the GParted project.

- Parted Magic – a commercial Linux distribution.

- SystemRescueCD – a Gentoo-based distribution with support for editing Windows registry.

In Space

SpaceX uses multiple redundant flight computers in a fault-tolerant design in the Falcon 9 rocket. Each Merlin engine is controlled by three voting computers, with two physical processors per computer that constantly check each other's operation. Linux is not inherently fault-tolerant (no operating system is, as it is a function of the whole system including the hardware), but the flight computer software makes it so for its purpose. For flexibility, commercial off-the-shelf parts and system-wide "radiation-tolerant" design are used instead of radiation hardened parts. As of June 2015, SpaceX has made 19 launches of the Falcon 9 since 2010, out of which 18 have successfully delivered their primary payloads to Earth orbit, including some support missions for the International Space Station.

In addition, Windows was used as an operating system on non-mission critical systems—laptops used on board the space station, for example—but it has been replaced with Linux; the first Linux-powered humanoid robot is also undergoing in-flight testing.

The Jet Propulsion Laboratory has used Linux for a number of years "to help with projects relating to the construction of unmanned space flight and deep space exploration"; NASA uses Linux in robotics in the Mars rover, and Ubuntu Linux to "save data from satellites".

Education

Linux distributions have been created to provide hands-on experience with coding and source code to students, on devices such as the Raspberry Pi. In addition to producing a practical device, the intention is to show students "how things work under the hood".

The Ubuntu derivatives Edubuntu and The Linux Schools Project, as well as the Debian derivative Skolelinux, provide education-oriented software packages. They also include tools for administering and building school computer labs and computer-based classrooms, such as the Linux Terminal Server Project (LTSP).

Others

Instant WebKiosk and Webconverger are browser-based Linux distributions often used in web kiosks and digital signage. Thinstation is a minimalist distribution designed for thin clients. Rocks Cluster Distribution is tailored for high-performance computing clusters.

There are general-purpose Linux distributions that target a specific audience, such as users of a specific language or geographical area. Such examples include Ubuntu Kylin for Chinese language users and BlankOn targeted at Indonesians. Profession-specific distributions include Ubuntu Studio for media creation and DNALinux for bioinformatics. There is also a Muslim-oriented distribution of the name Sabily, as well as an Arabic-focused distribution called Ojuba Linux that consequently also provides some Islamic tools. Certain organizations use slightly specialized Linux distributions internally, including GendBuntu used by the French National Gendarmerie, Goobuntu used internally by Google, and Astra Linux developed specifically for the Russian army.

Market Share and Uptake

Many quantitative studies of free/open-source software focus on topics including market share and reliability, with numerous studies specifically examining Linux. The Linux market is growing rapidly, and the revenue of servers, desktops, and packaged software running Linux was expected to exceed $35.7 billion by 2008. Analysts and proponents attribute the relative success of Linux to its security, reliability, low cost, and freedom from vendor lock-in.

Desktops and laptops

According to web server statistics, as of June 2016, the estimated market share of Linux on desktop computers is around 1.8%. In comparison, Microsoft Windows has a market share of around 89.7%, while Mac OS covers around 8.5%.

Web servers

W3Cook publishes stats that use the top 1,000,000 Alexa domains, which as of May 2015 estimate that 96.55% of web servers run Linux, 1.73% run Windows, and 1.72% run FreeBSD.

W3Techs publishes stats that use the top 10,000,000 Alexa domains, updated monthly and as of November 2016 estimate that 66.7% of web servers run Linux/Unix, and 33.4% run Microsoft Windows.

In September 2008, Microsoft's CEO Steve Ballmer stated that 60% of web servers ran Linux, versus 40% that ran Windows Server.

IDC's Q1 2007 report indicated that Linux held 12.7% of the overall server market at that time; this estimate was based on the number of Linux servers sold by various companies, and did not include server hardware purchased separately that had Linux installed on it later.

Mobile devices

Android, which is based on the Linux kernel, has become the dominant operating system for smartphones. During the second quarter of 2013, 79.3% of smartphones sold worldwide used Android. Android is also a popular operating system for tablets, being responsible for more than 60% of tablet sales as of 2013. According to web server statistics, as of December 2014 Android has a market share of about 46%, with iOS holding 45%, and the remaining 9% attributed to various niche platforms.

Film production

For years Linux has been the platform of choice in the film industry. The first major film produced on Linux servers was 1997's *Titanic*. Since then major studios including Dream-Works Animation, Pixar, Weta Digital, and Industrial Light & Magic have migrated to Linux. According to the Linux Movies Group, more than 95% of the servers and desktops at large animation and visual effects companies use Linux.

Use in government

Linux distributions have also gained popularity with various local and national governments. The federal government of Brazil is well known for its support for Linux. News of the Russian military creating its own Linux distribution has also surfaced, and has come to fruition as the

G.H.ost Project. The Indian state of Kerala has gone to the extent of mandating that all state high schools run Linux on their computers. China uses Linux exclusively as the operating system for its Loongson processor family to achieve technology independence. In Spain, some regions have developed their own Linux distributions, which are widely used in education and official institutions, like gnuLinEx in Extremadura and Guadalinex in Andalusia. France and Germany have also taken steps toward the adoption of Linux. North Korea's Red Star OS, developed since 2002, is based on a version of Fedora Linux.

Copyright, Trademark, and Naming

Linux kernel is licensed under the GNU General Public License (GPL), version 2. The GPL requires that anyone who distributes software based on source code under this license, must make the originating source code (and any modifications) available to the recipient under the same terms. Other key components of a typical Linux distribution are also mainly licensed under the GPL, but they may use other licenses; many libraries use the GNU Lesser General Public License (LGPL), a more permissive variant of the GPL, and the X.org implementation of the X Window System uses the MIT License.

Torvalds states that the Linux kernel will not move from version 2 of the GPL to version 3. He specifically dislikes some provisions in the new license which prohibit the use of the software in digital rights management. It would also be impractical to obtain permission from all the copyright holders, who number in the thousands.

A 2001 study of Red Hat Linux 7.1 found that this distribution contained 30 million source lines of code. Using the Constructive Cost Model, the study estimated that this distribution required about eight thousand man-years of development time. According to the study, if all this software had been developed by conventional proprietary means, it would have cost about $1.5 billion (2017 US dollars) to develop in the United States. Most of the source code (71%) was written in the C programming language, but many other languages were used, including C++, Lisp, assembly language, Perl, Python, Fortran, and various shell scripting languages. Slightly over half of all lines of code were licensed under the GPL. The Linux kernel itself was 2.4 million lines of code, or 8% of the total.

In a later study, the same analysis was performed for Debian version 4.0 (etch, which was released in 2007). This distribution contained close to 283 million source lines of code, and the study estimated that it would have required about seventy three thousand man-years and cost US$8.28 billion (in 2017 dollars) to develop by conventional means.

In the United States, the name *Linux* is a trademark registered to Linus Torvalds. Initially, nobody registered it, but on August 15, 1994, William R. Della Croce, Jr. filed for the trademark *Linux*, and then demanded royalties from Linux distributors. In 1996, Torvalds and some affected organizations sued him to have the trademark assigned to Torvalds, and, in 1997, the case was settled. The licensing of the trademark has since been handled by the Linux Mark Institute (LMI). Torvalds has stated that he trademarked the name only to prevent someone else from using it. LMI originally charged a nominal sublicensing fee for use of the Linux name as part of trademarks, but later changed this in favor of offering a free, perpetual worldwide sublicense.

The name "Linux" is also used for a laundry detergent made by Swiss company Rösch.

The Free Software Foundation (FSF) prefers *GNU/Linux* as the name when referring to the operating system as a whole, because it considers Linux distributions to be variants of the GNU operating system initiated in 1983 by Richard Stallman, president of the FSF. They explicitly take no issue over the name Android for the Android OS, which is also an operating system based on the Linux kernel, as GNU is not a part of it. However, they object to it on grounds of including proprietary components. The FSF holds this stance for any operating system with proprietary components, including Linux operating systems such as Red Hat Linux.

A minority of public figures and software projects other than Stallman and the FSF, notably Debian (which had been sponsored by the FSF up to 1996), also use *GNU/Linux* when referring to the operating system as a whole. Most media and common usage, however, refers to this family of operating systems simply as *Linux*, as do many large Linux distributions (for example, SUSE Linux and Red Hat Enterprise Linux). In contrast Linux distributions containing only free software use "GNU/Linux" or simply "GNU", such as Trisquel GNU/Linux, Parabola GNU/Linux-libre, BLAG Linux and GNU, and gNewSense.

As of May 2011, about 8% to 13% of a modern Linux distribution is made of GNU components (the range depending on whether GNOME is considered part of GNU), as determined by counting lines of source code making up Ubuntu's "Natty" release; meanwhile, 6% is taken by the Linux kernel, and 9% by the Linux kernel and its direct dependencies.

Microsoft Windows

Microsoft Windows (or simply Windows) is a metafamily of graphical operating systems developed, marketed, and sold by Microsoft. It consists of several families of operating systems, each of which cater to a certain sector of the computing industry with the OS typically associated with IBM PC compatible architecture. Active Windows families include Windows NT and Windows Embedded; these may encompass subfamilies, e.g. Windows Embedded Compact (Windows CE) or Windows Server. Defunct Windows families include Windows 9x, Windows Mobile and Windows Phone.

Microsoft introduced an operating environment named *Windows* on November 20, 1985, as a graphical operating system shell for MS-DOS in response to the growing interest in graphical user interfaces (GUIs). Microsoft Windows came to dominate the world's personal computer (PC) market with over 90% market share, overtaking Mac OS, which had been introduced in 1984. Apple came to see Windows as an unfair encroachment on their innovation in GUI development as implemented on products such as the Lisa and Macintosh (eventually settled in court in Microsoft's favor in 1993). On PCs, Windows is still the most popular operating system. However, in 2014, Microsoft admitted losing the majority of the overall operating system market to Android, because of the massive growth in sales of Android smartphones. In 2014, the number of Windows devices sold was less than 25% that of Android devices sold. This comparison however may not be fully relevant, as the two operating systems traditionally target different platforms.

As of September 2016, the most recent version of Windows for PCs, tablets, smartphones and embedded devices is Windows 10. The most recent versions for server computers is Windows Server 2016. A specialized version of Windows runs on the Xbox One game console.

Genealogy

By Marketing Role

Microsoft, the developer of Windows, has registered several trademarks each of which denote a family of Windows operating systems that target a specific sector of the computing industry. As of 2014, the following Windows families are being actively developed:

- Windows NT: Started as a family of operating system with Windows NT 3.1, an operating system for server computers and workstations. It now consists of three operating system subfamilies that are released almost at the same time and share the same kernel. It is almost impossible for someone unfamiliar with the subject to identify the members of this family by name because they do not adhere to any specific rule; e.g. Windows Vista, Windows 7, Windows 8/8.1 and Windows RT are members of this family but Windows 3.1 is not.

  o Windows: The operating system for mainstream personal computers, tablets and smartphones. The latest version is Windows 10. The main competitor of this family is macOS by Apple Inc. for personal computers and Android for mobile devices (c.f. Usage share of operating systems Market share by category).

  o Windows Server: The operating system for server computers. The latest version is Windows Server 2016. Unlike its clients sibling, it has adopted a strong naming scheme. The main competitor of this family is Linux. (c.f. Usage share of operating systems Market share by category).

  o Windows PE: A lightweight version of its Windows sibling meant to operate as a live operating system, used for installing Windows on bare-metal computers (especially on many computers at once), recovery or troubleshooting purposes. The latest version is Windows PE 10.0.10586.0.

- Windows Embedded: Initially, Microsoft developed Windows CE as a general-purpose operating system for every device that was too resource-limited to be called a full-fledged computer. Eventually, however, Windows CE was renamed Windows Embedded Compact and was folded under Windows Compact trademark which also consists of Windows Embedded Industry, Windows Embedded Professional, Windows Embedded Standard, Windows Embedded Handheld and Windows Embedded Automotive.

The following Windows families are no longer being developed:

- Windows 9x: An operating system that targeted consumers market. Discontinued because of suboptimal performance. (*PC World* called its last version, Windows ME, one of the worst products of all times.) Microsoft now caters to the consumers market with Windows NT.

- Windows Mobile: The predecessor to Windows Phone, it was a mobile phone operating system. The first version was called Pocket PC 2000; the third version, Windows Mobile 2003 is the first version to adopt the Windows Mobile trademark. The last version is Windows Mobile 6.5.

- Windows Phone: An operating system sold only to manufacturers of smartphones. The first version was Windows Phone 7, followed by Windows Phone 8, and the last version Windows Phone 8.1. It was succeeded by Windows 10 Mobile.

Version History

The term *Windows* collectively describes any or all of several generations of Microsoft operating system products. These products are generally categorized as follows:

Early Versions

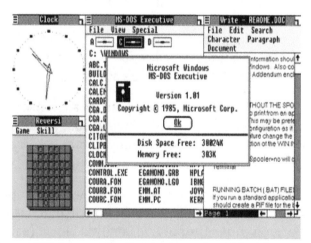

Windows 1.0, the first version, released in 1985

The history of Windows dates back to September 1981, when Chase Bishop, a computer scientist, designed the first model of an electronic device and project Interface Manager was started. It was announced in November 1983 (after the Apple Lisa, but before the Macintosh) under the name "Windows", but Windows 1.0 was not released until November 1985. Windows 1.0 was to compete with Apple's operating system, but achieved little popularity. Windows 1.0 is not a complete operating system; rather, it extends MS-DOS. The shell of Windows 1.0 is a program known as the MS-DOS Executive. Components included Calculator, Calendar, Cardfile, Clipboard viewer, Clock, Control Panel, Notepad, Paint, Reversi, Terminal and Write. Windows 1.0 does not allow overlapping windows. Instead all windows are tiled. Only modal dialog boxes may appear over other windows.

Windows 2.0 was released in December 1987, and was more popular than its predecessor. It features several improvements to the user interface and memory management. Windows 2.03 changed the OS from tiled windows to overlapping windows. The result of this change led to Apple Computer filing a suit against Microsoft alleging infringement on Apple's copyrights. Windows 2.0 also introduced more sophisticated keyboard shortcuts and could make use of expanded memory.

Windows 2.1 was released in two different versions: Windows/286 and Windows/386. Windows/386 uses the virtual 8086 mode of the Intel 80386 to multitask several DOS programs and the paged memory model to emulate expanded memory using available extended memory. Windows/286, in spite of its name, runs on both Intel 8086 and Intel 80286 processors. It runs in real mode but can make use of the high memory area.

In addition to full Windows-packages, there were runtime-only versions that shipped with early Windows software from third parties and made it possible to run their Windows software on MS-DOS and without the full Windows feature set.

The early versions of Windows are often thought of as graphical shells, mostly because they ran on top of MS-DOS and use it for file system services. However, even the earliest Windows versions already assumed many typical operating system functions; notably, having their own executable file format and providing their own device drivers (timer, graphics, printer, mouse, keyboard and sound). Unlike MS-DOS, Windows allowed users to execute multiple graphical applications at the same time, through cooperative multitasking. Windows implemented an elaborate, segment-based, software virtual memory scheme, which allows it to run applications larger than available memory: code segments and resources are swapped in and thrown away when memory became scarce; data segments moved in memory when a given application had relinquished processor control.

Windows 3.x

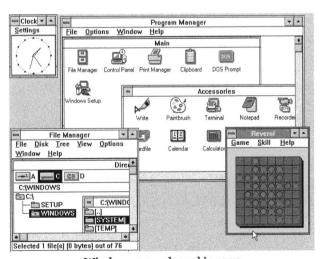

Windows 3.0, released in 1990

Windows 3.0, released in 1990, improved the design, mostly because of virtual memory and loadable virtual device drivers (VxDs) that allow Windows to share arbitrary devices between multitasked DOS applications. Windows 3.0 applications can run in protected mode, which gives them access to several megabytes of memory without the obligation to participate in the software virtual memory scheme. They run inside the same address space, where the segmented memory provides a degree of protection. Windows 3.0 also featured improvements to the user interface. Microsoft rewrote critical operations from C into assembly. Windows 3.0 is the first Microsoft Windows version to achieve broad commercial success, selling 2 million copies in the first six months.

Windows 3.1, made generally available on March 1, 1992, featured a facelift. In August 1993, Windows for Workgroups, a special version with integrated peer-to-peer networking features and a version number of 3.11, was released. It was sold along Windows 3.1. Support for Windows 3.1 ended on December 31, 2001.

Windows 3.2, released 1994, is an updated version of the Chinese version of Windows 3.1. The update was limited to this language version, as it fixed only issues related to the complex writing system of the Chinese language. Windows 3.2 was generally sold by computer manufacturers with a ten-disk version of MS-DOS that also had Simplified Chinese characters in basic output and some translated utilities.

Windows 9x

The next major consumer-oriented release of Windows, Windows 95, was released on August 24, 1995. While still remaining MS-DOS-based, Windows 95 introduced support for native 32-bit applications, plug and play hardware, preemptive multitasking, long file names of up to 255 characters, and provided increased stability over its predecessors. Windows 95 also introduced a redesigned, object oriented user interface, replacing the previous Program Manager with the Start menu, taskbar, and Windows Explorer shell. Windows 95 was a major commercial success for Microsoft; Ina Fried of CNET remarked that "by the time Windows 95 was finally ushered off the market in 2001, it had become a fixture on computer desktops around the world." Microsoft published four OEM Service Releases (OSR) of Windows 95, each of which was roughly equivalent to a service pack. The first OSR of Windows 95 was also the first version of Windows to be bundled with Microsoft's web browser, Internet Explorer. Mainstream support for Windows 95 ended on December 31, 2000, and extended support for Windows 95 ended on December 31, 2001.

Windows 95 was followed up with the release of Windows 98 on June 25, 1998, which introduced the Windows Driver Model, support for USB composite devices, support for ACPI, hibernation, and support for multi-monitor configurations. Windows 98 also included integration with Internet Explorer 4 through Active Desktop and other aspects of the Windows Desktop Update (a series of enhancements to the Explorer shell which were also made available for Windows 95). In May 1999, Microsoft released Windows 98 Second Edition, an updated version of Windows 98. Windows 98 SE added Internet Explorer 5.0 and Windows Media Player 6.2 amongst other upgrades. Mainstream support for Windows 98 ended on June 30, 2002, and extended support for Windows 98 ended on July 11, 2006.

On September 14, 2000, Microsoft released Windows ME (Millennium Edition), the last DOS-based version of Windows. Windows ME incorporated visual interface enhancements from its Windows NT-based counterpart Windows 2000, had faster boot times than previous versions (which however, required the removal of the ability to access a real mode DOS environment, removing compatibility with some older programs), expanded multimedia functionality (including Windows Media Player 7, Windows Movie Maker, and the Windows Image Acquisition framework for retrieving images from scanners and digital cameras), additional system utilities such as System File Protection and System Restore, and updated home networking tools. However, Windows ME was faced with criticism for its speed and instability, along with hardware compatibility issues and its removal of real mode DOS support. *PC World* considered Windows ME to be one of the worst operating systems Microsoft had ever released, and the 4th worst tech product of all time.

Windows NT

Early versions

In November 1988, a new development team within Microsoft (which included former Digital Equipment Corporation developers Dave Cutler and Mark Lucovsky) began work on a revamped version of IBM and Microsoft's OS/2 operating system known as "NT OS/2". NT OS/2 was intended to be a secure, multi-user operating system with POSIX compatibility and a modular, portable kernel with preemptive multitasking and support for multiple processor architectures. However, following the successful release of Windows 3.0, the NT development team decided to rework the project to use an extended 32-bit port of the Windows API known as Win32 instead of those of OS/2. Win32 maintained a similar structure to the Windows APIs (allowing existing Windows applications to easily be ported to the platform), but also supported the capabilities of the existing NT kernel. Following its approval by Microsoft's staff, development continued on what was now Windows NT, the first 32-bit version of Windows. However, IBM objected to the changes, and ultimately continued OS/2 development on its own.

The first release of the resulting operating system, Windows NT 3.1 (named to associate it with Windows 3.1) was released in July 1993, with versions for desktop workstations and servers. Windows NT 3.5 was released in September 1994, focusing on performance improvements and support for Novell's NetWare, and was followed up by Windows NT 3.51 in May 1995, which included additional improvements and support for the PowerPC architecture. Windows NT 4.0 was released in June 1996, introducing the redesigned interface of Windows 95 to the NT series. On February 17, 2000, Microsoft released Windows 2000, a successor to NT 4.0. The Windows NT name was dropped at this point in order to put a greater focus on the Windows brand.

Windows XP

The next major version of Windows NT, Windows XP, was released on October 25, 2001. The introduction of Windows XP aimed to unify the consumer-oriented Windows 9x series with the architecture introduced by Windows NT, a change which Microsoft promised would provide better performance over its DOS-based predecessors. Windows XP would also introduce a redesigned user interface (including an updated Start menu and a "task-oriented" Windows Explorer), streamlined multimedia and networking features, Internet Explorer 6, integration with Microsoft's .NET Passport services, modes to help provide compatibility with software designed for previous versions of Windows, and Remote Assistance functionality.

At retail, Windows XP was now marketed in two main editions: the "Home" edition was targeted towards consumers, while the "Professional" edition was targeted towards business environments and power users, and included additional security and networking features. Home and Professional were later accompanied by the "Media Center" edition (designed for home theater PCs, with an emphasis on support for DVD playback, TV tuner cards, DVR functionality, and remote controls), and the "Tablet PC" edition (designed for mobile devices meeting its specifications for a tablet computer, with support for stylus pen input and additional pen-enabled applications). Mainstream support for Windows XP ended on April 14, 2009. Extended support ended on April 8, 2014.

After Windows 2000, Microsoft also changed its release schedules for server operating systems; the server counterpart of Windows XP, Windows Server 2003, was released in April 2003. It was followed in December 2005, by Windows Server 2003 R2.

Windows Vista

After a lengthy development process, Windows Vista was released on November 30, 2006, for volume licensing and January 30, 2007, for consumers. It contained a number of new features, from a redesigned shell and user interface to significant technical changes, with a particular focus on security features. It was available in a number of different editions, and has been subject to some criticism, such as drop of performance, longer boot time, criticism of new UAC, and stricter license agreement. Vista's server counterpart, Windows Server 2008 was released in early 2008.

Windows 7

On July 22, 2009, Windows 7 and Windows Server 2008 R2 were released as RTM (release to manufacturing) while the former was released to the public 3 months later on October 22, 2009. Unlike its predecessor, Windows Vista, which introduced a large number of new features, Windows 7 was intended to be a more focused, incremental upgrade to the Windows line, with the goal of being compatible with applications and hardware with which Windows Vista was already compatible. Windows 7 has multi-touch support, a redesigned Windows shell with an updated taskbar, a home networking system called HomeGroup, and performance improvements.

Windows 8 and 8.1

Windows 8, the successor to Windows 7, was released generally on October 26, 2012. A number of significant changes were made on Windows 8, including the introduction of a user interface based around Microsoft's Metro design language with optimizations for touch-based devices such as tablets and all-in-one PCs. These changes include the Start screen, which uses large tiles that are more convenient for touch interactions and allow for the display of continually updated information, and a new class of apps which are designed primarily for use on touch-based devices. Other changes include increased integration with cloud services and other online platforms (such as social networks and Microsoft's own OneDrive (formerly SkyDrive) and Xbox Live services), the Windows Store service for software distribution, and a new variant known as Windows RT for use on devices that utilize the ARM architecture. An update to Windows 8, called Windows 8.1, was released on October 17, 2013, and includes features such as new live tile sizes, deeper OneDrive integration, and many other revisions. Windows 8 and Windows 8.1 has been subject to some criticism, such as removal of Start Menu.

Windows 10

On September 30, 2014, Microsoft announced Windows 10 as the successor to Windows 8.1. It was released on July 29, 2015, and addresses shortcomings in the user interface first introduced with Windows 8. Changes include the return of the Start Menu, a virtual desktop system, and the ability to run Windows Store apps within windows on the desktop rather than in full-screen mode. Windows 10 is said to be available to update from qualified Windows 7 with SP1 and Windows 8.1 computers from the Get Windows 10 Application (for Windows 7, Windows 8.1) or Windows Update (Windows 7).

On November 12, 2015, an update to Windows 10, version 1511, was released. This update can be activated with a Windows 7, 8 or 8.1 product key as well as Windows 10 product keys. Features include new icons and right-click context menus, default printer management, four times as many tiles allowed in the Start menu, Find My Device, and Edge updates.

Multilingual Support

Multilingual support is built into Windows. The language for both the keyboard and the interface can be changed through the Region and Language Control Panel. Components for all supported input languages, such as Input Method Editors, are automatically installed during Windows installation (in Windows XP and earlier, files for East Asian languages, such as Chinese, and right-to-left scripts, such as Arabic, may need to be installed separately, also from the said Control Panel). Third-party IMEs may also be installed if a user feels that the provided one is insufficient for their needs.

Interface languages for the operating system are free for download, but some languages are limited to certain editions of Windows. Language Interface Packs (LIPs) are redistributable and may be downloaded from Microsoft's Download Center and installed for any edition of Windows (XP or later) – they translate most, but not all, of the Windows interface, and require a certain base language (the language which Windows originally shipped with). This is used for most languages in emerging markets. Full Language Packs, which translates the complete operating system, are only available for specific editions of Windows (Ultimate and Enterprise editions of Windows Vista and 7, and all editions of Windows 8, 8.1 and RT except Single Language). They do not require a specific base language, and are commonly used for more popular languages such as French or Chinese. These languages cannot be downloaded through the Download Center, but available as optional updates through the Windows Update service (except Windows 8).

The interface language of installed applications are not affected by changes in the Windows interface language. Availability of languages depends on the application developers themselves.

Windows 8 and Windows Server 2012 introduces a new Language Control Panel where both the interface and input languages can be simultaneously changed, and language packs, regardless of type, can be downloaded from a central location. The PC Settings app in Windows 8.1 and Windows Server 2012 R2 also includes a counterpart settings page for this. Changing the interface language also changes the language of preinstalled Windows Store apps (such as Mail, Maps and News) and certain other Microsoft-developed apps (such as Remote Desktop). The above limitations for language packs are however still in effect, except that full language packs can be installed for any edition except Single Language, which caters to emerging markets.

Platform Support

Windows NT included support for several different platforms before the x86-based personal computer became dominant in the professional world. Windows NT 4.0 and its predecessors supported PowerPC, DEC Alpha and MIPS R4000. (Although some these platforms implement 64-bit computing, the operating system treated them as 32-bit.) However, Windows 2000, the successor of Windows NT 4.0, dropped support for all platforms except the third generation x86 (known as IA-32) or newer in 32-bit mode. The client line of Window NT family still runs on IA-32, although the Windows Server line has ceased supporting this platform with the release of Windows Server 2008 R2.

With the introduction of the Intel Itanium architecture (IA-64), Microsoft released new versions of Windows to support it. Itanium versions of Windows XP and Windows Server 2003 were released at the same time as their mainstream x86 counterparts. Windows XP 64-Bit Edition, released in 2005, is the last Windows client operating systems to support Itanium. Windows Server line continues to support this platform until Windows Server 2012; Windows Server 2008 R2 is the last Windows operating system to support Itanium architecture.

On April 25, 2005, Microsoft released Windows XP Professional x64 Edition and Windows Server 2003 x64 Editions to support the x86-64 (or simply x64), the eighth generation of x86 architecture. Windows Vista was the first client version of Windows NT to be released simultaneously in IA-32 and x64 editions. x64 is still supported.

An edition of Windows 8 known as Windows RT was specifically created for computers with ARM architecture and while ARM is still used for Windows smartphones with Windows 10, tablets with Windows RT will not be updated.

Windows CE

The latest current version of Windows CE, Windows Embedded Compact 7, displaying a concept media player UI

Windows CE (officially known as *Windows Embedded Compact*), is an edition of Windows that runs on minimalistic computers, like satellite navigation systems and some mobile phones. Windows Embedded Compact is based on its own dedicated kernel, dubbed Windows CE kernel. Microsoft licenses Windows CE to OEMs and device makers. The OEMs and device makers can modify and create their own user interfaces and experiences, while Windows CE provides the technical foundation to do so.

Windows CE was used in the Dreamcast along with Sega's own proprietary OS for the console. Windows CE was the core from which Windows Mobile was derived. Its successor, Windows Phone 7, was based on components from both Windows CE 6.0 R3 and Windows CE 7.0. Windows Phone 8 however, is based on the same NT-kernel as Windows 8.

Windows Embedded Compact is not to be confused with Windows XP Embedded or Windows NT 4.0 Embedded, modular editions of Windows based on Windows NT kernel.

Xbox OS

Xbox OS is an unofficial name given to the version of Windows that runs on the Xbox One. It is a more specific implementation with an emphasis on virtualization (using Hyper-V) as it is three operating systems running at once, consisting of the core operating system, a second implemented for games and a more Windows-like environment for applications. Microsoft updates Xbox One's OS every month, and these updates can be downloaded from the Xbox Live service to the Xbox and subsequently installed, or by using offline recovery images downloaded via a PC. The Windows 10-based Core had replaced the Windows 8-based one in this update, and the new system is sometimes referred to as "Windows 10 on Xbox One" or "OneCore". Xbox One's system also allows backward compatibility with Xbox 360, and the Xbox 360's system is backwards compatible with the original Xbox.

Timeline of Releases

Table of Windows versions

Legend:

Old version

Older version, still supported

Latest Version

Latest preview version

Future release

Product name	Latest version	General availability date	Codename	Support until		Latest version of		
				Mainstream	Extended	IE	DirectX	Edge
Windows 1.0	1.01	November 20, 1985	Interface Manager	December 31, 2001		N/A	N/A	N/A
Windows 2.0	2.03	December 9, 1987	N/A	December 31, 2001		N/A	N/A	N/A
Windows 2.1	2.11	May 27, 1988	N/A	December 31, 2001		N/A	N/A	N/A
Windows 3.0	3.0	May 22, 1990	N/A	December 31, 2001		N/A	N/A	N/A

Windows 3.1	3.1	April 6, 1992	Janus	December 31, 2001		5	N/A	N/A
Windows For Workgroups 3.1	3.1	October 1992	Sparta, Winball	December 31, 2001		5	N/A	N/A
Windows NT 3.1	NT 3.1.528	July 27, 1993	N/A	December 31, 2001		5	N/A	N/A
Windows For Workgroups 3.11	3.11	August 11, 1993	Sparta, Winball	December 31, 2001		5	N/A	N/A
Windows 3.2	3.2	November 22, 1993	N/A	December 31, 2001		5	N/A	N/A
Windows NT 3.5	NT 3.5.807	September 21, 1994	Daytona	December 31, 2001		5	N/A	N/A
Windows NT 3.51	NT 3.51.1057	May 30, 1995	N/A	December 31, 2001		5	N/A	N/A
Windows 95	4.0.950	August 24, 1995	Chicago, 4.0	December 31, 2000	December 31, 2001	5.5	6.1	N/A
Windows NT 4.0	NT 4.0.1381	July 31, 1996	Cairo	December 31, 2000	December 31, 2001	5	N/A	N/A
Windows 98	4.10.1998	June 25, 1998	Memphis, 97, 4.1	June 30, 2002	July 11, 2006	6	6.1	N/A
Windows 98 SE	4.10.2222	May 5, 1999	N/A	June 30, 2002	July 11, 2006	6	6.1	N/A
Windows 2000	NT 5.0.2195	December 15, 1999	N/A	June 30, 2005	July 13, 2010	5	N/A	N/A
Windows ME	4.90.3000	September 14, 2000	Millenium, 4.9	December 31, 2003	July 11, 2006	6	9.0c	N/A
Windows XP	NT 5.1.2600	October 25, 2001	Whistler	April 14, 2009	April 8, 2014	8	9.0c	N/A
Windows XP 64-bit Edition	NT 5.2.3790	March 28, 2003	N/A	April 14, 2009	April 8, 2014	6	9.0c	N/A
Windows Server 2003	NT 5.2.3790	April 24, 2003	N/A	July 13, 2010	July 14, 2015	8	9.0c	N/A
Windows XP Professional x64 Edition	NT 5.2.3790	April 25, 2005	N/A	April 14, 2009	April 8, 2014	8	9.0c	N/A
Windows Fundamentals for Legacy PCs	NT 5.1.2600	July 8, 2006	Eiger, Mönch	April 14, 2009	April 8, 2014	8	9.0c	N/A
Windows Vista	NT 6.0.6002	January 30, 2007	Longhorn	April 10, 2012	April 11, 2017	9	11	N/A
Windows Home Server	NT 5.2.4500	November 4, 2007	N/A	January 8, 2013		8	9.0c	N/A
Windows Server 2008	NT 6.0.6002	February 27, 2008	Longhorn Server	January 13, 2015	January 14, 2020	9	11	N/A
Windows 7	NT 6.1.7601	October 22, 2009	Blackcomb, Vienna	January 13, 2015	January 14, 2020	11	11	N/A
Windows Server 2008 R2	NT 6.1.7601	October 22, 2009	N/A	January 13, 2015	January 14, 2020	11	11	N/A

Windows Home Server 2011	NT 6.1.8400	April 6, 2011	Vail	April 12, 2016		9	11	N/A
Windows Server 2012	NT 6.2.9200	September 4, 2012	N/A	January 9, 2018	January 10, 2023	10	11.1	N/A
Windows 8	NT 6.2.9200	October 26, 2012	N/A	January 12, 2016		10	11.1	N/A
Windows 8.1	NT 6.3.9600	October 17, 2013	Blue	January 9, 2018	January 10, 2023	11	11.2	N/A
Windows Server 2012 R2	NT 6.3.9600	October 18, 2013	Server Blue	January 9, 2018	January 10, 2023	11	11.2	N/A
Windows 10	NT 10.0.14393	July 29, 2015	Threshold, Restone	October 13, 2020	October 14, 2025	11	12	25
Windows Server 2016	NT 10.0.14393	October 12, 2016	N/A	January 11, 2022	January 11, 2027	11	12	25

Windows timeline: Bar chart

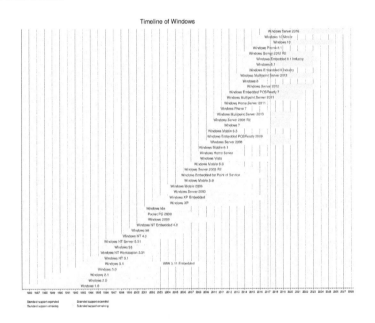

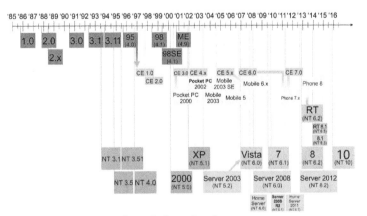

The Windows family tree

Usage Share and Device Sales

Market Share Overview

According to Net Applications and StatCounter data from March 2017

Desktop OS	Net Applications	StatCounter
Windows XP	7.44%	4.61%
Windows Vista	0.72%	0.91%
Windows 7	49.42%	39.70%
Windows 8	1.57%	2.06%
Windows 8.1	6.66%	8.11%
Windows 10	25.36%	28.89%
All listed versions	91.17%	84.28%

Mobile OS	Net Applications	StatCounter
Windows RT 8.1	—	0.03%
Windows Phone 7.5	0.03%	0.92%
Windows Phone 8	0.17%	
Windows Phone 8.1	0.79%	
Windows 10 Mobile	0.32%	
All listed versions	1.31%	0.95%

According to Net Applications, that tracks use based on web use, Windows is the most-used operating system family for personal computers as of June 2016 with close to 90% usage share. When including both personal computers of all kinds, e.g. mobile devices, in July 2016, according to StatCounter, that also tracks use based on web use, Windows OSes accounted for 46.87% of usage share, compared to 36.48% for Android, 12.26% for iOS, and 4.81% for macOS. The below 50% usage share of Windows, also applies to developed countries, such as the US, the UK and Ireland. These numbers are easiest (monthly numbers) to find that track real use, but they may not mirror installed base or sales numbers (in recent years) of devices.

In terms of the number of devices shipped with the operating system installed, on smartphones, Windows Phone was the third-most-shipped OS (2.6%) after Android (82.8%) and iOS (13.9%) in the second quarter of 2015 according IDC. Across both PCs and mobile devices, in 2014, Windows OSes were the second-most-shipped (333 million devices, or 14%) after Android (1.2 billion, 49%) and ahead of iOS and macOS combined (263 million, 11%).

Security

Consumer versions of Windows were originally designed for ease-of-use on a single-user PC without a network connection, and did not have security features built in from the outset. However, Windows NT and its successors are designed for security (including on a network) and multi-user

PCs, but were not initially designed with Internet security in mind as much, since, when it was first developed in the early 1990s, Internet use was less prevalent.

These design issues combined with programming errors (e.g. buffer overflows) and the popularity of Windows means that it is a frequent target of computer worm and virus writers. In June 2005, Bruce Schneier's *Counterpane Internet Security* reported that it had seen over 1,000 new viruses and worms in the previous six months. In 2005, Kaspersky Lab found around 11,000 malicious programs—viruses, Trojans, back-doors, and exploits written for Windows.

Microsoft releases security patches through its Windows Update service approximately once a month (usually the second Tuesday of the month), although critical updates are made available at shorter intervals when necessary. In versions of Windows after and including Windows 2000 SP3 and Windows XP, updates can be automatically downloaded and installed if the user selects to do so. As a result, Service Pack 2 for Windows XP, as well as Service Pack 1 for Windows Server 2003, were installed by users more quickly than it otherwise might have been.

While the Windows 9x series offered the option of having profiles for multiple users, they had no concept of access privileges, and did not allow concurrent access; and so were not true multi-user operating systems. In addition, they implemented only partial memory protection. They were accordingly widely criticised for lack of security.

The Windows NT series of operating systems, by contrast, are true multi-user, and implement absolute memory protection. However, a lot of the advantages of being a true multi-user operating system were nullified by the fact that, prior to Windows Vista, the first user account created during the setup process was an administrator account, which was also the default for new accounts. Though Windows XP did have limited accounts, the majority of home users did not change to an account type with fewer rights – partially due to the number of programs which unnecessarily required administrator rights – and so most home users ran as administrator all the time.

Windows Vista changes this by introducing a privilege elevation system called User Account Control. When logging in as a standard user, a logon session is created and a token containing only the most basic privileges is assigned. In this way, the new logon session is incapable of making changes that would affect the entire system. When logging in as a user in the Administrators group, two separate tokens are assigned. The first token contains all privileges typically awarded to an administrator, and the second is a restricted token similar to what a standard user would receive. User applications, including the Windows shell, are then started with the restricted token, resulting in a reduced privilege environment even under an Administrator account. When an application requests higher privileges or "Run as administrator" is clicked, UAC will prompt for confirmation and, if consent is given (including administrator credentials if the account requesting the elevation is not a member of the administrators group), start the process using the unrestricted token.

File Permissions

All Windows versions from Windows NT 3 have been based on a file system permission system referred to as AGLP (Accounts, Global, Local, Permissions) AGDLP which in essence where file permissions are applied to the file/folder in the form of a 'local group' which then has other 'global groups' as members. These global groups then hold other groups or users depending on different Windows versions used. This system varies from other vendor products such as Linux and NetWare due to the 'static' allocation of permission being applied directory to the file or folder. However using this process of AGLP/AGDLP/AGUDLP allows a small number of static permissions to be applied and allows for easy changes to the account groups without reapplying the file permissions on the files and folders.

Windows Defender

On January 6, 2005, Microsoft released a Beta version of Microsoft AntiSpyware, based upon the previously released Giant AntiSpyware. On February 14, 2006, Microsoft AntiSpyware became Windows Defender with the release of Beta 2. Windows Defender is a freeware program designed to protect against spyware and other unwanted software. Windows XP and Windows Server 2003 users who have genuine copies of Microsoft Windows can freely download the program from Microsoft's web site, and Windows Defender ships as part of Windows Vista and 7. In Windows 8, Windows Defender and Microsoft Security Essentials have been combined into a single program, named Windows Defender. It is based on Microsoft Security Essentials, borrowing its features and user interface. Although it is enabled by default, it can be turned off to use another anti-virus solution. Windows Malicious Software Removal Tool and the optional Microsoft Safety Scanner are two other free security products offered by Microsoft.

Third-party Analysis

In an section based on a report by Symantec, internetnews.com has described Microsoft Windows as having the "fewest number of patches and the shortest average patch development time of the five operating systems it monitored in the last six months of 2006."

A study conducted by Kevin Mitnick and marketing communications firm Avantgarde in 2004, found that an unprotected and unpatched Windows XP system with Service Pack 1 lasted only four minutes on the Internet before it was compromised, and an unprotected and also unpatched Windows Server 2003 system was compromised after being connected to the internet for 8 hours. The computer that was running Windows XP Service Pack 2 was not compromised. The AOL National Cyber Security Alliance Online Safety Study of October 2004, determined that 80% of Windows users were infected by at least one spyware/adware product. Much documentation is available describing how to increase the security of Microsoft Windows products. Typical suggestions include deploying Microsoft Windows behind a hardware or software firewall, running anti-virus and anti-spyware software, and installing patches as they become available through Windows Update.

Alternative Implementations

Owing to the operating system's popularity, a number of applications have been released that aim to provide compatibility with Windows applications, either as a compatibility layer for another operating system, or as a standalone system that can run software written for Windows out of the box. These include:

- Wine – a free and open-source implementation of the Windows API, allowing one to run many Windows applications on x86-based platforms, including UNIX, Linux and macOS. Wine developers refer to it as a "compatibility layer" and use Windows-style APIs to emulate Windows environment.

    o CrossOver – a Wine package with licensed fonts. Its developers are regular contributors to Wine, and focus on Wine running officially supported applications.

    o Cedega – a proprietary fork of Wine by TransGaming Technologies, designed specifically for running Microsoft Windows games on Linux. A version of Cedega known as Cider allows Windows games to run on macOS. Since Wine was licensed under the LGPL, Cedega has been unable to port the improvements made to Wine to their proprietary codebase. Cedega ceased its service in February 2011.

    o Darwine – a port of Wine for macOS and Darwin. Operates by running Wine on QEMU.

    o Linux Unified Kernel – a set of patches to the Linux kernel allowing many Windows executable files in Linux (using Wine DLLs); and some Windows drivers to be used.

- ReactOS – an open-source OS intended to run the same software as Windows, originally designed to simulate Windows NT 4.0, now aiming at Windows 7 compatibility. It has been in the development stage since 1996.

- Linspire – formerly LindowsOS, a commercial Linux distribution initially created with the goal of running major Windows software. Changed its name to Linspire after *Microsoft v. Lindows*. Discontinued in favor of Xandros Desktop, that was also later discontinued.

- Freedows OS – an open-source attempt at creating a Windows clone for x86 platforms, intended to be released under the GNU General Public License. Started in 1996, by Reece K. Sellin, the project was never completed, getting only to the stage of design discussions which featured a number of novel concepts until it was suspended in 2002.

Processes and Process Management

A process in execution needs resources like processing resource, memory and IO resources. Current machines allow several processes to share resources. In reality, one processor is shared amongst many processes. We indicated that the human computer interface provided by an OS involves supporting many concurrent processes like clock, icons and one or more windows.A system like a file server may even support processes from multiple users. And yet the owner of every process gets an illusion that the server (read processor) is available to their process without any interruption. This requires clever management and allocation of the processor as a resource.

What is a Process?

As we know a process is a *program in execution*. To understand the importance of this definition, let's imagine that we have written a program called *my_prog.c* in C. On execution, this program may read in some data and output some data. Note that when a program is written and a file is prepared, it is still a script. It has no dynamics of its own i.e, it cannot cause any input processing or output to happen. Once we compile, and still later when we run this program, the intended operations take place. In other words, a program is a text script with no dynamic behavior. When a program is in execution, the script is acted upon. It can result in engaging a processor for some processing and it can also engage in I/O operations. It is for this reason a process is differentiated from program. While the program is a text script, a program in execution is a process.

In other words, To begin with let us define what is a "process" and in which way a process differs from a program. A process is an executable entity – it's a program in execution. When we compile a C language program we get an a.out file which is an executable file. When we seek to run this file. Every process has its instruction sequence. Clearly, therefore, at any point in time there is a current instruction in execution.

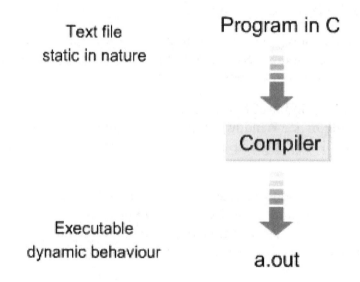

A program counter determines helps to identify the next instruction in the sequence. So process must have an inherent program counter. Referring back to the C language program – it's a text file. A program by it self is a passive entity and has no dynamic behavior of its own till we create the corresponding process. On the other hand, a process has a dynamic behavior and is an active entity.

Processes get created, may have to be suspended awaiting an event like completing a certain I/O. A process terminates when the task it is defined for is completed. During the life time of a process it may seek memory dynamically. In fact, the *malloc* instruction in C precisely does that. In any case, from the stand point of OS a process should be memory resident and, therefore, needs to be stored in specific area within the main memory. Processes during their life time may also seek to use I/O devices.

For instance, an output may have to appear on a monitor or a printed output may be needed. In other words, process management requires not only making the processor available for execution but, in addition, allocate main memory, files and IO. The process management component then requires coordination with the main memory management, secondary memory management, as well as, files and I/O. We shall examine the memory management and I/O management issues briefly here. These topics will be taken up for more detailed study later.

Main Memory Management

As we observed earlier in the systems operate using Von-Neumann's stored program concept. The basic idea is that an instruction sequence is required to be stored before it can be executed. Therefore, every executable file needs to be stored in the main memory. In addition, we noted that modern systems support multi-programming. This means that more than one executable process may be stored in the main memory. If there are several programs residing in the memory, it is imperative that these be appropriately assigned specific areas.

The OS needs to select one amongst these to execute. Further these processes have their data areas associated with them and may even dynamically seek more data areas.

In other words, the OS must cater to allocating and de-allocating memory to processes as well as to the data required by these processes. All processes need files for their operations and the OS must manage these as well.

Main Memory

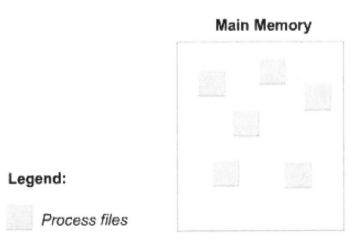

Legend:

Process files

Files and IO Management

On occasions processes need to operate on files. Typical file operations are:

1. Create: To create a file in the environment of operation.

2. Open: To open an existing file from the environment of operation.

3. Read: To read data from an opened file.

4. Write: To write into an existing file or into a newly created file or it may be to modify or append or write into a newly created file.

5. Append: Like write except that writing results in appending to an existing file.

6. Modify or rewrite: Essentially like write – results in rewriting a file.

7. Delete: This may be to remove or disband a file from further use.

OS must support all of these and many other file operations. For instance, there are other file operations like which applications or users may be permitted to access the files. Files may be "owned" or "shared". There are file operations that permit a user to specify this. Also, files may be of different types. For instance, we have already seen that we may have executable and text files. In addition, there may be image files or audio files. For now it suffices to know that one major task OSs perform related to management of files.

Process Management: Multi-Programming and Time Sharing

To understand processes and management, we begin by considering a simple system with only one processor and one user running only one program, prog_1 shown in fig (a).

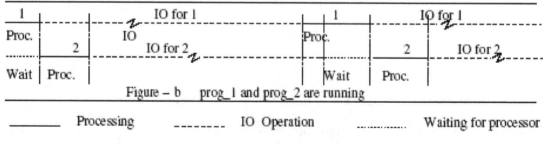

(a): Multiple-program Processing

We also assume that IO and processing takes place serially. So when an IO is required the processor waits for IO to be completed .When we input from a keyboard we are operating at a speed nearly a million times slower than that of a processor. So the processor is idle most of time. Even the fastest IO devices are at least 1000 times slower than processors, i.e, a processor is heavily underutilized as shown in figure.

Recall that Von Neumann computing requires a program to reside in main memory to run. Clearly, having just one program would result in gross under utilization of the processor.

Let us assume that we now have two ready to run programs

(b): Multiple-program Processing

Consider two programs prog_1 and prog_2 resident in the main memory. When prog_1 may be seeking the IO we make the processor available to run prog_2 that is we may schedule the operation of prog_2. Because the processor is very much faster compared to all other devices, we will till end up with processor waiting for IO to be completed as shown in figure (b). In this case we have two programs resident in main memory. A multi-programming OS allows and manages several programs to be simultaneously resident in main memory.

Processor Utilization

Processor Utilization: A processor is a central and a key element of a computer system. This is so because all information processing gets done in a processor. So a computer's throughput depends upon the extent of utilization of its processor. The greater the utilization of the processor, larger is the amount of information processed.

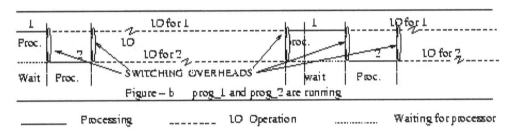

In the light of the above let us briefly review this figure above. In a uni-programming system (figure a) we have one program engaging the processor. In such a situation the processor is idling for very long periods of time. This is so because IO and communica- tion to devices (including memory) takes so much longer. In figure above we see that during intervals when prog_1 is not engaging the processor we can utilize the processor to run another ready to run program. The processor now processes two programs without significantly sacrificing the time required to process prog_1. Note that we may have a small overhead in switching the context of use of a processor. However, multiprogramming results in improving the utilization of computer's resources. In this example, with multiple programs residing in the memory, we enhance the memory utilization also.

When we invest in a computer system we invest in all its components. So if any part of the system is idling, it is a waste of resource. Ideally, we can get the maximum through put from a system when all the system components are busy all the time. That then is the goal. Multiprogramming support is essential to realize this goal because only those programs that are resident in the memory can engage devices within in a system.

Response Time

So far we have argued that use of multiprogramming increases utilization of processor and other elements within a computer system. So we should try to maximize the number of ready-to-run programs within a system. In fact, if these programs belong to different users then we have achieved sharing of the computer system resource amongst many users. Such a system is called a time sharing system.

We had observed that every time we switch the context of use of a processor we have some over head. For instance, we must know where in the instruction sequence was the program suspended. We need to know the program counter (or the instruction address) to resume a suspended program. In addition, we may have some intermediate values stored in registers at the time of suspension. These values may be critical for subsequent instructions. All this information also must be stored safely some where at the time of suspension (i.e. before context of use is switched). When we resume a suspended program we must reload all this information (before we can actually resume). In essence, a switch in the context of use has its overhead. When the number of resident user programs competing for the same resources increases, the frequency of storage, reloads and wait periods also increase. If the over heads are high or the context switching is too frequent, the users will have to wait longer to get their programs executed. In other words, response time of the system will become longer. Generally, the response time of a system is defined as the time interval which spans the time from the last character input to the first character of output. It is important that when we design a time sharing system we keep the response time at some acceptable level. Otherwise the advantage of giving access to, and sharing, the resource would be lost. A system which we use to access book information in a library is a time-shared system. Clearly, the response time should be such that it should be acceptable, say a few seconds. A library system is also an on-line system. In an online system, devices (which can include instrumentation in a plant) are continuously monitored (observed) by the computer system. If in an online system the response time is also within some acceptable limits then we say it is a real-time system. For instance, the airlines or railway booking office usually has a real-time online reservation system.

A major area of research in OS is performance evaluation. In performance evaluation we study the percentage utilization of processor time, capacity utilization of memory, response time and of course, the throughput of the over all computer system.

Process States

Process States: In the previous example we have seen a few possibilities with regards to the operational scenarios. For instance, we say that a process is in run state (or mode) when it is engaging the processor. It is in wait state (or mode) when it is waiting for an IO to be completed. It may be even in wait mode when it is ready-to-run but the processor may not be free as it is currently engaged by some other process.

Each of such identifiable states describe current operational conditions of a process. A study of process states helps to model the behavior for analytical studies.

For instance, in a simplistic model we may think of a five state model. The five states are: new-process, ready-to-run, running, waiting-on-IO and exit. The names are self- explanatory.

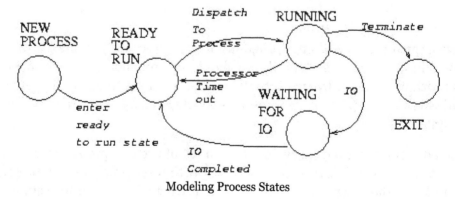

Modeling Process States

The new process is yet to be listed by an OS to be an active process that can be scheduled to execute. It enters the ready to run state when it is identified for future scheduling. Only then it may run. Once a processor is available then one of the ready to run processes may be chosen to run. It moves to the state "running". During this run it may be timed out or may have to wait for an IO to be completed. If it moves to the state of waiting for IO then it moves to ready to run state when the IO is completed. When a process terminates its operation it moves to exit state. All of these transitions are expressed in the figure.

Process States: Management Issues

Process states: Management issues An important point to ponder is: what role does an OS play as processes migrate from one state to another?

When a process is created the OS assigns it an id and also creates a data structure to record its progress. At some point in time OS makes this newly created process ready to run. This is a change in the state of this new process. With multiprogramming there are many ready to run processes in the main memory. The process data structure records state of a process as it evolves. A process marked as ready to run can be scheduled to run. The OS has a dispatcher module which chooses one of the ready to run processes and assigns it to the processor. The OS allocates a time slot to run this process. OS monitors the progress of every process during its life time. A process may, or may not, run for the entire duration of its allocated time slot. It may terminate well before the allocated time elapses or it may seek an IO. Some times a process may not be able to proceed till some event occurs. Such an event is detected as a synchronizing signal. Such a signal may even be received from some other process. When it waits for an IO to be completed, or some signal to arrive, the process is said to be blocked .OS must reallocate the processor now. OS marks this process as blocked for IO. OS must monitor all the IO activity to be able to detect completion of some IO or occurrence of some event. When that happens, the OS modifies the process data structure for one of the blocked processes and marks it ready to run. So, we see that OS maintains some data structures for management of processes. It modifies these data structures. In fact OS manages all the migrations between process states.

A Queuing Model

A Queuing Model: Data structures play an important role in management of processes. In general an OS may use more than one data structure in the management of processes. It may maintain a queue for all ready to run processes. It may maintain separate queues for blocked processes. It may even have a separate queue for each of the likely events (including completion of IO). This formulation shown in the figure below is a very flexible model useful in modeling computer system operations. This type of model helps in the study and analysis of chosen OS policies.

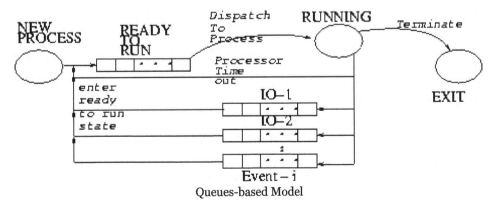

Queues-based Model

As an example, let us consider a first-come-first-served policy for ready-to-run queue. In such a case, processes enjoin the tail end of ready-to-run queue. Also, the processor is assigned to the process at the head of ready-to-run queue. Suppose we wish to compare this policy with another policy in which some processes have a higher priority over other processes. A comparison of these two policies can be used to study the following:

- The average and maximum delays experienced by the lowest priority process.

- Comparison of the best response times and throughputs in the two cases.

- Processor utilization in the two cases. And so on.

This kind of study can offer new insights. As an example, it is important to check what level of prioritization leads to a denial of service (also called starvation).The maxi mum delay for the lowest priority process increases as the range of priority difference increases. So at some threshold it may be unacceptably high. It may even become infinity. There may always be a higher priority process in the ready-to-run queue. As a result lower priority processes have no chance to run. That is starvation.

Scheduling: A Few Scenarios

The OS maintains the data for processes in various queues. The OS keeps the process identifications in each queue. These queues advance based on some policy. These are usually referred to as scheduling policies.

To understand the nature of OS's scheduling policies, let us examine a few situations we experience in daily life. When we wish to buy a railway ticket at the ticket window, the queue is processed using a "all customers are equal policy" i.e. first-come-first-served (FCFS). However, in a photocopy shop, customers with bulk copy requirements are often asked to wait. Some times their jobs are interrupted in favor of shorter jobs. The operators prefer to quickly service short job requests. This way they service a large number of customers quickly. The maximum waiting time for most of the customers is reduced considerably. This kind of scheduling is called shortest job first policy. In a university department, the secretary to the chairman of department always preempts any one's job to attend to the chairman's copy requests. Such a pre-emption is irrespective of the size of the job (or even its usefulness some times). The policy simply is priority based scheduling. The chairman has the highest priority. We also come across situations, typically in driving license offices and other bureaus, where applications are received till a certain time in the day (say 11:00 a.m.). All such applications are then taken as a batch. These are processed in the office and the out come is announced for all at the same time (say 2:00 p.m.). Next batch of applications are received the following day and that batch is processed next. This kind of scheduling is termed batch processing.

In the context of processes we also need to understand preemptive and non-preemptive operations. Non-preemptive operations usually proceed towards completion uninterrupted. In a non preemptive operation a process may suspend its operations temporarily or completely on its own. A process may suspend its operation for IO or terminate on completion. Note neither of these suspensions are forced upon it externally. On the other hand in a preemptive scheduling a suspension may be enforced by an OS. This may be to attend to an interrupt or because the process may have consumed its allocated time slot and OS must start execution of some other process. Note that each such policy affects the performance of the overall system in different ways.

Choosing a Policy

Depending upon the nature of operations the scheduling policy may differ. For instance, in a university set up, short job runs for student jobs may get a higher priority during assigned laboratory hours. In a financial institution processing of applications for investments may be processed in batches. In a design department projects nearing a dead- line may have higher priority. So an OS policy may be chosen to suit situations with specific requirements. In fact, within a computer system we need a policy to schedule access to processor, memory, disc, IO and shared resource (like printers). For the present we shall examine processor scheduling policies only. Other policy issues shall be studied later.

Policy Selection: A scheduling policy is often determined by a machine's configuration and usage. We consider processor scheduling in the following context:

- We have only one processor in the system.

- We have a multiprogramming system i.e. there may be more than one ready-to- run program resident in main memory.

- We study the effect (of the chosen scheduling policy) on the following:

    o   The response time to users

    o   The turn around time (The time to complete a task).

    o   The processor utilization.

    o   The throughput of the system (Overall productivity of the system)

    o   The fairness of allocation (includes starvation).

    o   The effect on other resources.

A careful examination of the above criterion indicates that the measures for response time and turn around are user centered requirements. The processor utilization and throughput are system centered considerations. Last two affect both the users and system. It is quite possible that a scheduling policy satisfies users needs but fails to utilize processor or gives a lower throughput. Some other policy may satisfy system centered requirements but may be poor from users point of view. This is precisely what we will like to study. Though ideally we strive to satisfy both the user's and system's requirements, it may not be always possible to do so. Some compromises have to be made. To illustrate the effect of the choice of a policy, we evaluate each policy for exactly the same operational scenario. So, we set to choose a set of processes with some pre-assigned characteristics and evaluate each policy. We try to find out to what extent it meets a set criterion. This way we can compare these policies against each other.

Comparison of Policies

We begin by assuming that we have 5 processes p1 through p5 with processing time requirements as shown in the figure below at (A).

- The jobs have run to completion.

- No new jobs arrive till these jobs are processed.

- Time required for each of the jobs is known apriori.

- During the run of jobs there is no suspension for IO operations.

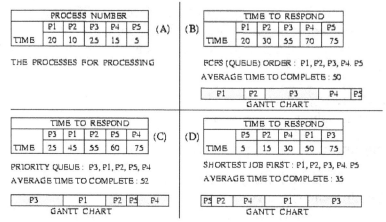

Comparison of three non-preemptive scheduling policies

We assume non-preemptive operations for comparison of all the cases. We show the processing of jobs on a Gantt chart. Let us first assume processing in the FCFS or internal queue order i.e. p1, p2, p3, p4 and p5). Next we assume that jobs are arranged in a priority queue order). Finally, we assume shortest job first order. We compare the figures of merit for each policy. Note that in all we process 5 jobs over a total time of 75 time units. So throughput for all the three cases is same. However, the results are the poorest (52 units) for priority schedule, and the best for Shortest-job-first schedule. In fact, it is well known that shortest-job-first policy is optimal.

Pre-emptive Policies

We continue with our example to see the application of pre-emptive policies. These policies are usually followed to ensure fairness. First, we use a Round-Robin policy i.e. allocate time slots in the internal queue order. A very good measure of fairness is the difference between the maximum and minimum time to complete. Also, it is a good idea to get some statistical measures of spread around the average value. In the figure below we compare four cases. These cases are:

- The Round-Robin allocation with time slice = 5 units. (CASE B)

- The Round-Robin allocation with time slice = 10 units. (CASE C)

- Shortest Job First within the Round-Robin; time slice = 5 units. (CASE D)

- Shortest Job First within the Round-Robin; time slice = 10 units. (CASE E)

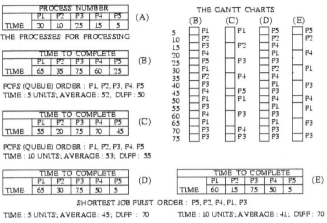

Comparison of Pre-emptive policy schedules

One of the interesting exercises is to find a good value for time slice for processor time allocation. OS designers spend a lot of time finding a good value for time slice.

Yet Another Variation

So far we had assumed that all jobs were present initially. However, a more realistic situation is processes arrive at different times. Each job is assumed to arrive with an estimate of time required to complete. Depending upon the arrival time and an estimated remaining time to complete jobs at hand, we can design an interesting variation of the shortest job first policy. It takes in to account the time which is estimated to be remaining to complete a job.

We could have used a job's service start time to compute the ``time required for com- pletion" as an alternative.

Also note that this policy may lead to starvation. This should be evident from the figure, the way job P3 keeps getting postponed. On the whole, though, this is a very good policy. However, some corrections need to be made for a job that has been denied service for a long period of time. This can be done by introducing some kind of priority (with jobs) which keeps getting revised upwards whenever a job is denied access for a long period of time. One simple way of achieving fairness is to keep a count of how often a job has been denied access to the processor. Whenever this count exceeds a certain threshold value this job must be scheduled during the next time slice.

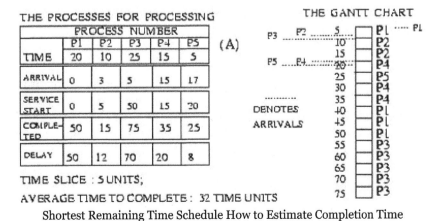

Shortest Remaining Time Schedule How to Estimate Completion Time

We made an assumption that OS knows the processing time required for a process. In practice an OS estimates this time. This is done by monitoring a process's current estimate and past activity. This can be done by monitoring a process's current estimate and past activity as explained in the following example.

First Scenario   Second Scenario

| 10 | 10 | 10 | 10 | 10 | 10 | | 1.7 | 2.9 | 1.9 | 3.7 | 2.5 | 1.8 |

Processor time utilisation

Consider we have a process P. The OS allocates it a fixed time slice of 10 ms each time P gets to run. As shown in the Figure in the first case it uses up all the time every time. The obvious conclusion would be that 10 ms is too small a time slice for the process P. May be it should be allocated higher time slices like 20 ms albeit at lower priority. In the second scenario we notice that except once, P never really uses more than 3 ms time. Our obvious conclusion would be that we are allocating P too much time.

The observation made on the above two scenario offers us a set of strategies. We could base our judgment for the next time allocation using one of the following methods:

- Allocate the next larger time slice to the time actually used. For example, if time slices could be 5, 10, 15 … ms then use 5 ms for the second scenario and 15 for the first (because 10 ms is always used up).

- Allocate the average over the last several time slice utilizations. This method gives all the previous utilizations equal weights to find the next time slice allocation.

- Use the entire history but give lower weights to the utilization in past, which means that the last utilization gets the highest, the previous to the last a little less and so on. This is what the exponential averaging technique does.

Exponential Averaging Technique

We denote our current, nth, CPU usage burst by tn. Also, we denote the average of all past usage bursts up to now by τ_n. Using a weighting factor $0 \leq \alpha \leq 1$ with tn and $1- \alpha$ with τ_n, we estimate the next CPU usage burst. The predicted value of τ_{n+1} is computed

as : $\tau_{n+1} = \alpha * t_n + (1-\alpha) * \tau_n$ This formula is called an exponential averaging formula.

Let us briefly examine the role of α. If it is equal to 1, then we note that the past history is ignored completely. The estimated next burst of usage is same as the immediate past utilization. If α is made 0 then we ignore the immediate past utilization altogether.

Obviously both would be undesirable choices. In choosing a value of α in the range of 0 to 1 we have an opportunity to weigh the immediate past usage, as well as, the previous history of a process with decreasing weight. It is worth while to expand the formula further.

$$\tau_{n+1} = \alpha * t_n + (1-\alpha)^* \tau_n = \alpha * t_n + \alpha *(1-\alpha)* t_{n-1} + (1-\alpha)^* \tau_{n-1}$$

which on full expansion gives the following expression:

$$t_{n+1} = \alpha *t_n + (1-\alpha)^* t_{n-1} + \alpha *(1-\alpha)2 *t_{n-2} + \alpha *(1-\alpha)3 * t_{n-3}...$$

A careful examination of this formula reveals that successive previous bursts in history get smaller weights.

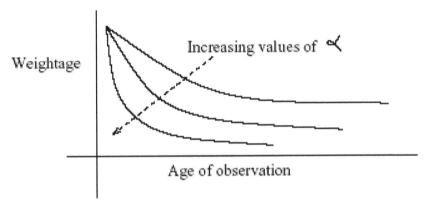

Processor time utilisation

In Figure we also see the effect of the choice of α has in determining the weights for past utilizations.

Multiple Queues Schedules It is a common practice to associate some priority depending upon where the process may have originated. For instance, systems programs may have a higher priority over the user programs. Within the users there may be level of importance. In an on-line system the priority may be determined by the criticality of the source or destination. In such a case, an OS may maintain many process queues, one for each level of priority. In a real-time system we may even follow an earliest deadline first schedule. This policy introduces a notion priority on the basis of the deadline. In general, OSs schedule processes with a mix of priority and fairness considerations.

Two Level Schedules It is also a common practice to keep a small number of processes as ready-to-run in the main memory and retain several others in the disks. As processes in the main memory block, or exit, processes from the disk may be loaded in the main memory. The process of moving processes in and out of main memory to disks is called swapping. The OSs have a swapping policy which may be determined by how "big" the process is. This may be determined by the amount of its storage requirement and how long it takes to execute. Also, what is its priority. We will learn more about on swapping in memory management chapter.

What Happens when Context is Switched?

We will continue to assume that we have a uni-processor multi-programming environment. We have earlier seen that only ready-to-run, main memory resident processes can be scheduled for execution. The OS usually manages the main memory by dividing it into two major partitions. In one partition, which is entirely for OS management, it keeps a record of all the processes which are currently resident in memory. This information may be organized as a single queue or a priority multiple queue or any other form that the designer may choose. In the other part, usually for user processes, all the processes that are presently active are resident.

An OS maintains, and keeps updating, a lot of information about the resources in use for a running process. For instance, each process in execution uses the program counter, registers and other resources within the CPU. So, whenever a process is switched, the OS moves out, and brings in, considerable amount of context switching information as shown in Figure. We see that process P_x is currently executing (note that the program counter is pointing in executable code area of P_x). Let us now switch the context in favor of running process P y. The following must happen:

- All the current context information about process P_x must be updated in its own context area.

- All context information about process P_y must be downloaded in its own context area.

- The program counter should have an address value to an instruction of process P_y. and process P_y must be now marked as "running".

The process context area is also called process control block. As an example when the process P_x is switched the information stored is:

1. Program counter

2. Registers (like stack, index etc.) currently in use

3. Changed state (changed from Running to ready-to-run)

4. The base and limit register values

5. IO status (files opened; IO blocked or completed etc.)

6. Accounting

7. Scheduling information

8. Any other relevant information.

When the process P_y is started its context must be loaded and then alone it can run.

Kernel Architecture: Shells

Most modern operating system distinguishes between a user process and a system process or utility. The user processes may have fewer privileges. For instance, the Unix and its derivatives permit user processes to operate within a shell.

This mode of operation shields the basic kernel of the operating system from direct access by a user process. The kernel is the one that provides OS services by processing system calls to perform IO or do any other form of process management activity – like delete a certain process. User processes can however operate within a shell and seek kernel services. The shell acts as a command interpreter. The command and its arguments are analyzed by the shell and a request is made to the kernel to provide the required service. There are times when a user needs to give a certain sequence of commands. These may form a batch file or a user may write a shell script to achieve the objective. This brings us essentially understand how operating systems handle system calls.

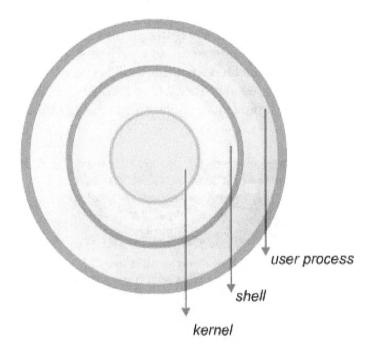

System Calls

As we explained earlier most user processes require a system call to seek OS services. Below we list several contexts in which user processes may need to employ a system call for getting OS services. The list below is only a representative list which shows a few user process activities that entail system calls. For instance it may need in process context (1-3), file and IO management context (4-6), or a network communication context (7-10).

1. To create or terminate processes.

2. To access or allocate memory.

3. To get or set process attributes.

4. To create, open, read, write files.

5. To change access rights on files.

6. To mount or un-mount devices in a file system.

7. To make network connections.

8. Set parameters for the network connection.

9. Open or close ports of communication.

10. To create and manage buffers for device or network communication.

Layered Design

A well known software engineering principle in the design of systems is: the separation of concerns. This application of this concept leads to structured and modular designs. Such are also quite often more maintainable and extensible. This principle was applied in the design of Unix systems. The result is the layered design as shown in the figure. In the context of the layered design of Unix it should be remarked that the design offers easy to user layers hiding unnecessary details as is evident from the figure. Unix has benefited from this design approach. With layering and modularization, faults can be easily isolated and traceable to modules in Unix. This makes Unix more maintainable. Also, this approach offers more opportunities to add utilities in Unix – thus making it an extensible system.

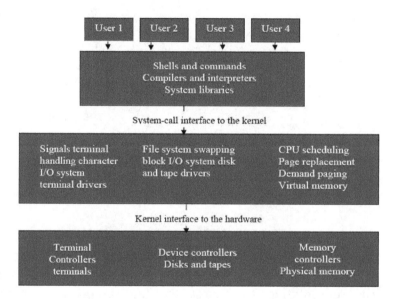

Unix Viewed as a Layered OS

The Virtual Machine Concept

One of the great innovations in the OS designs has been to offer a virtual machine. A virtual machine is an illusion of an actual machine by offering a form of replication of the same operating environment. This is achieved by clever scheduling as illustrated in the figure. As an illustration of such illusion consider spooling. Suppose a process seeks to output on a printer while the printer is busy. OS schedules it for later operation by spooling the output in an area of disk. This gives the process which sought the output, an impression that the print job has been attended to.

The figure depicts the manner in which the clever notion of virtual machine to support operation of multiple processes. OS ensures that each process gets an impression that all the resources of the system are available to each of the processes.

The notion of virtual machine has also been utilized to offer operating of one machine environment within the operative framework of another OS. For instance, it is a common knowledge that on a

Sun machine one can emulate an offer operational environment of Windows-on-Intel (WINTEL).

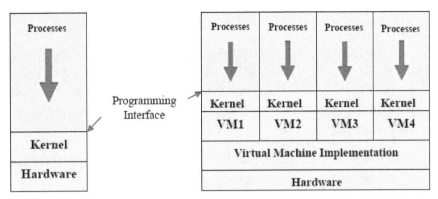

System models. (1) Non-virtual machine. (2) Virtual machine.

As an avid reader may have observed, each process operates in its own virtual machine environment, the system security is considerably enhanced. This a major advantage of employing the virtual machine concept. A good example of a high level virtual machine is when uses Java Virtual machine. It is an example which also offers interoperability.

System Generation

System generation is often employed at the time of installation as well as when upgrades are done. In fact, it reflects the ground reality to the OS. During system generation all the system resources are identified and mapped to the real resources so that the OS gets the correct characteristics of the resources. For instance, the type of modem used, its speed and protocol need to be selected during the system generation. The same applies for the printer, mouse and all the other resources used in a system. If we upgrade to augment RAM this also need to be reflected. In other words OS needs to selected the correct options to map to the actual devices used in a system.

Linux: An Introduction

Linux is a Unix like operating system for PCs. It is also POSIX complaint. It was first written by Linus Torvalds, a student from Finland, who started the work on it in 1991 as an academic project. His primary motivation was to learn more about the capabilities of a 386 processor for task switching. As for writing an OS, he was inspired by the Minix OS developed by Prof. Andrew Tanenbaum (from Vrije Universiteit, Amsterdam, The Netherlands Personal website. Minix was offered by Prof. Tanenbaum as a teaching tool to popularize teaching of OS course in Universities. Here are two mails Mr. Torvalds had sent to the Minix mail group and which provide the genesis of Linux.

Truly speaking, Linux is primarily the kernel of an OS. An operating system is not just the kernel. Its lots of "other things" as well. Today an OS supports a lot of other useful software within its operative environments. OS quite commonly support compilers, editors, text formatters, mail software and many other things. In this case of the "other things" were provided by Richard Stallman's GNU project. Richard Stallman started the GNU movement in 1983. His desire was to have a UNIX like free operating system.

Linux borrows heavily from ideas and techniques developed for Unix. Many programs that now run under Linux saw their first implementation in BSD. X-windows system that Linux uses, was developed at MIT. So maybe we could think of Linux as

Linux = Unix + Ideas from (BSD + GNU+ MIT+ ......) and still evolving.

Linux continues to evolve from the contributions of many independent developers who cooperate. The Linux repository is maintained by Linux Torvalds and can be accessed on the internet. Initially, Linux did not support many peripherals and worked only on a few processors. It is important to see how the Linux community has grown and how the contributions have evolved Linux into a full fledged OS in its own right.

The features have enhanced over time. The table below describes how incrementally the features got added, modified or deleted.

Version	Release Date	Features
Version 0.01	May 1991	- Linux kernel running on Intel 386 processor. - Supported by Minix file system. - No networking and very limited device support.
Version 1.00	March 1994	- Support for TCP/IP NETWORKING. - BSD sockets supported. - Enhanced file system support. (See the section on file systems) - Support for SCSI drives. - More hardware supported. - Still single processor x86 machines.
Version 1.2	March 1995	- Support added for several processors: (Alpha, Sparc, Mips) In Uni-processors configurations only.
Version 2.0	June 1996	- More platforms added. also, most importantly, support for multiprocessor architectures (SMP) added.
Version 2.2	January 1999	- More hardware devices supported. - More platforms: m68k Power PC. - Better CD ROM support............
Version	Release Date	Features
Version 2.4	January 2001	- This release is notable for making the large scale proliferation of Linux into the PC market. - Support was added for ISA (Industry Standard Architecture), USB Universal Serial Bus, PC Card Support.
Version 2.6	December 2003	- Partly preemptable kernel. More user responsive. Before this the Linux kernel was non-preemptable. - More easily adapted for embedded applications.(muLinux integrated) - More acceptable to large servers. (They got both design wins) - User mode Linux (port of Linux on Linux). - Better security.

The Linux Distribution

The best known distributions are from RedHat, Debian and Slackware. There are other distributions like SuSE and Caldera and Craftworks.

There are many free down loads available. It is advisable to look up the internet for these. We shall list some of the URLs at the end of the session as references and the reader is encouraged to look these up for additional information on Linux.

Linux Design Considerations

Linux is a Unix like system which implies it is a multi-user, multi-tasking system with its file system as well as networking environment adhering to the Unix semantics. From the very beginning Linux has been designed to be Posix compliant. One of the advantages today is the cluster mode of operation. Many organizations operate Linux clusters as servers, search engines. Linux clusters operate in multiprocessor environment. The most often cited and a very heavily used environment using Linux clusters is the famous Google search engine. Google uses geographically distributed clusters, each having any where up to 1000 Linux machines.

Components of Linux

Like Unix it has three main constituents. These are:

1. Kernel

2. System libraries

3. System utilities.

Amongst these the kernel is the core component. Kernel manages processes and also the virtual memory. System libraries define functions that applications use to seek kernel services without exercising the kernel code privileges. This isolation of privileges reduces the kernel overheads enormously. Like in Unix, the utilities are specialized functions like "sort" or daemons like login daemons or network connection management daemons.

system management programs	user processes	user utility programs	compilers
system shared libraries			
Linux kernel			
loadable kernel modules			

References

- Larabel, Michael (January 16, 2014). "Valve's VOGL OpenGL Debugger Should Be Great". Journal. Phoronix. Retrieved June 12, 2014

- Rubenstein, John. "Jon Rubinstein sends message to HP staff; Addresses TouchPad reviews". WebOS Nation. Retrieved 30 November 2015

- Clark, Don; Wingfield, Nick (May 23, 2005). "Apple Explores Use Of Chips From Intel For Macintosh Line". The Wall Street Journal. Dow Jones & Company. Retrieved February 8, 2009

- Editors, Macworld (2014-01-22). Total OS X Mavericks Superguide: Everything you need to know about Apple's newest operating system. IDG Consumer & SMB, Inc. ISBN 9781937821388

- Grothaus, Michael (April 12, 2011). "Mac OS X Lion to tone down the Aqua". The Unofficial Apple Weblog. AOL. Retrieved April 9, 2012

- Ritchie, D.M. (October 1984), "The UNIX System: The Evolution of the UNIX Time-sharing System", AT&T Bell Laboratories Technical Journal, 63 (8): 1577

- Torvalds, Linus and Diamond, David, Just for Fun: The Story of an Accidental Revolutionary, 2001, ISBN 0-06-662072-4

- Slivka, Eric (February 17, 2012). "Apple Removes X11 in OS X Mountain Lion, Shifts Support to Open Source

XQuartz". MacRumors. Retrieved February 23, 2012

- Stein, Scott (May 11, 2011). "First Take: Samsung Series 5 Chromebook, the future of Netbooks?". Journal. CNET. Retrieved June 12, 2014

- Linux Devices (November 28, 2006). "Trolltech rolls "complete" Linux smartphone stack". Archived from the original on May 25, 2012. Retrieved January 12, 2017

- Larabel, Michael (June 5, 2014). "There's Now 500 Games On Steam For Linux". Journal. Phoronix. Retrieved June 12, 2014

- Eckert, Jason W. (2012). Linux+ Guide to Linux Certification (Third ed.). Boston, Massachusetts: Cengage Learning. p. 33. ISBN 978-1111541538. Retrieved April 14, 2013

- John Foley (October 20, 2004). "Windows XP SP2 Distribution Surpasses 100 Million". InformationWeek. UBM TechWeb. Retrieved January 3, 2011

2

File System Management and Memory Management

The information stored in the non-volatile secondary memory amounts to files in a system. Since all information regardless of its type is a file, the storage system of a computer can contain huge number of files. File system does the needful in handling this problem. It controls the way data is stored and recovered. This chapter has been carefully written to provide an easy understanding of the varied facets of file system and management in an operating system.

File

What Are Files?

Suppose we are developing an application program. A program, which we prepare, is a file. Later we may compile this program file and get an object code or an executable. The executable is also a file. In other words, the output from a compiler may be an object code file or an executable file. When we store images from a web page we get an image file. If we store some music in digital format it is an audio file. So, in almost every situation we are engaged in using a file. Files are central to our view of communication with IO devices. So let us now ask again: What is a file?

Irrespective of the content any organized information is a file.

So be it a telephone numbers list or a program or an executable code or a web image or a data logged from an instrument we think of it always as a file. This formlessness and disassociation from content was emphasized first in Unix. The formlessness essentially means that files are arbitrary bit (or byte) streams. Formlessness in Unix follows from the basic design principle: keep it simple. The main advantage to a user is flexibility in organizing files. In addition, it also makes it easy to design a file system. A file system is that software which allows users and applications to organize their files. The organization of information may involve access, updates and movement of information between devices. We shall examine the user view of organizing files and the system view of managing the files of users and applications. We shall first look at the user view of files.

User's view of files: The very first need of a user is to be able to access some file he has stored in a non-volatile memory for an on-line access. Also, the file system should be able to locate the file sought by the user. This is achieved by associating an identification for a file i.e. a file must have a name. The name helps the user to identify the file. The file name also helps the file system to locate the file being sought by the user.

Let us consider the organization of my files for the Compilers course and the Operating Systems course on the web. Clearly, all files in compilers course have a set of pages that are related. Also, the pages of the OS system course are related. It is, therefore, natural to think of organizing the files of individual courses together. In other words, we would like to see that a file system supports grouping of related files. In addition, we would like that all such groups be put together under some general category.

This is essentially like making one file folder for the compilers course pages and other one for the OS course pages. Both these folders could be placed within another folder, say COURSES. This is precisely how MAC OS defines its folders. In Unix, each such group, with related files in it, is called a directory. So the COURSES directory may have subdirectories OS and COMPILERS to get a hierarchical file organization. All modern OSs support such a hierarchical file organization. In Figure we show a hierarchy of files. It must be noted that within a directory each file must have a distinct name. For instance, I tend to have ReadMe file in directories to give me the information on what is in each directory. At most there can be only one file with the name "ReadMe" in a directory. However, every subdirectory under this directory may also have its own ReadMe file. Unix emphasizes disassociation with content and form. So file names can be assigned any way.

Some systems, however, require specific name extensions to identify file type. MSDOS identifies executable files with a .COM or .EXE file name extension. Software systems like C or Pascal compilers expect file name extensions of .c or .p (or .pas) respectively. We see some common considerations in associating a file name extension to define a file type.

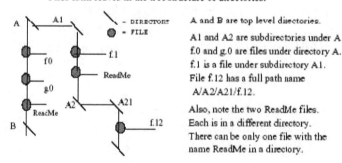

Directory and file orgenision

File Types and Operations

Many OSs, particularly those used in personal computers, tend to use a file type information within a name. Even Unix software support systems use standard file extension names, even though Unix as an OS does not require this. Most PC-based OSs associate file types with specific applications that generate them. For instance, a database generating program will leave explicit information with a file descriptor that it has been generated by a certain database program. A file descriptor is kept within the file structure and is often used by the file system software to help OS provide file management services. MAC OS usually stores this information in its resource fork which is a part of its file descriptors.

This is done to let OS display the icons of the application environment in which this file was created. These icons are important for PC users. The icons offer the operational clues as well. In Windows, for instance, if a file has been created using *notepad* or *word* or has been stored from the browser, a corresponding give away icon appears. In fact, the OS assigns it a file type. If the icon has an Adobe sign on it and we double click on it the acrobat reader opens it right away. Of course, if we choose to open any of the files differently, the OS provides us that as a choice (often using the right button).

For a user the extension in the name of a file helps to identify the file type. When a user has a very large number of files, it is very helpful to know the type of a file from its name extensions. In Table, we have many commonly used file name extensions. PDP-11 machines, on which Unix was originally designed, used an octal 0407 as a magic number to identify its executable files. This number actually was a machine executable jump instruction which would simply set the program counter to fetch the first executable instruction in the file. Modern systems use many magic numbers to identify which application created or will execute a certain file.

Usage	File extension used	Associated Functionality
An ASCII text file	.txt, .doc	A simple text file
A Word processing file	.wp, .tex	Usually for structured documents
Program files	.c, .p, .f77, .asm	C, Pascal, Fortran, or assembly code
Print of view	.ps, .gif, .dvi	Printing and viewing images, documents
Scripting	.pl, .BAT, .sh	For shell scripts or Web CGI
Program library	.lib	Library routines in packages
Archive generation	.arc, .zip, .tar	Compression and long-term storage
Files that execute	.exe, .out, .bin	Compiler generated executable files
Object codes	.o	Often need linking to execute

File extension and its context of use

In addition to the file types, a file system must have many other pieces of information that are important. For instance, a file system must know at which location a file is placed in the disk, it should know its size, when was it created, i.e. date and time of creation.

In addition, it should know who owns the files and who else may be permitted access to *read, write* or *execute*. We shall next dwell upon these operational issues.

File operations: As we observed earlier, a file is any organized information. So at that level of abstraction it should be possible for us to have some logical view of files, no matter how these may be stored. Note that the files are stored within the secondary storage. This is a physical view of a file. A file system (as a layer of software) provides a logical view of files to a user or to an application. Yet, at another level the file system offers the physical view to the OS. This means that the OS gets all the information it needs to physically locate, access, and do other file based operations whenever needed. Purely from an operational point of view, a user should be able to create a file. We will also assume that the creator owns the file. In that case he may wish to save or store this file. He should be able to read the contents of the file or even write into this file. Note that a user needs the write capability to update a file. He may wish to display or rename or append this file. He may even wish to make another copy or even delete this file. He may even wish to operate with two or more files. This may entail cut or copy from one file and paste information on the other.

Other management operations are like indicating who else has an authorization of an access to *read* or *write* or *execute* this file. In addition, a user should be able to move this file between his directories. For all of these operations the OS provides the services. These services may even be obtained from within an application like mail or a utility such as an editor. Unix provides a visual editor vi for ASCII file editing. It also provides another editor *sed* for stream editing. MAC OS and PCs provide a range of editors like SimpleText.

Usage	Editor based operation	OS terminology and description
Create	Under FILE menu NEW	A CREATE command is available with explicit read / write option
Open	Under FILE menu OPEN	An OPEN command is available with explicit read / write option
Close	Under FILE menu CLOSE Also when you choose QUIT	A file CLOSE option is available
Read	Open , to read	Specified at the time of open
Write	Save to write	Specified at the time of open
Rename or copy	Use SAVE AS	Can copy using a copy command
Cut and Paste	Via a buffer	Uses desk top environment CDE
Join file:		Concatenation possible or uses an append at shell level
Delete	Under FILE use delete	Use remove or delete command
Relocate		A move command is available
Alias		A symbolic link is possible
List files	OPEN offers selection	Use a list command in a shell

File operations.

With multimedia capabilities now with PCs we have editors for audio and video files too. These often employ MIDI capabilities. MAC OS has Claris works (or Apple works) and MSDOS-based systems have Office 2000 suite of packaged applications which provide the needed file oriented services.

For illustration of many of the basic operations and introduction of shell commands we shall assume that we are dealing with ASCII text files. One may need information on file sizes. More particularly, one may wish to determine the number of lines, words or characters in a file. For such requirements, a shell may have a suite of word counting programs. When there are many files, one often needs longer file names. Often file names may bear a common stem to help us categorize them. For instance, I tend to use "prog" as a prefix to identify my program text files. A programmer derives considerable support through use of regular expressions within file names. Use of regular expressions enhances programmer productivity in checking or accessing file names. For instance, prog* will mean all files prefixed with stem prog, while my file? may mean all the files with prefix my file followed by at most one character within the current directory. Now that we have seen the file operations, we move on to services. Table gives a brief description of the file-oriented services that are made available in a Unix OS. There are similar MS DOS commands. It is a very rewarding experience to try these commands and use regular expression operators like ? and * in conjunction with these commands.

Later we shall discuss some of these commands and other file-related issues in greater depth. Unix, as also the MS environment, allows users to manage the organization of their files. A command which helps viewing current status of files is the *ls* command in Unix (or the *dir* command in MS environment). This command is very versatile. It helps immensely to know various facets and usage options available under the *ls* command. The *ls* command: Unix's *ls* command which lists files and subdirectories in a directory is very revealing. It has many options that offer a wealth of information. It also offers an insight in to what is going on with the files i.e. how the file system is updating the information about files in "inode" which is a short form for an index node in Unix. We shall learn more about inode. In fact, it is very rewarding to study *ls* command in all its details. Table summarizes some of the options and their effects.

Usage	Unix shell command	MS DOS command
Copy a file	cp	COPY
Rename a file	mv	RENAME
Delete a file	rm	DEL
List Files	Is	DIR
Make a directory	mkdir	MKDIR
Change current directory	cd	CHDIR

File oriented Services.

Choose option	To get this information
None chosen	Lists files and directories in a single column list
-I	Lists long reveling file type, permissions, number of links, owner and group ids., file size in bytes, modification date time, name of the file
-d	For each named directory list directory information
-a	List files including those that start with . (period)
-s	Sizes of files in blocks occupied
-t	Print in time sorted order
-u	Print the access time instead of the modification time

Unix is command options.

Using regular expressions: Most operating systems allow use of regular expression operators in conjunction with the commands. This affords enormous flexibility in usage of a command. For instance, one may input a partial pattern and complete the rest by a * or a ? operator. This not only saves on typing but also helps you when you are searching a file after a long time gap and you do not remember the exact file names completely. Suppose a directory has files with names like Comp_page_1.gif, Comp_page_2.gif and Comp_page_1.ps and Comp_page_2.ps. Suppose you wish to list files for page_2. Use a partial name like *ls* C*p*2 or even *2* in *ls* command. We next illustrate the use of operator ?. For instance, use of *ls* my file? in *ls* command will list all files in the current directory with prefix my file followed by at most one character.

Besides these operators, there are command options that make a command structure very flexible. One useful option is to always use the *-i* option with the *rm* command in Unix. A *rm -i* my files* will interrogate a user for each file with prefix my file for a possible removal. This is very useful, as by itself *rm* my file* will remove all the files without any further prompts and this can be very dangerous. A powerful command option within the *rm* command is to use a *-r* option. This results in recursive removal, which means it removes all the files that are linked within a directory tree. It would remove files in the current, as well as, subdirectories all the way down. One should be careful in choosing the options, particularly for remove or delete commands, as information may be lost irretrievably.

It often happens that we may need to use a file in more than one context. For instance, we may need a file in two projects. If each project is in a separate directory then we have two possible solutions. One is to keep two copies, one in each directory or to create a symbolic link and keep one copy. If we keep two unrelated copies we have the problem of consistency because a change in one is not reflected in the other. The symbolic link helps to alleviate this problem. Unix provides the *ln* command to generate a link anywhere regardless of directory locations with the following structure and interpretation: *ln* fileName pseudonym.

Now fileName file has an alias in pseudonym too. Note that the two directories which share a file link should be in the same disk partition. Later, in the chapter on security, we shall observe how this simple facility may also become a security hazard.

File Access Rights

After defining a fairly wide range of possible operations on files we shall now look at the file system which supports all these services on behalf of the OS. In the preamble of this chapter we defined a file system as that software which allows users and applications to organize and manage their files. The organization of information may involve access, updates, and movement of information between devices. Our first major concern is access.

Access permissions: Typically a file may be accessed to read or write or execute.

The usage is determined usually by the context in which the file is created. For instance, a city bus timetable file is created by a transport authority for the benefit of its customers.

So this file may be accessed by all members of public. While they can access it for a read operation, they cannot write into it. An associated file may be available to the supervisor who assigns duties to drivers. He can, not only read but also write in to the files that assign drivers to bus routes. The management at the transport authority can read, write and even execute some files that generate the bus schedules. In other words, a file system must manage access by checking the access rights of users. In general, access is managed by keeping access rights information for each file in a file system.

Who can access files?: Unix recognizes three categories of users of files, e.g. user (usually the user who created it and owns it), the group, and others. The owner may be a person or a program (usually an application or a system-based utility). The notion of "group" comes from software engineering and denotes a team effort. The basic concept is that users in a group may share files for a common project. Group members often need to share files to support each other's activity. Others has the connotation of public usage as in the example above. Unix organizes access as a three bit information for each i.e. owner, group, and others. So the access rights are defined by 9 bits as *rwx rwx rwx* respectively for owner, group and others. The *rwx* can be defined as an octal number too. If all bits are set then we have a pattern 111 111 111 (or 777 in octal) which means the owner has read, write, and execute rights, and the group to which he belongs has also read, write and execute rights, and others have read, write and execute rights as well. A pattern of 111 110 100 (or 764 octal, also denoted as *rwx rw- r-*) means the owner has read, write, and execute permissions; the group has read and write permissions but no execute permission and others have only the read permission. Note that Unix group permissions are for all or none. Windows 2000 and NTFS permit a greater degree of refinement on a group of users. Linux allows individual users to make up groups.

File Access and Security Concerns

The owner of a file can alter the permissions using the *chmod* command in Unix. The commonly used format is *chmod* octalPattern fileName which results in assigning the permission interpreted from the octalPattern to the file named fileName. There are other alternatives to *chmod* command like *chmod* changePattern fileName where changePattern may be of the form *go-rw* to denote withdrawal of read write permission from group and others. Anyone can view all the currently applicable access rights using a *ls* command in Unix with *-l* option. This command lists all the files and subdirectories of the current directory with associated access permissions.

Security concerns: Access permissions are the most elementary and constitute a fairly effective form of security measure in a standalone single user system. In a system which may be connected in a network this can get very complex. We shall for now regard the access control as our first line of security. On a PC which is a single-user system there is no security as such as anyone with an access to the PC has access to all the files.

Windows 2000 and XP systems do permit access restriction amongst all the users of the system. These may have users with system administrator privileges. In Unix too, the super-user (root) has access to all the files of all the users. So there is a need for securing files for individual users. Some systems provide security by having a password for files. However, an enhanced level of security is provided by encryption of important files. Most systems provide some form of encryption facility. A user may use his own encryption key to encrypt his file. When someone else accesses an encrypted file he sees a garbled file which has no pattern or meaning. Unix provides a crypt command to encrypt files.

The format of the crypt command is:

crypt EncryptionKey < inputFileName > outputFileName

The EncryptionKey provides a symmetric key, so that you can use the same key to retrieve the old file (simply reverse the roles of inputFileName and outputFileName) We briefly mention about audit trails which are usually maintained in syslog files in Unix systems. In a chapter on security we shall discuss these issues in detail. So far we have dealt with the logical view of a file. Next, we shall address the issues involved in storage and management of files.

File System

In computing, a file system or filesystem is used to control how data is stored and retrieved. Without a file system, information placed in a storage medium would be one large body of data with no way to tell where one piece of information stops and the next begins. By separating the data into pieces and giving each piece a name, the information is easily isolated and identified. Taking its name from the way paper-based information systems are named, each group of data is called a "file". The structure and logic rules used to manage the groups of information and their names is called a "file system".

There are many different kinds of file systems. Each one has different structure and logic, properties of speed, flexibility, security, size and more. Some file systems have been designed to be used for specific applications. For example, the ISO 9660 file system is designed specifically for optical discs.

File systems can be used on numerous different types of storage devices that use different kinds of media. The most common storage device in use today is a hard disk drive. Other kinds of media that are used include flash memory, magnetic tapes, and optical discs. In some cases, such as with tmpfs, the computer's main memory (random-access memory, RAM) is used to create a temporary file system for short-term use.

Some file systems are used on local data storage devices; others provide file access via a network protocol (for example, NFS, SMB, or 9P clients). Some file systems are "virtual", meaning that the supplied "files" (called virtual files) are computed on request (e.g. procfs) or are merely a mapping into a different file system used as a backing store. The file system manages access to both the content of files and the metadata about those files. It is responsible for arranging storage space; reliability, efficiency, and tuning with regard to the physical storage medium are important design considerations.

Origin of the Term

Before the advent of computers the term *file system* was used to describe a method of storing and retrieving paper documents. By 1961 the term was being applied to computerized filing alongside the original meaning. By 1964 it was in general use.

Architecture

A file system consists of two or three layers. Sometimes the layers are explicitly separated, and sometimes the functions are combined.

The *logical file system* is responsible for interaction with the user application. It provides the application program interface (API) for file operations — OPEN, CLOSE, READ, etc., and passes the requested operation to the layer below it for processing. The logical file system "manage[s] open file table entries and per-process file descriptors." This layer provides "file access, directory operations, [and] security and protection."

The second optional layer is the *virtual file system*. "This interface allows support for multiple concurrent instances of physical file systems, each of which is called a file system implementation."

The third layer is the *physical file system*. This layer is concerned with the physical operation of the storage device (e.g.disk). It processes physical blocks being read or written. It handles buffering and memory management and is responsible for the physical placement of blocks in specific locations on the storage medium. The physical file system interacts with the device drivers or with the channel to drive the storage device.

Aspects of File Systems

Space Management

File systems allocate space in a granular manner, usually multiple physical units on the device.

The file system is responsible for organizing files and directories, and keeping track of which areas of the media belong to which file and which are not being used. For example, in Apple DOS of the early 1980s, 256-byte sectors on 140 kilobyte floppy disk used a *track/sector map*.

Name ▲	Size
🗎 99998.txt	1 KB
🗎 99999.txt	1 KB
🗎 100000.txt	1 KB
🗎 mkfile.bat	1 KB
🗎 source.txt	1 KB

Type:	File Folder
Location:	C:\
Size:	488 KB (500,059 bytes)
Size on disk:	390 MB (409,608,192 bytes)
Contains:	100,002 Files, 0 Folders

An example of slack space, demonstrated with 4,096-byte NTFS clusters: 100,000 files, each five bytes per file, which equal to 500,000 bytes of actual data but require 409,600,000 bytes of disk space to store

This results in unused space when a file is not an exact multiple of the allocation unit, sometimes referred to as *slack space*. For a 512-byte allocation, the average unused space is 256 bytes. For 64 KB clusters, the average unused space is 32 KB. The size of the allocation unit is chosen when the file system is created. Choosing the allocation size based on the average size of the files expected to be in the file system can minimize the amount of unusable space. Frequently the default allocation may provide reasonable usage. Choosing an allocation size that is too small results in excessive overhead if the file system will contain mostly very large files.

F (Second Allocation)

File systems may become fragmented

File system fragmentation occurs when unused space or single files are not contiguous. As a file system is used, files are created, modified and deleted. When a file is created the file system allocates space for the data. Some file systems permit or require specifying an initial space allocation and subsequent incremental allocations as the file grows. As files are deleted the space they were allocated eventually is considered available for use by other files. This creates alternating used and unused areas of various sizes. This is free space fragmentation. When a file is created and there is not an area of contiguous space available for its initial allocation the space must be assigned in fragments. When a file is modified such that it becomes larger it may exceed the space initially allocated to it, another allocation must be assigned elsewhere and the file becomes fragmented.

Filenames

A filename (or file name) is used to identify a storage location in the file system. Most file systems have restrictions on the length of filenames. In some file systems, filenames are not case sensitive (i.e., filenames such as FOO and foo refer to the same file); in others, filenames are case sensitive (i.e., the names FOO, Foo and foo refer to three separate files).

Most modern file systems allow filenames to contain a wide range of characters from the Unicode character set. However, they may have restrictions on the use of certain special characters, disallowing them within filenames; those characters might be used to indicate a device, device type, directory prefix, file path separator, or file type.

Directories

File systems typically have directories (also called folders) which allow the user to group files into separate collections. This may be implemented by associating the file name with an index in a table of contents or an inode in a Unix-like file system. Directory structures may be flat (i.e. linear), or allow hierarchies where directories may contain subdirectories. The first file system to support arbitrary hierarchies of directories was used in the Multics operating system. The native file systems of Unix-like systems also support arbitrary directory hierarchies, as do, for example, Apple's Hierarchical File System, and its successor HFS+ in classic Mac OS (HFS+ is still used in macOS), the FAT file system in MS-DOS 2.0 and later versions of MS-DOS and in Microsoft Windows, the NTFS file system in the Windows NT family of operating systems, and the ODS-2 (On-Disk Structure-2) and higher levels of the Files-11 file system in OpenVMS.

Metadata

Other bookkeeping information is typically associated with each file within a file system. The length of the data contained in a file may be stored as the number of blocks allocated for the file or as a byte count. The time that the file was last modified may be stored as the file's timestamp. File systems might store the file creation time, the time it was last accessed, the time the file's metadata was changed, or the time the file was last backed up. Other information can include the file's device type (e.g. block, character, socket, subdirectory, etc.), its owner user ID and group ID, its access permissions and other file attributes (e.g. whether the file is read-only, executable, etc.).

A file system stores all the metadata associated with the file—including the file name, the length of the contents of a file, and the location of the file in the folder hierarchy—separate from the contents of the file.

Most file systems store the names of all the files in one directory in one place—the directory table for that directory—which is often stored like any other file. Many file systems put only some of the metadata for a file in the directory table, and the rest of the metadata for that file in a completely separate structure, such as the inode.

Most file systems also store metadata not associated with any one particular file. Such metadata includes information about unused regions—free space bitmap, block availability map—and information about bad sectors. Often such information about an allocation group is stored inside the allocation group itself.

Additional attributes can be associated on file systems, such as NTFS, XFS, ext2, ext3, some versions of UFS, and HFS+, using extended file attributes. Some file systems provide for user defined attributes such as the author of the document, the character encoding of a document or the size of an image.

Some file systems allow for different data collections to be associated with one file name. These separate collections may be referred to as *streams* or *forks*. Apple has long used a forked file system on the Macintosh, and Microsoft supports streams in NTFS. Some file systems maintain multiple past revisions of a file under a single file name; the filename by itself retrieves the most recent version, while prior saved version can be accessed using a special naming convention such as "filename;4" or "filename(-4)" to access the version four saves ago.

File System as an Abstract User Interface

In some cases, a file system may not make use of a storage device but can be used to organize and represent access to any data, whether it is stored or dynamically generated (e.g. procfs).

Utilities

File systems include utilities to initialize, alter parameters of and remove an instance of the file system. Some include the ability to extend or truncate the space allocated to the file system.

Directory utilities may be used to create, rename and delete *directory entries*, which are also known as *dentries* (singular: *dentry*), and to alter metadata associated with a directory. Directory utilities may also include capabilities to create additional links to a directory (hard links in Unix), to rename parent links (".." in Unix-like operating systems), and to create bidirectional links to files.

File utilities create, list, copy, move and delete files, and alter metadata. They may be able to truncate data, truncate or extend space allocation, append to, move, and modify files in-place. Depending on the underlying structure of the file system, they may provide a mechanism to prepend to, or truncate from, the beginning of a file, insert entries into the middle of a file or delete entries from a file.

Utilities to free space for deleted files, if the file system provides an undelete function, also belong to this category.

Some file systems defer operations such as reorganization of free space, secure erasing of free space, and rebuilding of hierarchical structures by providing utilities to perform these functions at times of minimal activity. An example is the file system defragmentation utilities.

Some of the most important features of file system utilities involve supervisory activities which may involve bypassing ownership or direct access to the underlying device. These include high-performance backup and recovery, data replication and reorganization of various data structures and allocation tables within the file system.

Restricting and Permitting Access

There are several mechanisms used by file systems to control access to data. Usually the intent is to prevent reading or modifying files by a user or group of users. Another reason is to ensure data is modified in a controlled way so access may be restricted to a specific program. Examples include passwords stored in the metadata of the file or elsewhere and file permissions in the form of permission bits, access control lists, or capabilities. The need for file system utilities to be able to access the data at the media level to reorganize the structures and provide efficient backup usually means that these are only effective for polite users but are not effective against intruders.

Methods for encrypting file data are sometimes included in the file system. This is very effective since there is no need for file system utilities to know the encryption seed to effectively manage the data. The risks of relying on encryption include the fact that an attacker can copy the data and use brute force to decrypt the data. Losing the seed means losing the data.

Maintaining Integrity

One significant responsibility of a file system is to ensure that, regardless of the actions by programs accessing the data, the structure remains consistent. This includes actions taken if a program modifying data terminates abnormally or neglects to inform the file system that it has completed its activities. This may include updating the metadata, the directory entry and handling any data that was buffered but not yet updated on the physical storage media.

Other failures which the file system must deal with include media failures or loss of connection to remote systems.

In the event of an operating system failure or "soft" power failure, special routines in the file system must be invoked similar to when an individual program fails.

The file system must also be able to correct damaged structures. These may occur as a result of an operating system failure for which the OS was unable to notify the file system, power failure or reset.

The file system must also record events to allow analysis of systemic issues as well as problems with specific files or directories.

User Data

The most important purpose of a file system is to manage user data. This includes storing, retrieving and updating data.

Some file systems accept data for storage as a stream of bytes which are collected and stored in a manner efficient for the media. When a program retrieves the data, it specifies the size of a memory buffer and the file system transfers data from the media to the buffer. A runtime library routine may sometimes allow the user program to define a *record* based on a library call specifying a length. When the user program reads the data, the library retrieves data via the file system and returns a *record*.

Some file systems allow the specification of a fixed record length which is used for all writes and reads. This facilitates locating the nth record as well as updating records.

An identification for each record, also known as a key, makes for a more sophisticated file system. The user program can read, write and update records without regard to their location. This requires complicated management of blocks of media usually separating key blocks and data blocks. Very efficient algorithms can be developed with pyramid structure for locating records.

Using a File System

Utilities, language specific run-time libraries and user programs use file system APIs to make requests of the file system. These include data transfer, positioning, updating metadata, managing directories, managing access specifications, and removal.

Multiple file Systems within a Single System

Frequently, retail systems are configured with a single file system occupying the entire storage device.

Another approach is to partition the disk so that several file systems with different attributes can be used. One file system, for use as browser cache, might be configured with a small allocation size. This has the additional advantage of keeping the frantic activity of creating and deleting files typical of browser activity in a narrow area of the disk and not interfering with allocations of other files. A similar partition might be created for email. Another partition, and file system might be created for the storage of audio or video files with a relatively large allocation. One of the file systems may normally be set *read-only* and only periodically be set writable.

A third approach, which is mostly used in cloud systems, is to use "disk images" to house additional file systems, with the same attributes or not, within another (host) file system as a file. A common example is virtualization: one user can run an experimental Linux distribution (using the ext4 file system) in a virtual machine under his/her production Windows environment (using NTFS). The ext4 file system resides in a disk image, which is treated as a file (or multiple files, depending on the hypervisor and settings) in the NTFS host file system.

Having multiple file systems on a single system has the additional benefit that in the event of a corruption of a single partition, the remaining file systems will frequently still be intact. This includes virus destruction of the *system* partition or even a system that will not boot. File system utilities which require dedicated access can be effectively completed piecemeal. In addition, defragmentation may be more effective. Several system maintenance utilities, such as virus scans and backups, can also be processed in segments. For example, it is not necessary to backup the file system containing videos along with all the other files if none have been added since the last backup. As for the image files, one can easily "spin off" differential images which contain only "new" data written to the master (original) image. Differential images can be used for both safety concerns (as a "disposable" system - can be quickly restored if destroyed or contaminated by a virus, as the old image can be removed and a new image can be created in matter of seconds, even without automated procedures) and quick virtual machine deployment (since the differential images can be quickly spawned using a script in batches).

Design Limitations

All file systems have some functional limit that defines the maximum storable data capacity within that system. These functional limits are a best-guess effort by the designer based on how large the storage systems are right now and how large storage systems are likely to become in the future. Disk storage has continued to increase at near exponential rates, so after a few years, file systems have kept reaching design limitations that require computer users to repeatedly move to a newer system with ever-greater capacity.

File system complexity typically varies proportionally with the available storage capacity. The file systems of early 1980s home computers with 50 KB to 512 KB of storage would not be a reasonable choice for modern storage systems with hundreds of gigabytes of capacity. Likewise, modern file systems would not be a reasonable choice for these early systems, since the complexity of modern file system structures would quickly consume or even exceed the very limited capacity of the early storage systems.

Types of File Systems

File system types can be classified into disk/tape file systems, network file systems and special-purpose file systems.

Disk File Systems

A *disk file system* takes advantages of the ability of disk storage media to randomly address data in a short amount of time. Additional considerations include the speed of accessing data following that initially requested and the anticipation that the following data may also be requested. This permits multiple users (or processes) access to various data on the disk without regard to the sequential location of the data. Examples include FAT (FAT12, FAT16, FAT32), exFAT, NTFS, HFS and HFS+, HPFS, APFS, UFS, ext2, ext3, ext4, XFS, btrfs, ISO 9660, Files-11, Veritas File System, VMFS, ZFS, ReiserFS and UDF. Some disk file systems are journaling file systems or versioning file systems.

Optical Discs

ISO 9660 and Universal Disk Format (UDF) are two common formats that target Compact Discs, DVDs and Blu-ray discs. Mount Rainier is an extension to UDF supported since 2.6 series of the Linux kernel and since Windows Vista that facilitates rewriting to DVDs.

Flash File Systems

A *flash file system* considers the special abilities, performance and restrictions of flash memory devices. Frequently a disk file system can use a flash memory device as the underlying storage media but it is much better to use a file system specifically designed for a flash device.

Tape File Systems

A *tape file system* is a file system and tape format designed to store files on tape in a self-describing form. Magnetic tapes are sequential storage media with significantly longer random data access times than disks, posing challenges to the creation and efficient management of a general-purpose file system.

In a disk file system there is typically a master file directory, and a map of used and free data regions. Any file additions, changes, or removals require updating the directory and the used/free maps. Random access to data regions is measured in milliseconds so this system works well for disks.

Tape requires linear motion to wind and unwind potentially very long reels of media. This tape motion may take several seconds to several minutes to move the read/write head from one end of the tape to the other.

Consequently, a master file directory and usage map can be extremely slow and inefficient with tape. Writing typically involves reading the block usage map to find free blocks for writing, updating the usage map and directory to add the data, and then advancing the tape to write the data in the correct spot. Each additional file write requires updating the map and directory and writing the data, which may take several seconds to occur for each file.

Tape file systems instead typically allow for the file directory to be spread across the tape intermixed with the data, referred to as *streaming*, so that time-consuming and repeated tape motions are not required to write new data.

However, a side effect of this design is that reading the file directory of a tape usually requires scanning the entire tape to read all the scattered directory entries. Most data archiving software that works with tape storage will store a local copy of the tape catalog on a disk file system, so that adding files to a tape can be done quickly without having to rescan the tape media. The local tape catalog copy is usually discarded if not used for a specified period of time, at which point the tape must be re-scanned if it is to be used in the future.

IBM has developed a file system for tape called the Linear Tape File System. The IBM implementation of this file system has been released as the open-source IBM Linear Tape File System — Single Drive Edition (LTFS-SDE) product. The Linear Tape File System uses a separate partition on the tape to record the index meta-data, thereby avoiding the problems associated with scattering directory entries across the entire tape.

Tape Formatting

Writing data to a tape, erasing, or formatting a tape is often a significantly time-consuming process and can take several hours on large tapes. With many data tape technologies it is not necessary to format the tape before over-writing new data to the tape. This is due to the inherently destructive nature of overwriting data on sequential media.

Because of the time it can take to format a tape, typically tapes are pre-formatted so that the tape user does not need to spend time preparing each new tape for use. All that is usually necessary is to write an identifying media label to the tape before use, and even this can be automatically written by software when a new tape is used for the first time.

Database File Systems

Another concept for file management is the idea of a database-based file system. Instead of, or in addition to, hierarchical structured management, files are identified by their characteristics, like type of file, topic, author, or similar rich metadata.

IBM DB2 for i (formerly known as DB2/400 and DB2 for i5/OS) is a database file system as part of the object based IBM i operating system (formerly known as OS/400 and i5/OS), incorporating a single level store and running on IBM Power Systems (formerly known as AS/400 and iSeries), designed by Frank G. Soltis IBM's former chief scientist for IBM i. Around 1978 to 1988 Frank G. Soltis and his team at IBM Rochester have successfully designed and applied technologies like the database file system where others like Microsoft later failed to accomplish. These technologies are informally known as 'Fortress Rochester' and were in few basic aspects extended from early Mainframe technologies but in many ways more advanced from a technological perspective.

Some other projects that aren't "pure" database file systems but that use some aspects of a database file system:

- Many Web content management systems use a relational DBMS to store and retrieve files. For example, XHTML files are stored as XML or text fields, while image files are stored as blob fields; SQL SELECT (with optional XPath) statements retrieve the files, and allow the use of a sophisticated logic and more rich information associations than "usual file systems". Many CMSs also have the option of storing only metadata within the database, with the standard filesystem used to store the content of files.

- Very large file systems, embodied by applications like Apache Hadoop and Google File System, use some *database file system* concepts.

Transactional File Systems

Some programs need to update multiple files "all at once". For example, a software installation may write program binaries, libraries, and configuration files. If the software installation fails, the program may be unusable. If the installation is upgrading a key system utility, such as the command shell, the entire system may be left in an unusable state.

Transaction processing introduces the isolation guarantee, which states that operations within a transaction are hidden from other threads on the system until the transaction commits, and that interfering operations on the system will be properly serialized with the transaction. Transactions also provide the atomicity guarantee, ensuring that operations inside of a transaction are either all committed or the transaction can be aborted and the system discards all of its partial results. This means that if there is a crash or power failure, after recovery, the stored state will be consistent. Either the software will be completely installed or the failed installation will be completely rolled back, but an unusable partial install will not be left on the system.

Windows, beginning with Vista, added transaction support to NTFS, in a feature called Transactional NTFS, but its use is now discouraged. There are a number of research prototypes of transactional file systems for UNIX systems, including the Valor file system, Amino, LFS, and a transactional ext3 file system on the TxOS kernel, as well as transactional file systems targeting embedded systems, such as TFFS.

Ensuring consistency across multiple file system operations is difficult, if not impossible, without file system transactions. File locking can be used as a concurrency control mechanism for individual files, but it typically does not protect the directory structure or file metadata. For instance, file locking cannot prevent TOCTTOU race conditions on symbolic links. File locking also cannot automatically roll back a failed operation, such as a software upgrade; this requires atomicity.

Journaling file systems are one technique used to introduce transaction-level consistency to file system structures. Journal transactions are not exposed to programs as part of the OS API; they are only used internally to ensure consistency at the granularity of a single system call.

Data backup systems typically do not provide support for direct backup of data stored in a transactional manner, which makes recovery of reliable and consistent data sets difficult. Most backup software simply notes what files have changed since a certain time, regardless of the transactional state shared across multiple files in the overall dataset. As a workaround, some database systems simply produce an archived state file containing all data up to that point, and the backup software only backs that up and does not interact directly with the active transactional databases at all. Recovery requires separate recreation of the database from the state file, after the file has been restored by the backup software.

Network File Systems

A *network file system* is a file system that acts as a client for a remote file access protocol, providing access to files on a server. Programs using local interfaces can transparently create, manage and access hierarchical directories and files in remote network-connected computers. Examples of network file systems include clients for the NFS, AFS, SMB protocols, and file-system-like clients for FTP and WebDAV.

Shared Disk File Systems

A *shared disk file system* is one in which a number of machines (usually servers) all have access to the same external disk subsystem (usually a SAN). The file system arbitrates access to that subsystem, preventing write collisions. Examples include GFS2 from Red Hat, GPFS from IBM, SFS from DataPlow, CXFS from SGI and StorNext from Quantum Corporation.

Special File Systems

A *special file system* presents non-file elements of an operating system as files so they can be acted on using file system APIs. This is most commonly done in Unix-like operating systems, but devices are given file names in some non-Unix-like operating systems as well.

Device File Systems

A *device file system* represents I/O devices and pseudo-devices as files, called device files. Examples in Unix-like systems include devfs and, in Linux 2.6 systems, udev. In non-Unix-like systems, such as TOPS-10 and other operating systems influenced by it, where the full filename or pathname of a file can include a device prefix, devices other than those containing file systems are referred to by a device prefix specifying the device, without anything following it.

Other Special File Systems

- In the Linux kernel, configfs and sysfs provide files that can be used to query the kernel for information and configure entities in the kernel.

- procfs maps processes and, on Linux, other operating system structures into a filespace.

Minimal File System / audio-cassette Storage

The late 1970s saw the development of the microcomputer. Disk and digital tape devices were too expensive for hobbyists. An inexpensive basic data storage system was devised that used common audio cassette tape.

When the system needed to write data, the user was notified to press "RECORD" on the cassette recorder, then press "RETURN" on the keyboard to notify the system that the cassette recorder was recording. The system wrote a sound to provide time synchronization, then modulated sounds that encoded a prefix, the data, a checksum and a suffix. When the system needed to read data, the user was instructed to press "PLAY" on the cassette recorder. The system would *listen* to the sounds on the tape waiting until a burst of sound could be recognized as the synchronization. The system would then interpret subsequent sounds as data. When the data read was complete, the system would notify the user to press "STOP" on the cassette recorder. It was primitive, but it worked (a lot of the time). Data was stored sequentially, usually in an unnamed format, although some systems (such as the Commodore PET series of computers) did allow the files to be named. Multiple sets of data could be written and located by fast-forwarding the tape and observing at the tape counter to find the approximate start of the next data region on the tape. The user might have to listen to the sounds to find the right spot to begin playing the next data region. Some implementations even included audible sounds interspersed with the data.

Flat File Systems

In a flat file system, there are no subdirectories, directory entries for all files are stored in a single directory.

When floppy disk media was first available this type of file system was adequate due to the relatively small amount of data space available. CP/M machines featured a flat file system, where files could be assigned to one of 16 *user areas* and generic file operations narrowed to work on one instead of defaulting to work on all of them. These user areas were no more than special attributes associated with the files, that is, it was not necessary to define specific quota for each of these areas and files could be added to groups for as long as there was still free storage space on the disk. The early Apple Macintosh also featured a flat file system, the Macintosh File System. It was unusual in that the file management program (Macintosh Finder) created the illusion of a partially hierarchical filing system on top of EMFS. This structure required every file to have a unique name, even if it appeared to be in a separate folder. IBM DOS/360 and OS/360 store entries for all files on a disk pack (*volume*) in a directory on the pack called a *Volume Table of Contents* (VTOC).

While simple, flat file systems become awkward as the number of files grows and makes it difficult to organize data into related groups of files.

A recent addition to the flat file system family is Amazon's S3, a remote storage service, which is intentionally simplistic to allow users the ability to customize how their data is stored. The only constructs are buckets (imagine a disk drive of unlimited size) and objects (similar, but not identical to the standard concept of a file). Advanced file management is allowed by being able to use nearly any character (including '/') in the object's name, and the ability to select subsets of the bucket's content based on identical prefixes.

File Systems and Operating Systems

Many operating systems include support for more than one file system. Sometimes the OS and the file system are so tightly interwoven that it is difficult to separate out file system functions.

There needs to be an interface provided by the operating system software between the user and the file system. This interface can be textual (such as provided by a command line interface, such as the Unix shell, or OpenVMS DCL) or graphical (such as provided by a graphical user interface, such as file browsers). If graphical, the metaphor of the *folder*, containing documents, other files, and nested folders is often used.

Unix and Unix-like Operating Systems

Unix-like operating systems create a virtual file system, which makes all the files on all the devices appear to exist in a single hierarchy. This means, in those systems, there is one root directory, and every file existing on the system is located under it somewhere. Unix-like systems can use a RAM disk or network shared resource as its root directory.

Unix-like systems assign a device name to each device, but this is not how the files on that device are accessed. Instead, to gain access to files on another device, the operating system must first be informed where in the directory tree those files should appear. This process is called mounting a file system. For example, to access the files on a CD-ROM, one must tell the operating system "Take the file system from this CD-ROM and make it appear under such-and-such directory". The directory given to the operating system is called the *mount point* – it might, for example, be /media. The /media directory exists on many Unix systems (as specified in the Filesystem Hierarchy Standard) and is intended specifically for use as a mount point for removable media such as CDs, DVDs, USB drives or floppy disks. It may be empty, or it may contain subdirectories for mounting individual devices. Generally, only the administrator (i.e. root user) may authorize the mounting of file systems.

Unix-like operating systems often include software and tools that assist in the mounting process and provide it new functionality. Some of these strategies have been coined "auto-mounting" as a reflection of their purpose.

- In many situations, file systems other than the root need to be available as soon as the operating system has booted. All Unix-like systems therefore provide a facility for mounting file systems at boot time. System administrators define these file systems in the configuration file fstab (*vfstab* in Solaris), which also indicates options and mount points.

- In some situations, there is no need to mount certain file systems at boot time, although their use may be desired thereafter. There are some utilities for Unix-like systems that allow the mounting of predefined file systems upon demand.

- Removable media have become very common with microcomputer platforms. They allow programs and data to be transferred between machines without a physical connection. Common examples include USB flash drives, CD-ROMs, and DVDs. Utilities have therefore been developed to detect the presence and availability of a medium and then mount that medium without any user intervention.

- Progressive Unix-like systems have also introduced a concept called supermounting the Linux supermount-ng project. For example, a floppy disk that has been supermounted can be physically removed from the system. Under normal circumstances, the disk should have been synchronized and then unmounted before its removal. Provided synchronization has occurred, a different disk can be inserted into the drive. The system automatically notices that the disk has changed and updates the mount point contents to reflect the new medium.

- An automounter will automatically mount a file system when a reference is made to the directory atop which it should be mounted. This is usually used for file systems on network servers, rather than relying on events such as the insertion of media, as would be appropriate for removable media.

Linux

Linux supports numerous file systems, but common choices for the system disk on a block device include the ext* family (ext2, ext3 and ext4), XFS, JFS, ReiserFS and btrfs. For raw flash without a flash translation layer (FTL) or Memory Technology Device (MTD), there are UBIFS, JFFS2 and YAFFS, among others. SquashFS is a common compressed read-only file system.

Solaris

Solaris in earlier releases defaulted to (non-journaled or non-logging) UFS for bootable and supplementary file systems. Solaris defaulted to, supported, and extended UFS.

Support for other file systems and significant enhancements were added over time, including Veritas Software Corp. (Journaling) VxFS, Sun Microsystems (Clustering) QFS, Sun Microsystems (Journaling) UFS, and Sun Microsystems (open source, poolable, 128 bit compressible, and error-correcting) ZFS.

Kernel extensions were added to Solaris to allow for bootable Veritas VxFS operation. Logging or Journaling was added to UFS in Sun's Solaris 7. Releases of Solaris 10, Solaris Express, OpenSolaris, and other open source variants of the Solaris operating system later supported bootable ZFS.

Logical Volume Management allows for spanning a file system across multiple devices for the purpose of adding redundancy, capacity, and/or throughput. Legacy environments in Solaris may use Solaris Volume Manager (formerly known as Solstice DiskSuite). Multiple operating systems (including Solaris) may use Veritas Volume Manager. Modern Solaris based operating systems eclipse the need for Volume Management through leveraging virtual storage pools in ZFS.

macOS

macOS (formerly Mac OS X) uses a file system inherited from classic Mac OS called HFS Plus. Apple also uses the term "Mac OS Extended". HFS Plus is a metadata-rich and case-preserving but (usually) case-insensitive file system. Due to the Unix roots of macOS, Unix permissions were added to HFS Plus. Later versions of HFS Plus added journaling to prevent corruption of the file system structure and introduced a number of optimizations to the allocation algorithms in an attempt to defragment files automatically without requiring an external defragmenter.

Filenames can be up to 255 characters. HFS Plus uses Unicode to store filenames. On macOS, the filetype can come from the type code, stored in file's metadata, or the filename extension.

HFS Plus has three kinds of links: Unix-style hard links, Unix-style symbolic links and aliases. Aliases are designed to maintain a link to their original file even if they are moved or renamed; they are not interpreted by the file system itself, but by the File Manager code in userland.

macOS also supported the UFS file system, derived from the BSD Unix Fast File System via NeXT-STEP. However, as of Mac OS X Leopard, macOS could no longer be installed on a UFS volume, nor can a pre-Leopard system installed on a UFS volume be upgraded to Leopard. As of Mac OS X Lion UFS support was completely dropped.

Newer versions of macOS are capable of reading and writing to the legacy FAT file systems (16 & 32) common on Windows. They are also capable of *reading* the newer NTFS file systems for Windows. In order to *write* to NTFS file systems on macOS versions prior to Mac OS X Snow Leopard third party software is necessary. Mac OS X 10.6 (Snow Leopard) and later allow writing to NTFS file systems, but only after a non-trivial system setting change (third party software exists that automates this).

Finally, macOS supports reading and writing of the exFAT file system since Mac OS X Snow Leopard, starting from version 10.6.5.

OS/2

OS/2 1.2 introduced the High Performance File System (HPFS). HPFS supports mixed case file names in different code pages, long file names (255 characters), more efficient use of disk space, an architecture that keeps related items close to each other on the disk volume, less fragmentation of data, extent-based space allocation, a B+ tree structure for directories, and the root directory located at the midpoint of the disk, for faster average access. A Journaled filesystem (JFS) was shipped in 1999.

PC-BSD

PC-BSD is a desktop version of FreeBSD, which inherits FreeBSD's ZFS support, similarly to FreeNAS. The new graphical installer of PC-BSD can handle / *(root) on ZFS* and RAID-Z pool installs and disk encryption using Geli right from the start in an easy convenient (GUI) way. The current PC-BSD 9.0+ 'Isotope Edition' has ZFS filesystem version 5 and ZFS storage pool version 28.

Plan 9

Plan 9 from Bell Labs treats everything as a file and accesses all objects as a file would be accessed (i.e., there is no ioctl or mmap): networking, graphics, debugging, authentication, capabilities, encryption, and other services are accessed via I/O operations on file descriptors. The 9P protocol removes the difference between local and remote files. File systems in Plan 9 are organized with the help of private, per-process namespaces, allowing each process to have a different view of the many file systems that provide resources in a distributed system.

The Inferno operating system shares these concepts with Plan 9.

Microsoft Windows

```
C:\Temp> dir
 Volume in drive C is C
 Volume Serial Number is 74F5-B93C

 Directory of C:\Temp

2009-08-25  11:59    <DIR>          .
2009-08-25  11:59    <DIR>          ..
2007-03-01  11:37         2,321,600 AdobeUpdater12345.exe
2009-04-03  10:01            27,988 dd_depcheckdotnetfx30.txt
2009-04-03  10:01               764 dd_dotnetfx3error.txt
2009-04-03  10:01            32,572 dd_dotnetfx3install.txt
2009-06-09  13:46            35,145 GenProfile.log
2009-08-05  12:11               155 KB969856.log
2009-04-20  08:37               402 MSI29e0b.LOG
2009-04-09  16:34            38,895 offcln11.log
2009-04-03  16:02    <DIR>          OfficePatches
2009-07-14  14:30    <DIR>          OHotfix
2009-08-25  10:52            16,384 Perflib_Perfdata_c30.dat
2009-04-03  10:01             1,744 uxeventlog.txt
2009-08-25  11:42        50,245,632 WFV2F.tmp
2009-04-20  10:07             1,397 {AC76BA86-7AD7-1033-7B44-A81200000003}.ini
2009-04-20  10:13               617 {AC76BA86-7AD7-1033-7B44-A81300000003}.ini
              13 File(s)     52,723,295 bytes
               4 Dir(s)  83,570,208,768 bytes free
```

Directory listing in a Windows command shell

Windows makes use of the FAT, NTFS, exFAT, Live File System and ReFS file systems (the last of these is only supported and usable in Windows Server 2012, Windows Server 2016, Windows 8, Windows 8.1, and Windows 10; Windows cannot boot from it).

Windows uses a *drive letter* abstraction at the user level to distinguish one disk or partition from another. For example, the path C:\WINDOWS represents a directory WINDOWS on the partition represented by the letter C. Drive C: is most commonly used for the primary hard disk drive partition, on which Windows is usually installed and from which it boots. This "tradition" has become so firmly ingrained that bugs exist in many applications which make assumptions that the drive that the operating system is installed on is C. The use of drive letters, and the tradition of using "C" as the drive letter for the primary hard disk drive partition, can be traced to MS-DOS, where the letters A and B were reserved for up to two floppy disk drives. This in turn derived from CP/M in the 1970s, and ultimately from IBM's CP/CMS of 1967.

FAT

The family of FAT file systems is supported by almost all operating systems for personal computers, including all versions of Windows and MS-DOS/PC DOS and DR-DOS. (PC DOS is an OEM version of MS-DOS, MS-DOS was originally based on SCP's 86-DOS. DR-DOS was based on Digital Research's Concurrent DOS, a successor of CP/M-86.) The FAT file systems are therefore well-suited as a universal exchange format between computers and devices of most any type and age.

The FAT file system traces its roots back to an (incompatible) 8-bit FAT precursor in Standalone Disk BASIC and the short-lived MDOS/MIDAS project.

Over the years, the file system has been expanded from FAT12 to FAT16 and FAT32. Various features have been added to the file system including subdirectories, codepage support, extended attributes, and long filenames. Third parties such as Digital Research have incorporated optional support for deletion tracking, and volume/directory/file-based multi-user security schemes to support file and directory passwords and permissions such as read/write/execute/delete access rights. Most of these extensions are not supported by Windows.

The FAT12 and FAT16 file systems had a limit on the number of entries in the root directory of the file system and had restrictions on the maximum size of FAT-formatted disks or partitions.

FAT32 addresses the limitations in FAT12 and FAT16, except for the file size limit of close to 4 GB, but it remains limited compared to NTFS.

FAT12, FAT16 and FAT32 also have a limit of eight characters for the file name, and three characters for the extension (such as .exe). This is commonly referred to as the 8.3 filename limit. VFAT, an optional extension to FAT12, FAT16 and FAT32, introduced in Windows 95 and Windows NT 3.5, allowed long file names (LFN) to be stored in the FAT file system in a backwards compatible fashion.

NTFS

NTFS, introduced with the Windows NT operating system in 1993, allowed ACL-based permission control. Other features also supported by NTFS include hard links, multiple file streams, attribute indexing, quota tracking, sparse files, encryption, compression, and reparse points (directories working as mount-points for other file systems, symlinks, junctions, remote storage links).

exFAT

exFAT is a proprietary and patent-protected file system with certain advantages over NTFS with regard to file system overhead.

exFAT is not backward compatible with FAT file systems such as FAT12, FAT16 or FAT32. The file system is supported with newer Windows systems, such as Windows Server 2003, Windows Vista, Windows 2008, Windows 7, Windows 8, and more recently, support has been added for Windows XP.

exFAT is supported in OS X starting with version 10.6.5 (Snow Leopard). Support in other operating systems is sparse since Microsoft has not published the specifications of the file system and implementing support for exFAT requires a license. exFAT is the only file system that is fully supported on both OS X and Windows that can hold files bigger than 4 GB.

OpenVMS

MVS [IBM Mainframe]

Prior to the introduction of VSAM, OS/360 systems implemented an unusual hybrid file system. The system was designed to easily support removable disk packs, so the information relating to all files on one disk (*volume* in IBM terminology) is stored on that disk in a flat system file called the *Volume Table of Contents* (VTOC). The VTOC stores all metadata for the file. Later a hierarchical directory structure was imposed with the introduction of the *System Catalog*, which can optionally catalog files (datasets) on resident and removable volumes. The catalog only contains information to relate a dataset to a specific volume. If the user requests access to a dataset on an offline volume, and he has suitable privileges, the system will attempt to mount the required volume. Cataloged and non-cataloged datasets can still be accessed using information in the VTOC, bypassing the catalog, if the required volume id is provided to the OPEN request.

Conversational Monitor System

The IBM Conversational Monitor System (CMS) component of VM/370 uses a separate flat file system for each virtual disk (*minidisk*). File data and control information are scattered and intermixed.

The anchor is a record called the *Master File Directory* (MFD), always located in the fourth block on the disk. Originally CMS used fixed-length 800-byte blocks, but later versions used larger size blocks up to 4K. Access to a data record requires two levels of indirection, where the file's directory entry (called a *File Status Table* (FST) entry) points to blocks containing a list of addresses of the individual records.

AS/400 File System

Data on the AS/400 and its successors consists of system objects mapped into the system virtual address space in a single-level store. Many types of AS/400 objects are defined including the directories and files found in other file systems. File objects, along with other types of objects, form the basis of the As/400's support for an integrated relational database.

Other File Systems

- The Prospero File System is a file system based on the Virtual System Model. The system was created by Dr. B. Clifford Neuman of the Information Sciences Institute at the University of Southern California.

- RSRE FLEX file system - written in ALGOL 68.

- The file system of the Michigan Terminal System (MTS) is interesting because: (i) it provides "line files" where record lengths and line numbers are associated as metadata with each record in the file, lines can be added, replaced, updated with the same or different length records, and deleted anywhere in the file without the need to read and rewrite the entire file; (ii) using program keys files may be shared or permitted to commands and programs in addition to users and groups; and (iii) there is a comprehensive file locking mechanism that protects both the file's data and its metadata.

Limitations

Converting the Type of a File System

It may be advantageous or necessary to have files in a different file system than they currently exist. Reasons include the need for an increase in the space requirements beyond the limits of the current file system. The depth of path may need to be increased beyond the restrictions of the file system. There may be performance or reliability considerations. Providing access to another operating system which does not support existing file system is another reason.

In-place Conversion

In some cases conversion can be done in-place, although migrating the file system is more conservative, as it involves a creating a copy of the data and is recommended. On Windows, FAT and FAT32 file systems can be converted to NTFS via the convert.exe utility, but not the reverse. On Linux, ext2 can be converted to ext3 (and converted back), and ext3 can be converted to ext4 (but not back), and both ext3 and ext4 can be converted to btrfs, and converted back until the undo information is deleted. These conversions are possible due to using the same format for the file data itself, and relocating the metadata into empty space, in some cases using sparse file support.

Migrating to a Different File System

Migration has the disadvantage of requiring additional space although it may be faster. The best case is if there is unused space on media which will contain the final file system.

For example, to migrate a FAT32 file system to an ext2 file system. First create a new ext2 file system, then copy the data to the file system, then delete the FAT32 file system.

An alternative, when there is not sufficient space to retain the original file system until the new one is created, is to use a work area (such as a removable media). This takes longer but a backup of the data is a nice side effect.

Long File Paths and Long File Names

In hierarchical file systems, files are accessed by means of a *path* that is a branching list of directories containing the file. Different file systems have different limits on the depth of the path. File systems also have a limit on the length of an individual filename.

Copying files with long names or located in paths of significant depth from one file system to another may cause undesirable results. This depends on how the utility doing the copying handles the discrepancy.

File Storage Management

An operating system needs to maintain several pieces of information that can assist in management of files. For instance, it is important to record when the file was last used and by whom. Also, which are the current processes (recall a process is a program in execution) accessing a particular file. This helps in management of access. One of the important files from the system point of view is the audit trail which indicates who accessed when and did what. As mentioned earlier, these trails are maintained in syslog files under Unix. Audit trail is very useful in recovering from a system crash. It also is useful to detect un-authorized accesses to the system. There is an emerging area within the security community which looks up the audit trails for clues to determine the identity of an intruder.

In Table we list the kind of information which may be needed to perform proper file management. While Unix emphasizes formlessness, it recognizes four basic file types internally. These are ordinary, directory, special, and named. Ordinary files are those that are created by users, programs or utilities. Directory is a file type that organizes files hierarchically, and the system views them differently from ordinary files. All IO communications are conducted as communications to and from special files. For the present we need not concern ourselves with named files. Unix maintains much of this information in a data structure called inode which is a short form for an index node. All file management operations in Unix are controlled and maintained by the information in the inode structure.

We shall now briefly study the structure of inode.

Inode in Unix

In Table we describe typical inode contents. Typically, it offers all the information about access rights, file size, its date of creation, usage and modification. All this information is useful for the management in terms of allocation of physical space, securing information from malicious usage and providing services for legitimate user needs to support applications.

Nature of Information	Its significance	Its use in management
File name	Chosen by its Creator user or a program	To check its uniqueness within a directory
File type	Text, binary, program, etc.	To check its correct usage
Date of creation and last usage	Time and date	Useful for recording identity of user(s)
Current usage	Time and date	identity of all current users
Back-up info.	Time and date	Useful for recovery following a crash
Permissions	rwx information	Controls rw execute + useful for network access
Starting address	Physical mapping	Useful for access
Size	The user must operate within the allocated space	Internal allocation of disk blocks
File structure	Useful in data manipulation	To check its usage

Information required for management of files

Typically, a disk shall have inode tables which point to data blocks. In Figure we show how a disk may have data and inode tables organized. We also show how a typical Unix-based system provides for a label on the disk.

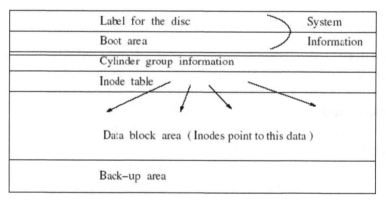

Organistion of inodes.

Item	Description
File type	16 bit information
	Bits 14 - 12 : file type (ordinary; directory; character, etc.)
	Bits 11 - 9 : Execution flags
	Bits 8 - 6 : Owner's rwx information
	Bits 5 - 3 : group's rwx information
	Bits 2 - 0 : other's rwx information
Link count	Number of symbolic references to this file
Owner's id	Login id of the individual who owns this file

Group's id	Group id of the user
File size	Expressed in number of bytes
File address	39 bytes of addressing information
Last access to File	Date and time of last access
Last modified	Date and time of last modification
Last inode modification	Date and time of last inode modification

Inode structure in unix

File Control Blocks

In MS environment the counterpart of inode is FCB, which is a short form for File Control Block. The FCBs store file name, location of secondary storage, length of file in bytes, date and time of its creation, last access, etc. One clear advantage MS has over Unix is that it usually maintains file type by noting which application created it. It uses extension names like *doc, txt, dll,* etc. to identify how the file was created. Of course, notepad may be used to open any file (one can make sense out of it when it is a text file). MS environment uses a simple chain of clusters which is easy to manage files.

The Root File System

At this stage it would be worthwhile to think about the organization and management of files in the root file system. When an OS is installed initially, it creates a root file system. The OS not only ensures, but also specifies how the system and user files shall be distributed for space allocation on the disk storage. Almost always the root file system has a directory tree structure. This is just like the users file organization which we studied earlier in Figure. In OSs with Unix flavors the root of the root file system is a directory. The root is identified by the directory '/'. In MS environment it is identified by 'n'. The root file system has several subdirectories. OS creates disk partitions to allocate files for specific usages. A certain disk partition may have system files and some others may have other user files or utilities. The system files are usually programs that are executable with . bin in Unix and .EXE extension in MS environment.

Under Unix the following convention is commonly employed.

- Subdirectory usr contain shareable binaries. These may be used both by users and the system. Usually these are used in read-only mode.

- Under subdirectories bin (found at any level of directory hierarchy) there are executables. For instance, the Unix commands are under /usr/bin. Clearly, these are shareable executables.

- Subdirectory sbin contains some binaries for system use. These files are used during boot time and on power-on.

- Subdirectories named lib anywhere usually contain libraries. A lib subdirectory may appear at many places. For example, as we explain a little later the graphics library which supports the graphics user interface (GUI) uses the X11 graphics library, and there shall be a lib subdirectory under directory X11.

- Subdirectory etc contains the host related files. It usually has many subdirectories to store device, internet and configuration related information. Subdirectory hosts stores internet addresses of hosts machines which may access this host. Similarly, config subdirectory maintains system configuration information and inet subdirectory maintains internet configuration related information. Under subdirectory dev, we have all the IO device related utilities.

- Subdirectories mnt contain the device mount information (in Linux).

- Subdirectories tmp contain temporary files created during file operation. When you use an editor the OS maintains a file in this directory keeping track of all the edits. Clearly this is its temporary residence.

- Subdirectories var contain files which have variable data. For instance, mail and system log information keeps varying over time. It may also have subdirectories for spools. Spools are temporary storages. For instance, a file given away for printing may be spooled to be picked up by the printer. Even mails may be spooled temporarily.

- All X related file support is under a special directory X11. One finds all X11 library files under a lib directory within this directory.

- A user with name u name would find that his files are under /home/u name. This is also the home directory for the user u name.

- Subdirectories include contain the C header include files.

- A subdirectory marked as yp (a short form for yellow pages) has network information. Essentially, it provides a database support for network operations.

One major advantage of the root file system is that the system knows exactly where to look for some specific routines. For instance, when we give a command, the system looks for a path starting from the root directory and looks for an executable file with the command name specified (usually to find it under one of the bin directories). Users can customize their operational environment by providing a definition for an environment variable PATH which guides the sequence in which the OS searches for the commands. Unix, as also the MS environment, allows users to manage the organization of their files.

One of the commands which helps to view the current status of files is the *ls* command in Unix or the command dir in MS environment.

Block-based File Organization

Recall we observed in chapter 1 that disks are bulk data transfer devices (as opposed to character devices like a keyboard). So data transfer takes place from disks in blocks as large as 512 or 1024 bytes at a time. Any file which a user generates (or retrieves), therefore, moves in blocks. Each operating system has its own block management policy. We shall study the general principles underlying allocation policies. These policies map each linear byte stream into disk blocks. We consider a very simple case where we need to support a file system on one disk. Note a policy on storage management can heavily influence the performance of a file system (which in turn affects the throughput of an OS). File Storage allocation policy: Let us assume we know apriori the sizes of files before their creation. So this information can always be given to OS before a file is created. Consequently, the OS can simply make space available. In such a situation it is possible to follow a pre-allocation policy: find a suitable starting block so that the file can be accommodated in a contiguous sequence of disk blocks. A simple solution would be to allocate a sequence of contiguous blocks as shown in Figure.

The numbers 1, 2, 3 and 4 denote the starting blocks for the four files. One clear advantage of such a policy is that the retrieval of information is very fast. However, note that pre-allocation policy requires apriori knowledge. Also, it is a static policy. Often users' needs develop over time and files undergo changes. Therefore, we need a dynamic policy.

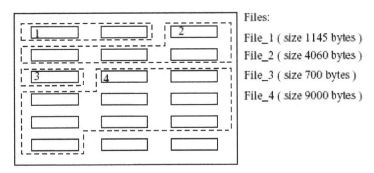

Contiguous allocation

Chained list Allocation : There are two reasons why a dynamic block allocation policy is needed. The first is that in most cases it is not possible to know apriori the size of a file being created. The second is that there are some files that already exist and it is not easy to find contiguous regions. For instance, even though there may be enough space in the disk, yet it may not be possible to find a single large enough chunk to accommodate an incoming file. Also, users' needs evolve and a file during its lifetime undergoes changes. Contiguous blocks leave no room for such changes. That is because there may be already allocated files occupying the contiguous space.

In a dynamic situation, a list of free blocks is maintained. Allocation is made as the need arises. We may even allocate one block at a time from a free space list. The OS maintains a chain of free blocks and allocates next free block in the chain to an incoming file. This way the finally allocated files may be located at various positions on the disk. The obvious overhead is the maintenance of chained links. But then we now have a dynamically allocated disk space. An example is shown in Figure.

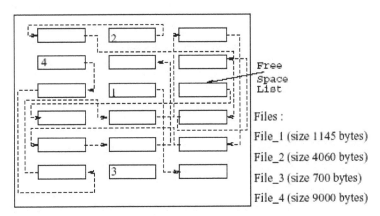

Chained allocation

Chained list allocation does not require apriori size information. Also, it is a dynamic allocation method. However, it has one major disadvantage: random access to blocks is not possible.

Indexed allocation: In an indexed allocation we maintain an index table for each file in its very first block. Thus it is possible to obtain the address information for each of the blocks with only one level of indirection, i.e. from the index. This has the advantage that there is a direct access to every block of the file. This means we truly operate in the direct access mode at the block level.

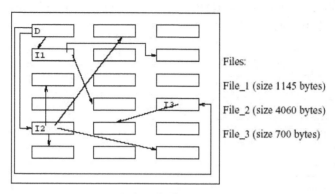

Indexed allocation

In Figure we see that File-2 occupies four blocks. Suppose we use a block I2 to store the starting addresses of these four blocks, then from this index we can access any of the four parts of this file. In a chained list arrangement we would have to traverse the links. In Figure we have also shown D to denote the file's current directory. All files have their own index blocks. In terms of storage the overhead of storing the indices is more than the overhead of storing the links in the chained list arrangements. However, the speed of access compensates for the extra overhead.

Internal and external Fragmentation: In mapping byte streams to blocks we assumed a block size of 1024 bytes. In our example, a file (File 1) of size 1145 bytes was allocated two blocks. The two blocks together have 2048 bytes capacity. We will fill the first block completely but the second block will be mostly empty. This is because only 121 bytes out of 1024 bytes are used. As the assignment of storage is by blocks in size of 1024 bytes the remaining bytes in the second block can not be used. Such non-utilization of space caused internally (as it is within a file's space) is termed as internal fragmentation. We note that initially the whole disk is a free-space list of connected blocks. After a number of file insertions and deletion or modifications the free-space list becomes smaller in size. This can be explained as follows. For instance, suppose we have a file which was initially spread over 7 blocks. Now after a few edits the file needs only 4 blocks. This space of 3 blocks which got released is now not connected anywhere. It is not connected with the free storage list either. As a result, we end up with a hole of 3 blocks which is not connected anywhere. After many file edits and operations many such holes of various sizes get created. Suppose we now wish to insert a moderately large sized file thinking that adequate space should be still available. Then it may happen that the free space list has shrunk so much that enough space is not available. This may be because there are many unutilized holes in the disk. Such non-utilization, which is outside of file space, is regarded as external fragmentation. A file system, therefore, must periodic all perform an operation to rebuild free storage list by collecting all the unutilized holes and linking them back to free storage list. This process is called compaction. When you boot a system, often the compaction gets done automatically. This is usually a part of file system management check. Some run-time systems, like LISP and Java, support periodic automatic compaction. This is also referred to as run-time garbage collection.

Policies In Practice

MS DOS and OS2 (the PC-based systems) use a FAT (file allocation table) strategy. FAT is a table that has entries for files for each directory. The file name is used to get the starting address of the first block of a file. Each file block is chain linked to the next block till an EOF (end of file) is stored in some block. MS uses the notion of a cluster in place of blocks, i.e. the concept of cluster in MS is same as that of blocks in Unix. The cluster size is different for different sizes of disks. For instance, for a 256 MB disk the cluster may have a size of 4 KB and for a disk with size of 1 GB it may be 32 KB. The formula used for determining the cluster size in MS environment is disk-size/64K.

FAT was created to keep track of all the file entries. To that extent it also has the information similar to the index node in Unix. Since MS environment uses chained allocation, FAT also maintains a list of "free" block chains. Earlier, the file names under MS DOS were restricted to eight characters and a three letter extension often indicating the file type like BAT or EXE, etc. Usually FAT is stored in the first few blocks of disk space.

An updated version of FAT, called FAT32, is used in Windows 98 and later systems. FAT32 additionally supports longer file names and file compression. File compression may be used to save on storage space for less often used files. Yet another version of the Windows is available under the Windows NT. This file system is called NTFS. Rather than having one FAT in the beginning of disk, the NTFS file system spreads file tables throughout the disks for efficient management. Like FAT32, it also supports long file names and file compression. Windows 2000 uses NTFS. Other characteristics worthy of note are the file access permissions supported by NTFS.

Unix always supported long file names and most Unix based systems such as Solaris and almost all Linux versions automatically compress the files that have not been used for long. Unix uses indexed allocation. Unix was designed to support truly large files. We next describe how large can be large files in Unix.

Unix file sizes: Unix was designed to support large-scale program development with team effort. Within this framework, it supports group access to very large files at very high speeds. It also has a very flexible organization for files of various sizes. The information about files is stored in two parts. The first part has information about the mode of access, the symbolic links, owner and times of creation and last modification. The second part is a 39 byte area within the inode structure. These 39 bytes are 13, 3 byte address pointers. Of the 39 bytes, first 10 point to the first 10 blocks of a file. If the files are longer then the other 3, 3 byte addresses are used for indirect indexing. So the 11th 3 byte address points to a block that has pointers to real data. In case the file is still larger then the 12th 3 byte address points to an index. This index in turn points to another index table which finally point to data. If the files are still larger then the 13th 3 byte address is used to support a triple indirect indexing. Obviously, Unix employs the indexed allocation.

In Figure we assume a data block size of 1024 bytes. We show the basic scheme and also show the size of files supported as the levels of indirection increase. Physical Layout of Information on Media: In our discussions on file storage and management we have concentrated on logical storage of files. We, however, ignored one very important aspect. And that concerns the physical layout of information on the disk media. Of course, we shall revisit aspects of information map on physical medium later in the chapter on IO device management. For now, we let us examine Figures to see how information is stored, read, and written in to a disk.

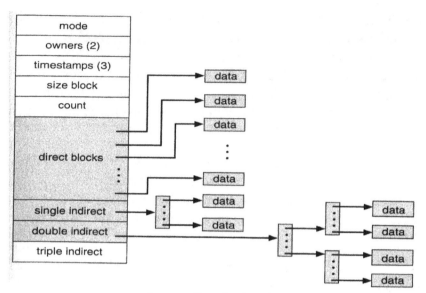

Storage allocation in unix.

In Figure, tracks may be envisaged as rings on a disk platter. Each ring on a platter is capable of storing 1 bit along its width. These 1 bit wide rings are broken into sectors, which serve as blocks. We essentially referred to these as blocks.

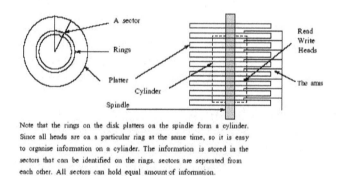

Note that the rings on the disk platters on the spindle form a cylinder. Since all heads are on a particular ring at the same time, so it is easy to organise information on a cylinder. The information is stored in the sectors that can be identified on the rings. sectors are seperated from each other. All sectors can hold equal amount of information.

Figure 2.7: Information storage organisation on disks.

Preamble			Sync		Sync	ECC	
25	8	1	25	1	512	6	22
Header			Pre–amble		Data bytes	Post–amble	

The numbers are in bytes

Information storage in sectors.

This break up into sectors is necessitated because of the physical nature of control required to let the system recognize, where within the tracks blocks begin in a disk. With disks moving at a very high speed, it is not possible to identify individual characters as they are laid out. Only the beginning of a block of information can be detected by hardware control to initiate a stream of bits for either input or output. The read-write heads on the tracks read or write a stream of data along the track in the identified sectors. With multiple disks mounted on a spindle as shown in Figure, it helps to think of a cylinder formed by tracks that are equidistant from the center. Just imagine a large number of tracks, one above the other, and you begin to see a cylinder. These cylinders can be given contiguous block sequence numbers to store information. In fact, this is desirable because then one can access these blocks in sequence without any additional head movement in a head per track disk. The question of our interest for now is: where is inode (or FAT block) located and how it helps to locate the physical file which is mapped on to sectors on tracks which form cylinders.

Disk Partitions

Disk-partitioning is an important notion. It allows a better management of disk space. The basic idea is rather simple. If you think of a disk as a large space then simply draw some boundaries to keep things in specific areas for specific purposes. In most cases the disk partitions are created at the time the disc is formatted. So a formatted disk has information about the partition size.

In Unix oriented systems, a physical partition of a disk houses a file system. Unix also allows creating a logical partition of disk space which may extend over multiple disk drives. In either case, every partition has its own file system management information.

This information is about the files in that partition which populate the file system. Unix ensures that the partitions for the system kernel and the users files are located in different partitions (or file systems). Unix systems identify specific partitions to store the root file system, usually in root partition. The root partition may also co-locate other system functions with variable storage requirements which we discussed earlier. The user files may be in another file system, usually called home. Under Linux, a proc houses all the executable processes.

Under the Windows system too, a hard disk is partitioned. One interesting conceptual notion is to make each such partition that can be taken as a logical drive. In fact, one may have one drive and by partitioning, a user can make the OS offer a possibility to write into each partition as if it was writing in to a separate drive. There are many third-party tools for personal computer to help users to create partitions on their disks. Yet another use in the PC world is to house two operating system, one in each partition. For instance, using two partitions it is possible to have Linux on one and Windows on another partition in the disk. This gives enormous flexibility of operations. Typically, a 80 GB disk in modern machines may be utilized to house Windows XP and Linux with nearly 40 GB disk available for each.

Yet another associated concept in this context, is the way the disk partitions are mounted on a file system. Clearly, a disk partition, with all its contents, is essentially a set of organized information. It has its own directory structure. Hence, it is a tree by itself. This tree gets connected to some node in the overall tree structure of the file system and forks out. This is precisely what mounting means. The partition is regarded to be mounted in the file system. This basic concept is also carried to the file servers on a network. The network file system may have remote partitions which are mounted on it. It offers seamless file access as if all of the storage was on the local disk. In modern systems, the file servers are located on networks somewhere without the knowledge of the user. From a user's standpoint all that is important to note is that as a user, his files are a part of a large tree structure which is a file system.

Portable Storage

There are external media like tapes, disks, and floppies. These storage devices can be physically ported. Most file systems recognize these as on-line files when these are mounted on an IO device like a tape drive or a floppy drive. Unix treats these as special files. PCs and MAC OS recognize these as external files and provide an icon when these are mounted.

In this chapter we have covered considerable ground. Files are the entities that users deal with all the time. Users create files, manage them and seek system support in their file management activity. The discussion here has been to help build up a conceptual basis and leaves much to be covered with respect to specific instructions. For specifics, one should consult manuals. In this very rapidly advancing field, while the concept does not change, the practice does and does at a phenomenal pace.

File System Fragmentation

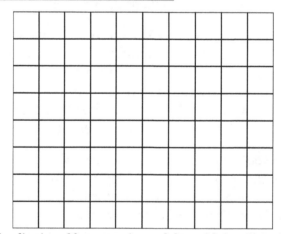

Visualization of fragmentation and then of defragmentation

In computing, file system fragmentation, sometimes called file system aging, is the tendency of a file system to lay out the contents of files non-contiguously to allow in-place modification of their contents. It is a special case of data fragmentation. File system fragmentation increases disk head movement or seek time, which are known to hinder throughput. In addition, file systems cannot sustain unlimited fragmentation. The correction to existing fragmentation is to reorganize files and free space back into contiguous areas, a process called defragmentation.

Causes

When a file system is first initialized on a partition, it contains only a few small internal structures and is otherwise one contiguous block of empty space. This means that the file system is able to place newly created files anywhere on the partition. For some time after creation, files can be laid out near-optimally. When the operating system and applications are installed or archives are unpacked, separate files end up occurring sequentially so related files are positioned close to each other.

As existing files are deleted or truncated, new regions of free space are created. When existing files are appended to, it is often impossible to resume the write exactly where the file used to end, as another file may already be allocated there; thus, a new fragment has to be allocated. As time goes on, and the same factors are continuously present, free space as well as frequently appended files tend to fragment more. Shorter regions of free space also mean that the file system is no longer able to allocate new files contiguously, and has to break them into fragments. This is especially true when the file system becomes full and large contiguous regions of free space are unavailable.

Example

(1)	A	B	C	D	E	Free Space
(2)	A		C	D	E	Free Space
(3)	A	F	C	D	E	Free Space
(4)	A	F G	C	D	E	Free Space
(5)	A	F G	C	D	E	Free Space

F (Second *extent*, or allocation) ┘

Oversimplified example of how free space fragmentation and file fragmentation occur

The following example is a simplification of an otherwise complicated subject. Consider the following scenario: A new disk has had five files, named A, B, C, D and E, saved continuously and sequentially in that order. Each file is using 10 *blocks* of space. (Here, the block size is unimportant.) The remainder of the disk space is one free block. Thus, additional files can be created and saved after the file E.

If the file B is deleted, a second region of ten blocks of free space is created, and the disk becomes fragmented. The empty space is simply left there, marked as and available for later use, then used again as needed. The file system *could* defragment the disk immediately after a deletion, but doing so would incur a severe performance penalty at unpredictable times.

Now, a new file called F, which requires seven blocks of space, can be placed into the first seven blocks of the newly freed space formerly holding the file B, and the three blocks following it will remain available. If another new file called G, which needs only three blocks, is added, it could then occupy the space after F and before C.

If subsequently F needs to be expanded, since the space immediately following it is occupied, there are three options for the file system:

1. Adding a new block somewhere else and indicating that F has a second extent

2. Moving files in the way of the expansion elsewhere, to allow F to remain contiguous

3. Moving file F so it can be one contiguous file of the new, larger size

The second option is probably impractical for performance reasons, as is the third when the file is very large. The third option is impossible when there is no single contiguous free space large enough to hold the new file. Thus the usual practice is simply to create an *extent* somewhere else and chain the new extent onto the old one.

Material added to the end of file F would be part of the same extent. But if there is so much material that no room is available after the last extent, then *another* extent would have to be created, and so on. Eventually the file system has free segments in many places and some files may be spread over many extents. Access time for those files (or for all files) may become excessively long.

Necessity

Some early file systems were unable to fragment files. One such example was the Acorn DFS file system used on the BBC Micro. Due to its inability to fragment files, the error message *can't extend* would at times appear, and the user would often be unable to save a file even if the disk had adequate space for it.

DFS used a very simple disk structure and files on disk were located only by their length and starting sector. This meant that all files had to exist as a continuous block of sectors and fragmentation was not possible. Using the example in the table above, the attempt to expand file F in step five would have failed on such a system with the *can't extend* error message. Regardless of how much free space might remain on the disk in total, it was not available to extend the data file.

Standards of error handling at the time were primitive and in any case programs squeezed into the limited memory of the BBC Micro could rarely afford to waste space attempting to handle errors gracefully. Instead, the user would find themselves dumped back at the command prompt with the *Can't extend* message and all the data which had yet to be appended to the file would be lost. The resulting frustration would be greater if the user had taken the trouble to check the free space on the disk beforehand and found free space. While free space on the disk may exist, the fact that it was not in the place where it was needed was not apparent without analyzing the numbers presented by the disk catalog and so would escape the user's notice. In addition, DFS users had almost without exception previously been accustomed to cassette file storage, which does not suffer from this error. The upgrade to a floppy disk system was expensive performance upgrade, and it was a shock to make the sudden and unpleasant discovery that the upgrade might without warning cause data loss.

Types

File system fragmentation may occur on several levels:

- Fragmentation within individual files
- Free space fragmentation
- The decrease of locality of reference between separate, but related files

File Fragmentation

Individual file fragmentation occurs when a single file has been broken into multiple pieces (called extents on extent-based file systems). While disk file systems attempt to keep individual files contiguous, this is not often possible without significant performance penalties. File system check and defragmentation tools typically only account for file fragmentation in their "fragmentation percentage" statistic.

Free Space Fragmentation

Free (unallocated) space fragmentation occurs when there are several unused areas of the file system where new files or metadata can be written to. Unwanted free space fragmentation is generally caused by deletion or truncation of files, but file systems may also intentionally insert fragments ("bubbles") of free space in order to facilitate extending nearby files.

File Scattering

File segmentation, also called related-file fragmentation, or application-level (file) fragmentation, refers to the lack of locality of reference (within the storing medium) between related files. Unlike the previous two types of fragmentation, file scattering is a much more vague concept, as it heavily depends on the access pattern of specific applications. This also makes objectively measuring or estimating it very difficult. However, arguably, it is the most critical type of fragmentation, as studies have found that the most frequently accessed files tend to be small compared to available disk throughput per second.

To avoid related file fragmentation and improve locality of reference (in this case called *file contiguity*), assumptions or active observations about the operation of applications have to be made. A very frequent assumption made is that it is worthwhile to keep smaller files within a single directory together, and lay them out in the natural file system order. While it is often a reasonable assumption, it does not always hold. For example, an application might read several different files, perhaps in different directories, in exactly the same order they were written. Thus, a file system that simply orders all writes successively, might work faster for the given application.

Negative Consequences

File system fragmentation is more problematic with consumer-grade hard disk drives because of the increasing disparity between sequential access speed and rotational latency (and to a lesser extent seek time) on which file systems are usually placed. Thus, fragmentation is an important problem in file system research and design. The containment of fragmentation not only depends on the on-disk format of the file system, but also heavily on its implementation. File system fragmentation has less performance impact upon solid-state drives, as there is no mechanical seek time involved. However, the file system needs to store one additional piece of metadata for the corresponding file. Each piece of metadata itself occupies space and requires processing power and processor time. If the maximum fragmentation limit is reached, write requests fail.

In simple file system benchmarks, the fragmentation factor is often omitted, as realistic aging and fragmentation is difficult to model. Rather, for simplicity of comparison, file system benchmarks are often run on empty file systems. Thus, the results may vary heavily from real-life access patterns.

Mitigation

Several techniques have been developed to fight fragmentation. They can usually be classified into two categories: *preemptive* and *retroactive*. Due to the difficulty of predicting access patterns these techniques are most often heuristic in nature and may degrade performance under unexpected workloads.

Preventing Fragmentation

Preemptive techniques attempt to keep fragmentation at a minimum at the time data is being written on the disk. The simplest is appending data to an existing fragment in place where possible, instead of allocating new blocks to a new fragment.

Many of today's file systems attempt to preallocate longer chunks, or chunks from different free space fragments, called extents to files that are actively appended to. This largely avoids file fragmentation when several files are concurrently being appended to, thus avoiding their becoming excessively intertwined.

If the final size of a file subject to modification is known, storage for the entire file may be preallocated. For example, the Microsoft Windows swap file (page file) can be resized dynamically under normal operation, and therefore can become highly fragmented. This can be prevented by specifying a page file with the same minimum and maximum sizes, effectively preallocating the entire file.

BitTorrent and other peer-to-peer filesharing applications limit fragmentation by preallocating the full space needed for a file when initiating downloads.

A relatively recent technique is delayed allocation in XFS, HFS+ and ZFS; the same technique is also called allocate-on-flush in reiser4 and ext4. When the file system is being written to, file system blocks are reserved, but the locations of specific files are not laid down yet. Later, when the file system is forced to flush changes as a result of memory pressure or a transaction commit, the allocator will have much better knowledge of the files' characteristics. Most file systems with this approach try to flush files in a single directory contiguously. Assuming that multiple reads from a single directory are common, locality of reference is improved. Reiser4 also orders the layout of files according to the directory hash table, so that when files are being accessed in the natural file system order (as dictated by readdir), they are always read sequentially.

Defragmentation

Retroactive techniques attempt to reduce fragmentation, or the negative effects of fragmentation, after it has occurred. Many file systems provide defragmentation tools, which attempt to reorder fragments of files, and sometimes also decrease their scattering (i.e. improve their contiguity, or locality of reference) by keeping either smaller files in directories, or directory trees, or even file sequences close to each other on the disk.

The HFS Plus file system transparently defragments files that are less than 20 MiB in size and are broken into 8 or more fragments, when the file is being opened.

The now obsolete Commodore Amiga Smart File System (SFS) defragmented itself while the filesystem was in use. The defragmentation process is almost completely stateless (apart from the location it is working on), so that it can be stopped and started instantly. During defragmentation data integrity is ensured for both metadata and normal data.

Memory Management

The von Neumann principle for the design and operation of computers requires that a program has to be primary memory resident to execute. Also, a user requires to revisit his programs often during its evolution. However, due to the fact that primary memory is volatile, a user needs to store his program in some non-volatile store. All computers provide a non-volatile secondary memory available as an online storage. Programs and files may be disk resident and downloaded whenever their execution is required. Therefore, some form of memory management is needed at both primary and secondary memory levels.

Secondary memory may store program scripts, executable process images and data files. It may store applications, as well as, system programs. In fact, a good part of all OS, the system programs which provide services (the utilities for instance) are stored in the secondary memory. These are requisitioned as needed.

The main motivation for management of main memory comes from the support for multi- programming. Several executables processes reside in main memory at any given time. In other words, there are several programs using the main memory as their address space. Also, programs move into, and out of, the main memory as they terminate, or get suspended for some IO, or new executables are required to be loaded in main memory.

So, the OS has to have some strategy for main memory management. In this chapter we shall discuss the management issues and strategies for both main memory and secondary memory.

Main Memory Management

Let us begin by examining the issues that prompt the main memory management.

- Allocation: First of all the processes that are scheduled to run must be resident in the memory. These processes must be allocated space in main memory.

- Swapping, fragmentation and compaction: If a program is moved out or terminates, it creates a hole, (i.e. a contiguous unused area) in main memory. When a new process is to be moved in, it may be allocated one of the available holes. It is quite possible that main memory has far too many small holes at a certain time. In such a situation none of these holes is really large enough to be allocated to a new process that may be moving in. The main memory is too fragmented. It is, therefore, essential to attempt compaction. Compaction means OS re-allocates the existing programs in contiguous regions and creates a large enough free area for allocation to a new process.

- Garbage collection: Some programs use dynamic data structures. These programs dynamically use and discard memory space. Technically, the deleted data items (from a dynamic data structure) release memory locations. However, in practice the OS does not collect such free space immediately for allocation. This is because that affects performance. Such areas, therefore, are called garbage. When such garbage exceeds a certain threshold, the OS would not have enough memory available for any further allocation. This entails compaction (or garbage collection), without severely affecting performance.

- Protection: With many programs residing in main memory it can happen that due to a programming error (or with malice) some process writes into data or instruction area of some other process. The OS ensures that each process accesses only to its own allocated area, i.e. each process is protected from other processes.

- Virtual memory: Often a processor sees a large logical storage space (a virtual storage space) though the actual main memory may not be that large. So some facility needs to be provided to translate a logical address available to a processor into a physical address to access the desired data or instruction.

- IO support: Most of the block-oriented devices are recognized as specialized files. Their buffers need to be managed within main memory alongside the other processes. The considerations stated above motivate the study of main memory management.

One of the important considerations in locating an executable program is that it should be possible to relocate it any where in the main memory. We shall dwell upon the concept of relocation next.

Memory Relocation Concept

Relocation is an important concept. To understand this concept we shall begin with a linear map (one-dimensional view) of main memory. If we know an address we can fetch its contents. So, a process residing in the main memory, we set the program counter to an absolute address of its first instruction and can initiate its run. Also, if we know the locations of data then we can fetch those too. All of this stipulates that we know the absolute addresses for a program, its data and process context etc. This means that we can load a process with only absolute addresses for instructions and data, only when those specific addresses are free in main memory. This would mean we loose flexibility with regard to loading a process. For instance, we cannot load a process, if some other process is currently occupying that area which is needed by this process. This may happen even though we may have enough space in the memory. To avoid such a catastrophe, processes are generated to be relocatable. In Figure we see a process resident in main memory.

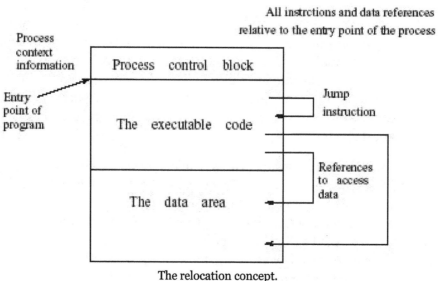

The relocation concept.

Initially, all the addresses in the process are relative to the start address. With this flexibility we can allocate any area in the memory to load this process. Its instruction, data, process context (process control block) and any other data structure required by the process can be accessed easily if the addresses are relative. This is most helpful when processes move in and out of main memory. Suppose a process created a hole on moving out. In case we use non-relocatable addresses, we have the following very severe problem.

When the process moves back in, that particular hole (or area) may not be available any longer. In case we can relocate, moving a process back in creates no problem. This is so because the process can be relocated in some other free area. We shall next examine the linking and loading of programs to understand the process of relocation better.

Compiler Generated Bindings

The advantage of relocation can also be seen in the light of binding of addresses to variables in a program. Suppose we have a program variable x in a program P. Suppose the compiler allocated a fixed address to x. This address allocation by the compiler is called binding. If x is bound to a fixed location then we can execute program P only when x could be put in its allocated memory location. Otherwise, all address references to x will be incorrect.

If, however, the variable can be assigned a location relative to an assumed origin (or first address in program P) then, on relocating the program's origin anywhere in main memory, we will still be able to generate a proper relative address reference for x and execute the program. In fact, compilers generate relocatable code.

Linking and Loading Concepts

In Figure we depict the three stages of the way a HLL program gets processed.

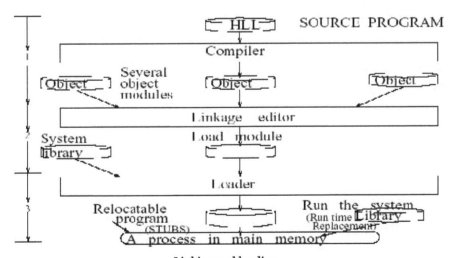

Linking and loading.

The three stages of the processing are:

- Stage 1: In the first stage the HLL source program is compiled and an object code is produced. Technically, depending upon the program, this object code may by itself be sufficient to generate a relocatable process. However many programs are compiled in parts, so this object code may have to link up with other object modules. At this stage the compiler may also insert stub at points where run time library modules may be linked.

- Stage 2: All those object modules which have sufficient linking information (generated by the compiler) for static linking are taken up for linking. The linking editor generates a re-locatable code. At this stage, however, we still do not replace the stubs placed by compilers for a run time library link up.

- Stage3: The final step is to arrange to make substitution for the stubs with run time library code which is a relocatable code.

When all the three stages are completed we have an executable. When this executable is resident in the main memory it is a runnable process.

The compiler uses a symbol table to generate addresses. These addresses are not bound, i.e. these do not have absolute values but do have information on sizes of data. The binding produced at compile time is generally relative. Some OSs support a linking loader which translates the relative addresses to relocatable addresses. In any event, the relocatable process is finally formed as an output of a loader.

Process and Main Memory Management

Once processes have been created, the OS organizes their execution. This requires interaction between process management and main memory management. To understand this interaction better, we shall create a scenario requiring memory allocations. For the operating environment we assume the following:

- A uni-processor, multi-programming operation.

- A Unix like operating system environment.

With a Unix like OS, we can assume that main memory is partitioned in two parts. One part is for user processes and the other is for OS. We will assume that we have a main memory of 20 units (for instance it could be 2 or 20 or 200 MB). We show the requirements and time of arrival and processing requirements for 6 processes in Table.

	P1	P2	P3	P4	P5	P6
Time of arrival	0	0	0	0	10	15
Processing time required	8	5	20	12	10	5
Memory required	3 units	7 units	2 units	4 units	2 units	2 units

The given data.

We shall assume that OS requires 6 units of space. To be able to compare various policies, we shall repeatedly use the data in table for every policy option.

With these requirements we can now trace the emerging scenario for the given data. We shall assume round robin allocation of processor time slots with no context switching over-heads. We shall trace the events as they occur giving reference to the corresponding part in Table. This table also shows a memory map as the processes move in and out of the main memory.

Time units	Programs in main memory	Programs on disk	Holes with sizes	Figures	Comments
0	P1, P2, P3	P4	H1=2	(a)	P4 requires more space than H1
5	P1, P4, P3		H1=2; H2=3	(b)	P2 is finished P4 is loaded Hole H2 is Created
8	P4, P3		H1=2; H2=3; H3=3	(c)	New hole created
10	P4, P3	P5			P5 arrives
10+	P5, P4, P3		H1=2; H2=3; H3=1	(d)	P5 is allocated P1's space
15	P5, P4, P3	P6	H1=2; H2=3; H3=1		P6 has arrived
15+	P5, P4, P6, P3		H1=2; H2=1; H3=1	(e)	P6 is allocated

FCFS memory allocation.

The First Fit Policy: Memory Allocation

In this example we make use of a policy called first fit memory allocation policy. The first fit policy suggests that we use the first available hole, which is large enough to accommodate an incoming process. In Figure, it is important to note that we are following first-come first-served (process management) and first fit (memory allocation) policies. The process index denotes its place in the queue. As per first-come first-served policies the queue order determines the order in which the processes are allocated areas. In addition, as per first-fit policy allocation we scan the memory always from one end and find the first block of free space which is large enough to accommodate the incoming process.

In our example, initially, processes P1, P2, P3 and P4 are in the queue. The allocations for processes P1, P2, P3 are shown in 4.3(a). At time 5, process P2 terminates. So, process P4 is allocated in the hole created by process P2. This is shown at 4.3(b) in the figure. It still leaves a hole of size 3. Now on advancing time further we see that at time 8, process P1 terminates. This creates a hole of size 3 as shown at 4.3(c) in the figure.

This hole too is now available for allocation. We have 3 holes at this stage. Two of these 3 holes are of size 3 and one is of size 2. When process P5 arrives at time 10, we look for the first hole which can accommodate it. This is the one created by the departure of process P1. Using the first-fit argument this is the hole allocated to process P5 as shown in Figure(d). The final allocation status is shown in Figure. The first-fit allocation policy is very easy to implement and is fast in execution.

Program P1	Program P1	Hole 3 units	Program P5	Program P5
			Hole 1 unit	Hole 1 unit
Program P2	Program P4	Program P4	Program P4	Program P4
	Hole 3 units	Hole 3 units	Hole 3 units	Program P6
				Hole 1 unit
Program P3	Program P3	Program P3	Program P3	Program P3
Hole 2 units	Hole 2 units	Hole 2 units	Hole 2 units	Hole 2 units
Operting system's area	Operting system's area	Operting system's area	Operting system's area	Operting system's area
(a)	(b)	(c)	(d)	(e)

First-fit policy allocation.

The Best Fit Policy: Memory Allocation

The main criticism of first-fit policy is that it may leave many smaller holes. For instance, let us trace the allocation for process P5. It needs 2 units of space. At the time it moves into the main memory there is a hole with 2 units of space. But this is the last hole when we scan the main memory from the top (beginning). The first hole is 3 units. Using the first-fit policy process P5 is allocated this hole. So when we used this hole we also created a still smaller hole. Note that smaller holes are less useful for future allocations.

In the best-fit policy we scan the main memory for all the available holes. Once we have information about all the holes in the memory then we choose the one which is closest to the size of the requirement of the process. In our example we allocate the hole with size 2 as there is one available. Table follows best-fit policy for the current example.

Also, as we did for the previous example, we shall again assume round-robin allocation of the processor time slots. With these considerations we can now trace the possible emerging scenario.

In Figure, we are following first-come first-served (process management) and best fit (memory allocation) policies. The process index denotes its place in the queue. Initially, processes P1, P2, P3 and P4 are in the queue. Processes P1, P2 and P3 are allocated as shown in Figure (a). At time 5, P2 terminates and process P4 is allocated in the hole so created. This is shown in Figure (b). This is the best fit. It leaves a space of size 3 creating a new hole. At time 8, process P1 terminates. We now have 3 holes. Two of these holes are of size 3 and one is of size 2. When process P5 arrives at time 10, we look for a hole whose size is nearest to 2 and can accommodate P5. This is the last hole.

Program P1	Program P1	H3 Hole 3 units	H3 Hole 3 units	Program P6 Hole 1 unit H4
Program P2	Program P4	Program P4	Program P4	Program P4
	H2 Hole 3 units	H2 Hole 3 units	H2 Hole 3 units	H2 Hole 3 units
Program P3	Program P3	Program P3	Program P3	Program P3
H1 Hole 2 units	H1 Hole 2 units	H1 Hole 2 units	Program P5	Program P5
Operating System's area	Operating System's area	Operating System's area	Operating System's area	Operating System's area
(a)	(b)	(c)	(d)	(e)

Best-fit policy allocation

Clearly, the best-fit (and also the worst-fit) policy should be expected to be slow in execution. This is so because the implementation requires a time consuming scan of all of main memory. There is another method called the next-fit policy. In the next-fit method the search pointer does not start at the top (beginning), instead it begins from where it ended during the previous search. Like the first-fit policy it locates the next first-fit hole that can be used. Note that unlike the first-fit policy the next-fit policy can be expected to distribute small holes uniformly in the main memory. The first-fit policy would have a tendency to create small holes towards the beginning of the main memory scan. Both first-fit and next-fit methods are very fast and easy to implement.

In conclusion, first-fit and next-fit are the fastest and seem to be the preferred methods. One of the important considerations in main memory management is: how should an OS allocate a chunk of main memory required by a process. One simple approach would be to somehow create partitions and then different processes could reside in different partitions. We shall next discuss how the main memory partitions may be created.

Time units	Programs in Main memory	Programs on disk	Holes with sizes	Figure 4.4	Comments
0	P1, P2, P3	P4	H1=2	(a)	P4 requires more space than H1
5	P1, P4, P3		H1=2; H2=3	(b)	P2 is finished P4 is loaded Hole H2 is created
8	P4, P3		H1=2; H2=3; H3=3	(c)	Creates a new hole
10	P4, P3	P5			P5 arrives
10+	P4, P3, P5		H2=3; H3=3	(d)	P5 is allocated the best fit hole
15	P4, P3, P5	P6	H2=3; H3=3		P6 arrives
15+	P6, P4, P3, P5		H2=3; H4=1	(e)	P6 takes the hole left by P1

Best-fit policy memory allocation.

Fixed and Variable Partitions

In a fixed size partitioning of the main memory all partitions are of the same size. The memory resident processes can be assigned to any of these partitions. Fixed sized partitions are relatively simple to implement. However, there are two problems. This scheme is not easy to use when a program requires more space than the partition size. In this situation the programmer has to resort to overlays. Overlays involve moving data and program segments in and out of memory essentially reusing the area in main memory. The second problem has to do with internal fragmentation. No matter what the size of the process is, a fixed size of memory block is allocated as shown in Figure (a). So there will always be some space which will remain unutilized within the partition.

In a variable-sized partition, the memory is partitioned into partitions with different sizes. Processes are loaded into the size nearest to its requirements. It is easy to always ensure the best-fit. One may organize a queue for each size of the partition as shown in the Figure (b). With best-fit policy, variable partitions minimize internal fragmentation.

However, such an allocation may be quite slow in execution. This is so because a process may end up waiting (queued up) in the best-fit queue even while there is space available elsewhere. For example, we may have several jobs queued up in a queue meant for jobs that require 1 unit of memory, even while no jobs are queued up for jobs that require say 4 units of memory.

Both fixed and dynamic partitions suffer from external fragmentation whenever there are partitions that have no process in it. One of techniques that have been used to keep both internal and external fragmentations low is dynamic partitioning. It is basically a variable partitioning with a variable number of partitions determined dynamically (i.e. at run time).

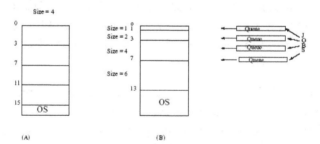

Fixed and variable sized partitions.

Such a scheme is difficult to implement. Another scheme which falls between the fixed and dynamic partitioning is a buddy system described next.

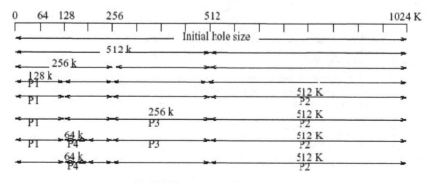

Buddy system allocation.

The Buddy system of partitioning: The buddy system of partitioning relies on the fact that space allocations can be conveniently handled in sizes of power of 2. There are two ways in which the buddy system allocates space. Suppose we have a hole which is the closest power of two. In that case, that hole is used for allocation. In case we do not have

that situation then we look for the next power of 2 hole size, split it in two equal halves and allocate one of these. Because we always split the holes in two equal sizes, the two are \buddies". Hence, the name buddy system. We shall illustrate allocation using a buddy system. We assume that initially we have a space of 1024 K. We also assume that processes arrive and are allocated following a time sequence as shown in figure.

With 1024 K or (1 M) storage space we split it into buddies of 512 K, splitting one of them to two 256 K buddies and so on till we get the right size. Also, we assume scan of memory from the beginning. We always use the first hole which accommodates the process. Otherwise, we split the next sized hole into buddies. Note that the buddy system begins search for a hole as if we had a fixed number of holes of variable sizes but turns into a dynamic partitioning scheme when we do not find the best-fit hole. The buddy system has the advantage that it minimizes the internal fragmentation. However, it is not popular because it is very slow. In Figure we assume the requirements as (P1:80 K); (P2:312 K); (P3:164 K); (P4:38 K). These processes arrive in the order of their index and P1 and P3 finish at the same time.

Virtual Storage Space and Main Memory Partitions

Programming models assume the presence of main memory only. Therefore, ideally we would like to have an unlimited (infinite) main memory available. In fact, an unlimited main memory shall give us a Turing machine capability. However, in practice it is infeasible. So the next best thing is attempted. CPU designers support and generate a very large logical addressable space to support programming concerns. However, the directly addressable main memory is limited and is quite small in comparison to the logical addressable space. The actual size of main memory is referred as the physical memory. The logical addressable space is referred to as virtual memory. The notion of virtual memory is a bit of an illusion. The OS supports and makes this illusion possible. It does so by copying chunks of disk memory into the main memory as shown in Figure. In other words, the processor is fooled into believing that it is accessing a large addressable space. Hence, the name virtual storage space. The disk area may map to the virtual space requirements and even beyond.

Besides the obvious benefit that virtual memory offers a very large address space, there is one other major benefit derived from the use of virtual storage. We now can have many more main memory resident active processes. This can be explained as follows. During much of the lifetime of its execution, a process operates on a small set of instructions within a certain neighborhood. The same applies for the data as well. In other words a process makes use of a very small memory area for doing most of the instructions and making references to the data. This is primarily due to the locality of reference. So, technically, at any time we need a very small part of a process to really be memory resident. For a moment, let us suppose that this small part is only 1/10th of the process's overall requirements. Note in that case, for the same size of physical main memory, we can service 10 times as many memory resident programs. The next question then is how do we organize and allocate these small chunks of often required areas to be in memory. In fact, this is where paging and segmentation become important. In this context we need to understand some of the techniques of partitioning of main memory into pages or segments.

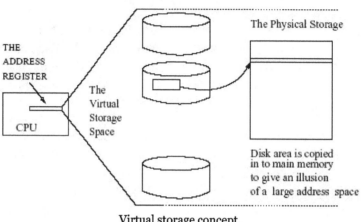

Virtual storage concept.

In addition, we need to understand virtual addressing concepts with paging and/or segmentation. We begin with some simple techniques of partitioning both these memories and management of processes.

Virtual Memory: Paging

In some sense, paging of virtual memory has an underlying mechanism which resembles reading of a book. When we read a book we only need to open only the current page to read. All the other pages are not visible to us. In the same manner, we can argue that even when we may have a large online main memory available, the processor only needs a small set of instructions to execute at any time. In fact, it often happens that for a brief while, all the instructions which the processor needs to execute are within a small proximity of each other. That is like a page we are currently reading in a book. Clearly, this kind of situation happens quite frequently.

Essentially virtual memory is a large addressable space supported by address generating mechanisms in modern CPUs. Virtual address space is much larger than the physical main memory in a computer system. During its execution, a process mostly generates instruction and data references from within a small range. This is referred to as the locality of reference. Examples of locality of reference abound. For instance, we have locality of reference during execution of a *for* or *while* loop, or a call to a procedure. Even in a sequence of assignment statements, the references to instructions and data are usually within a very small range. Which means, during bursts of process execution, only small parts of all of the instruction and data space are needed, i.e. only these parts need be in the main memory. The remaining process, instructions and data, can be anywhere in the virtual space (i.e. it must remain accessible by CPU but not necessarily in main memory). If we are able to achieve that, then we can actually follow a schedule, in which we support a large address space and keep bringing in that part of process which is needed. This way we can comfortably support (a) multi-programming (b) a large logical addressable space giving enormous freedom to a programmer. Note, however, that this entails mapping of logical addresses into physical address space. Such a mapping assures that the instruction in sequence is fetched or the data required in computation is correctly used.

If this translation were to be done in software, it would be very slow. In fact, nowadays this address translation support is provided by hardware in CPUs. Paging is one of the popular memory management schemes to implement such virtual memory management schemes. OS software and the hardware address translation between them achieve this.

Mapping the Pages

Paging stipulates that main memory is partitioned into frames of sufficiently small sizes. Also, we require that the virtual space is divided into pages of the same size as the frames. This equality facilitates movement of a page from anywhere in the virtual space (on disks) to a frame anywhere in the physical memory. The capability to map "any page" to "any frame" gives a lot of flexibility of operation as shown in Figure.

Division of main memory into frames is like fixed partitioning. So keeping the frame size small helps to keep the internal fragmentation small. Often, the page to frame movement is determined by a convenient size (usually a power of two) which disks also use for their own DMA data transfer. The usual frame size is 1024 bytes, though it is not unusual to have 4 K frame sizes as well. Paging supports multi-programming. In general there can be many processes in main memory, each with a different number of pages. To that extent, paging is like dynamic variable partitioning.

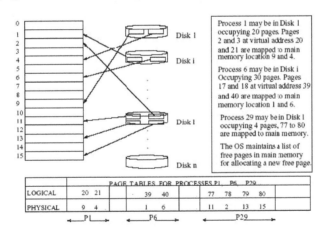

Paging implementation.

Paging: Implementation

Paging implementation requires CPU (HW) and OS (SW) support. In Figure, we assume presence of three active processes. These processes need to have their pages mapped to the main memory page frames. The OS maintains a page table for every process to translate its logical to physical addresses. The page table may itself be resident in main memory.

For a process, which is presently active, there are a number of pages that are in the main memory. This set of pages (being used by the process) forms its resident set. With the locality of reference generally observed, most of the time, the processes make reference within the resident set. We define the set of pages needed by a process at any time as the working set. The OS makes every effort to have the resident set to be the same as the working set. However, it does happen (and happens quite often), that a page required for continuing the process is not in the resident set. This is called a page fault. In normal course of operation, though whenever a process makes virtual address reference, its page table is looked up to find if that page is in main memory. Often it is there. Let us now suppose that the page is not in main memory, i.e. a page fault has occurred. In that case, the OS accesses the required page on the disk and loads it in a free page frame. It then makes an entry for this page in process page table. Similarly, when a page is swapped out, the OS deletes its entry from the page table. Sometimes it may well happen that all the page frames in main memory are in use. If a process now needs a page which is not in main memory, then a page must be forced out to make way for the new page. This is done using a page replacement policy discussed next.

Paging: Replacement

Page replacement policies are based on the way the processes use page frames. In our example shown in Figure, process P29 has all its pages present in main memory. Process P6 does not have all its pages in main memory. If a page is present we record 1 against its entry. The OS also records if a page has been referenced to read or to write. In both these cases a reference is recorded. If a page frame is written into, then a modified bit is set. In our example frames 4, 9, 40, 77, 79 have been referenced and page frames 9 and 13 have been modified. Sometimes OS may also have some information about protection using *rwe* information. If a reference is made to a certain virtual address and its corresponding page is not present in main memory, then we say a page fault has occurred. Typically, a page fault is followed by moving in a page. However, this may require that we move a page out to create a space for it. Usually this is done by using an appropriate page replacement policy to ensure that the throughput of a system does not suffer. We shall later see how a page replacement policy can affect performance of a system.

Page tables for processes P1, .. P6, .. P29 ...

	P1		P6				P29			
Logical	20 21		39 40		· ·	77	78	79	80	
Physical	9 4		1 6		·	11	2	13	15	
Present	0 1 1 0	0 0 1	1 0	1 1 1	1	1	1	1		
Referenced	1 1		0 1			1	0	1	0	
Modified	1 0		0 0			0	0	1	0	
Protection	rw— rw—					r—		r—		

Replacement policy.

Page Replacement Policy

Towards understanding page replacement policies we shall consider a simple example of a process P which gets an allocation of four pages to execute. Further, we assume that the OS collects some information about the use of these pages as this process progresses in execution. Let us examine the information depicted in figure

- In some detail to determine how this may help in evolving a page replacement policy. Note that we have the following information available about P.

- The time of arrival of each page. We assume that the process began at some time with value of time unit 100. During its course of progression we now have pages that have been loaded at times 112, 117 119, and 120.

- The time of last usage. This indicates when a certain page was last used. This entirely depends upon which part of the process P is being executed at any time.

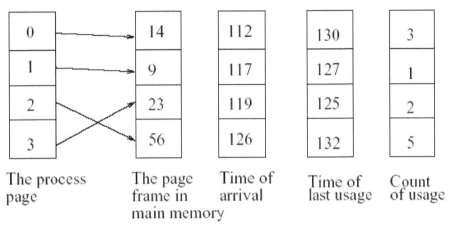

The process page	The page frame in main memory	Time of arrival	Time of last usage	Count of usage
0	14	112	130	3
1	9	117	127	1
2	23	119	125	2
3	56	126	132	5

Information on page usage policy.

- The frequency of use. We have also maintained the frequency of use over some fixed interval of time T in the immediate past. This clearly depends upon the nature of control flow in process P.

As an example we may say that page located at 23 which was installed at time 119, was last used at time unit 125 and over the time period T the process P made two references to it. Based on the above pieces of information if we now assume that at time unit 135 the process P experiences a page-fault, what should be done. Based on the choice of the policy and the data collected for P, we shall be able to decide which page to swap out to bring in a new page.

FIFO policy: This policy simply removes pages in the order they arrived in the main memory. Using this policy we simply remove a page based on the time of its arrival in the memory. Clearly, use of this policy would suggest that we swap page located at 14 as it arrived in the memory earliest.

LRU policy: LRU expands to least recently used. This policy suggests that we remove a page whose last usage is farthest from current time. Note that the current time is 135 and the least recently used page is the page located at 23. It was used last at time unit 125 and every other page is more recently used. So, page 23 is the least recently used page and so it should be swapped if LRU replacement policy is employed.

NFU policy: NFU expands to not frequently used. This policy suggests to use the criterion of the count of usage of page over the interval T. Note that process P has not made use of page located at 9. Other pages have a count of usage like 2, 3 or even 5 times. So the basic argument is that these pages may still be needed as compared to the page at 9. So page 9 should be swapped.

Let us briefly discuss the merits of choices that one is offered. FIFO is a very simple policy and it is relatively easy to implement. All it needs is the time of arrival. However, in following such a policy we may end up replacing a page frame that is referred often during the lifetime of a process. In other words, we should examine how useful a certain page is before we decide to replace it. LRU and NFU policies are certainly better in that regard but as is obvious we need to keep the information about the usage of the pages by the process. In following the not frequently used (NFU) and least recently used (LRU) page replacement policies, the OS needs to define *recency*. As we saw recency is defined as a fixed time interval proceeding the current time. With a definition of recency, we can implement the policy framework like least recently used (LRU). So one must choose a proper interval of time. Depending upon the nature of application environment and the work load a choice of duration of recency will give different throughput from the system. Also, this means that the OS must keep a tab on the pages which are being used and how often these are in use. It is often the case that the most recently used pages are likely to be the ones used again. On the whole one can sense that the LRU policy should be statistically better than FIFO.

A more advanced technique of page replacement policy may look-up the likely future references to pages. Such a policy frame would require use of some form of predictive techniques. In that case, one can prevent too many frequent replacements of pages which prevents thrashing as discussed in the subsection.

Let us for now briefly pay our attention to page references resulting in a page hit and a page miss. When we find that a page frame reference is in the main memory then we have a page hit and when page fault occurs we say we have a page miss. As is obvious from the discussion, a poor choice of policy may result in lot of page misses. We should be able to determine how it influences the throughput of a system. Let us assume that we have a system with the following characteristics.

- Time to look-up page table: 10 time units.

- Time to look-up the information from a page frame (case of a page hit): 40 time units.

- Time to retrieve a page from disk and load it and finally access the page frame (case of a page miss): 190 time units.

Now let us consider the following two cases when we have 50% and 80% page hits. We shall compute the average time to access.

- Case 1: With 50% page hits the average access time is $((10+40) * 0.5) + (10+190)$

    * $0.5 = 125$ time units.

- Case 2: With 80% page hits the average access time is $(10+40) * 0.8) + (10+190)$

    * $0.2 = 80$ time units.

Clearly, the case 2 is better. The OS designers attempt to offer a page replacement policy which will try to minimize the page miss. Also, sometimes the system programmers have to tune an OS to achieve a high efficacy in performance by ensuring that page miss cases are within some tolerable limits. It is not unusual to be able to achieve over 90% page hits when the application profile is very well known.

There is one other concern that may arise with regard to page replacement. It may be that while a certain process is operative, some of the information may be often required. These may be definitions globally defined in a program, or some terminal related IO information in a monitoring program. If this kind of information is stored in certain pages then these have to be kept at all times during the lifetime of the process. Clearly, this requires that we have these pages identified. Some programming environments allow directives like keep to specify such information to be available at all the time during the lifetime of the process. In Windows there is a keep function that allows one to specify which programs must be kept at all the time. The Windows environment essentially uses the keep function to load TSR (terminate and stay resident) programs to be loaded in the memory 1. Recall, earlier we made a reference to thrashing which arises from the overheads generated from frequent page replacement. We shall next study that.

Thrashing

Suppose there is a process with several pages in its resident set. However, the page replacement policy results in a situation such that two pages alternatively move in and out of the resident set. Note that because pages are moved between main memory and disk, this has an enormous overhead. This can adversely affect the throughput of a system. The drop in the level of system throughput resulting from frequent page replacement is called thrashing. Let us try to comprehend when and how it manifests. Statistically, on introducing paging we can hope to enhance multi-programming as well as locality of reference. The main consequence of this shall be enhanced processor utilization and hence, better throughput. Note that the page size influences the number of pages and hence it determines the number of resident sets we may support. With more programs in main memory or more pages of a program we hope for better locality of reference. This is seen to happen (at least initially) as more pages are available. This is because, we may have more effective locality of reference as well as multi-programming. However, when the page size becomes too small we may begin to witness more page-faults.

Incidentally, a virus writer may employ this to mount an attack. For instance, the keep facility may be used to have a periodic display of some kind on the victim's screen. More page-faults would result in more frequent disk IO. As disk IO happens more often the throughput would drop. The point when this begins to happen, we say thrashing has occurred. In other words, the basic advantage of higher throughput from a greater level of utilization of processor and more effective multi-programming does not accrue any more. When the advantage derived from locality of reference and multi-programming begins to vanish, we are at the point when thrashing manifests. This is shown in Figure.

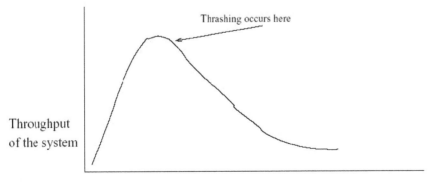

Thrashing on numerous page fault.

Paging: HW support

Recall we emphasized that we need HW within CPU to support paging. The CPU generates a logical address which must get translated to a physical address. In figure we indicate the basic address generation and translation.

Let us trace the sequence of steps in the generation of address.

- The process generates a logical address. This address is interpreted in two parts.

- The first part of the logical address identifies the virtual page.

- The second part of the logical address gives the offset within this page.

- The first part is used as an input to the page table to find out the following:

  * Is the page in the main memory?

  * What is the page frame number for this virtual page?

- The page frame number is the first part of the physical memory address.

- The offset is the second part of the correct physical memory location.

Address generation and translation

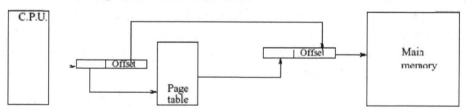

The Offset is same because the page and frame size are same
The page table provides the mapping of virutal page to frame number

Hardware support for paging.

If the page is not in the physical memory, a page-fault is generated. This is treated as a trap. The trap then suspends the regular sequence of operations and fetches the required page from the disk into main memory.

We next discuss a relatively simple extension of the basic paging scheme with hardware support. This scheme results in considerable improvement in page frame access.

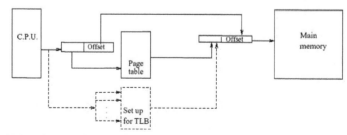

The dotted lines show the Translation lookaside buffer operation

Paging with translation look-aside buffer.

The TLB scheme

The basic idea in the translation look-aside buffer access is quite simple. The scheme is very effective in improving the performance of page frame access. The scheme employs a cache buffer to keep copies of some of the page frames in a cache buffer. This buffer is also interrogated for the presence of page frame copy. Note that a cache buffer is implemented in a technology which is faster than the main memory technology. So, a retrieval from the cache buffer is faster than that from the main memory. The hardware signal which looks up the page table is also used to look up (with address translation) to check if the cache buffer on a side has the desired page. This nature of look-up explains why this scheme is called Translation Look-aside Buffer (TLB) scheme. The basic TLB buffering scheme is shown in Figure. Note that the figure replicates the usual hardware support for page table look-up. So, obviously the scheme cannot be worse than the usual page table look-up schemes. However, since a cache buffer is additionally maintained to keep some of the frequently accessed pages, one can expect to achieve an improvement in the access time required for those pages which obtain a page hit for presence in the buffer. Suppose we wish to access page frame p. The following three possibilities may arise:

1. Cache presence: There is a copy of the page frame p. In this case it is procured from the look-aside buffer which is the cache.

2. Page table presence: The cache does not have a copy of the page frame p, but page table access results in a page hit. The page is accessed from the main memory.

3. Not in page table: This is a case when the copy of the page frame is neither in the cache buffer nor does it have an entry in the page table. Clearly, this is a case of page-fault. It is handled exactly as the page-fault is normally handled.

Note that if a certain page frame copy is available in the cache then the cache look-up takes precedence and the page frame is fetched from the cache instead of fetching it from the main memory. This obviously saves time to access the page frame. In the case the page hit occurs for a page not in cache then the scheme ensures its access from the main memory. So it is at least as good as the standard paging scheme with a possibility of improvement whenever a page frame copy is in cache buffer.

Some Additional Points

Since page frames can be loaded anywhere in the main memory, we can say that paging mechanism supports dynamic relocation. Also, there are other schemes like multi-level page support systems which support page tables at multiple levels of hierarchy. In addition, there are methods to identify pages that may be shared amongst more than one process. Clearly, such shareable pages involve additional considerations to maintain consistency of data when multiple processes try to have read and write access. These are usually areas of research and beyond the scope of this book.

Segmentation

Like paging, segmentation is also a scheme which supports virtual memory concept. Segmentation can be best understood in the context of a program's storage requirements. One view could be that each part like its code segment, its stack requirements (of data, nested procedure calls), its different object modules, etc. has a contiguous space. This space would then define a process's space requirement as an integrated whole (or complete space). As a view, this is very uni-dimensional.

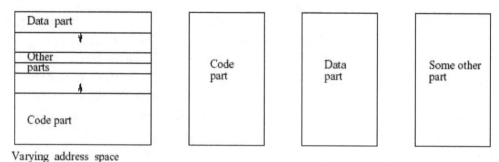

Segmentation scheme: A two dimensional view

In using segmentation, one recognizes various segments such as the stack, object code, data area etc. Each segment has requirements that vary over time. For instance, stacks grow and shrink the memory requirements of object and data segments may change during the lifetime of the process. This may depend on which functions have been called and are currently active. It is, therefore, best to take a two-dimensional view of a process's memory requirement. In this view, each of the process segments has an opportunity to acquire a variable amount of space over time. This ensures that one area does not run into the space of any other segment. The basic scheme is shown in Figure. The implementation of segmentation is similar to paging, except that we now have segment table (in place of a page table) look-ups to identify addresses in each of the segments. HW supports a table look-up for a segment and an offset within that segment. We may now compare paging with segmentation.

- Paging offers the simplest mechanism to effect virtual addressing.

- While paging suffers from internal fragmentation, segmentation suffers from external fragmentation.

- One of the advantages segmentation clearly offers is separate compilation of each segment with a view to link up later. This has another advantage. A user may develop a code segment and share it amongst many applications. He generates the required links at the time of launching the application. However, note that this also places burden on the programmer to manage linking. To that extent paging offers greater transparency in usage.

- In paging, a process address space is linear. Hence, it is uni-dimensional. In a segment based scheme each procedure and data segment has its own virtual space mapping. Thus the segmentation assures a much greater degree of protection.

- In case a program's address space fluctuates considerably, paging may result in frequent page faults. Segmentation does not suffer from such problems.

- Paging partitions a program and data space uniformly and is, therefore, much simpler to manage. However, one cannot easily distinguish data space from program space in paging. Segmentation partitions process space requirements according to a logical division of the segments that make up the process. Generally, this simplifies protection.

Clearly, a clever scheme with advantages of both would be: segmentation with paging. In such a scheme each segment would have a descriptor with its pages identified. Such a scheme is shown in Figure. Note that we have to now use three sets of offsets. First, a segment offset helps to identify the set of pages. Next, within the corresponding page table (for the segment), we need to identify the exact page table. This is done by using the page table part of the virtual address. Once the exact page has been identified, the offset is used to obtain main memory address reference.

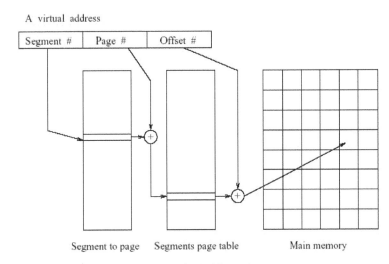

Segmentation with paging.

In practice, there are segments for the code(s), data, and stack. Each segment carries the *rwe* information as well. Usually the stack and data have read write permissions but no execute permissions. Code rarely has write permission but would have a read and execute permission.

References

- Disc File Applications: Reports Presented at the Nation's First Disc File Symposium. American Data Processing. 1964. Retrieved August 1, 2016

- "OS X Mountain Lion: What is a Mac OS Extended (Journaled) volume?". Apple. August 8, 2013. Retrieved February 7, 2014

- McGill, Florence E. (1922). Office Practice and Business Procedure. Gregg Publishing Company. p. 197. Retrieved August 1, 2016

- Singh, Amit (2007). "12 The HFS Plus File System". Mac OS X Internals: A Systems Approach. Addison Wesley. ISBN 0321278542

- Reiser, Hans (2006-02-06). "The Reiser4 Filesystem". Google TechTalks. Archived from the original on 22 August 2012. Retrieved 2006-12-14

- Douceur, John R.; Bolosky, William J. (June 1999). "A Large-Scale Study of File-System Contents". ACM SIGMETRICS Performance Evaluation Review. Association for Computing Machinery. 27 (1): 59–70. doi:10.1145/301464.301480

- Smith, Keith Arnold (January 2001). "Workload-Specific File System Benchmarks" (PDF). Cambridge, Massachusetts: Harvard University. Retrieved 2006-12-14

3

Real Time Operating Systems: An Integrated Study

Owing to time constraint in some data processing applications, it becomes necessary that system responses reach within the stipulated time. This time period, however, can be generalized as it depends on the application and its urgency. These data processing application include online banking, tele-ticketing, online stock trading, etc. and are known as real time systems. The major components of real time operating systems are discussed in this chapter.

Real Time Operating Systems

In some data processing applications system responses are meaningful, if these are within a certain stipulated time period. System responses that arrive later than the expected time are usually irrelevant or meaningless. In fact, sometimes, it's no better than being simply wrong. Therefore, the system response must be generated well within the stipulated time. This is true particularly of on-line stock trading, tele-ticketing and similar other transactions. These systems are generally recognized to be real-time systems. For interactive systems the responses ought to match human reaction times to be able to see the effects as well (as in on line banking or video games).

Real-time systems may be required in life critical applications such as patient monitoring systems. They may also be applied in safety critical systems such as reactor control systems in a power plant. Let us consider a safety critical application like anti-lock braking system (ABS), where control settings have to be determined in real-time. A passenger car driver needs to be able to control his automobile under adverse driving conditions.

In a car without ABS, the driver has to cleverly pump and release the brake pedal to prevent skids. Cars, with ABS control, regulate pumping cycle of brakes automatically. This is achieved by modifying the pressure applied on brake pedals by a driver in panic. A real-time control system gives a timely response. Clearly, what is a timely response is determined by the context of application. Usually, one reckons that a certain response is timely, if it allows for enough time to set the needed controller(s) appropriately, i.e. before it is too late. In safety critical, or life critical situations a delay may even result in a catastrophe. Operating systems are designed keeping in mind the context of use. As we have seen, the OS designers ensure high resource utilization and throughput in the general purpose computing context. However, for a system which both monitors and responds to events from its operative environment, the system responses are required to be timely. For such an OS, the minimalist kernel design is required. In fact, since all IO requires use of communications through kernel, it is important that kernel overheads are minimal. This has resulted in emergence of micro-kernels. Micro-kernels are minimal kernels which offer kernel services with minimum overheads. The kernels used in hard real-time systems 1 are often micro-kernels. In this chapter, we shall cover the relevant issues and strategies to design an OS which can service real-time requirements.

A real-time operating system (RTOS) is an operating system (OS) intended to serve real-time applications that process data as it comes in, typically without buffering delays. Processing time requirements (including any OS delay) are measured in tenths of seconds or shorter increments of time. They either are event driven or time sharing. Event driven systems switch between tasks based on their priorities while time sharing systems switch the task based on clock interrupts.

A key characteristic of an RTOS is the level of its consistency concerning the amount of time it takes to accept and complete an application's task; the variability is *jitter*. A *hard* real-time operating system has less jitter than a *soft* real-time operating system. The chief design goal is not high throughput, but rather a guarantee of a soft or hard performance category. An RTOS that can usually or *generally* meet a *deadline* is a soft real-time OS, but if it can meet a deadline deterministically it is a hard real-time OS.

An RTOS has an advanced algorithm for scheduling. Scheduler flexibility enables a wider, computer-system orchestration of process priorities, but a real-time OS is more frequently dedicated to a narrow set of applications. Key factors in a real-time OS are minimal interrupt latency and minimal thread switching latency; a real-time OS is valued more for how quickly or how predictably it can respond than for the amount of work it can perform in a given period of time.

Design Philosophies

The most common designs are:

- Event-driven – switches tasks only when an event of higher priority needs servicing; called preemptive priority, or priority scheduling.

- Time-sharing – switches tasks on a regular clocked interrupt, and on events; called round robin.

Time sharing designs switch tasks more often than strictly needed, but give smoother multitasking, giving the illusion that a process or user has sole use of a machine.

Early CPU designs needed many cycles to switch tasks, during which the CPU could do nothing else useful. For example, with a 20 MHz 68000 processor (typical of the late 1980s), task switch times are roughly 20 microseconds. (In contrast, a 100 MHz ARM CPU (from 2008) switches in less than 3 microseconds.) Because of this, early OSes tried to minimize wasting CPU time by avoiding unnecessary task switching.

Scheduling

In typical designs, a task has three states:

1. Running (executing on the CPU);

2. Ready (ready to be executed);

3. Blocked (waiting for an event, I/O for example).

Most tasks are blocked or ready most of the time because generally only one task can run at a time per CPU. The number of items in the ready queue can vary greatly, depending on the number of tasks the system needs to perform and the type of scheduler that the system uses. On simpler non-preemptive but still multitasking systems, a task has to give up its time on the CPU to other tasks, which can cause the ready queue to have a greater number of overall tasks in the ready to be executed state (resource starvation).

Usually the data structure of the ready list in the scheduler is designed to minimize the worst-case length of time spent in the scheduler's critical section, during which preemption is inhibited, and, in some cases, all interrupts are disabled. But the choice of data structure depends also on the maximum number of tasks that can be on the ready list.

If there are never more than a few tasks on the ready list, then a doubly linked list of ready tasks is likely optimal. If the ready list usually contains only a few tasks but occasionally contains more, then the list should be sorted by priority. That way, finding the highest priority task to run does not require iterating through the entire list. Inserting a task then requires walking the ready list until reaching either the end of the list, or a task of lower priority than that of the task being inserted.

Care must be taken not to inhibit preemption during this search. Longer critical sections should be divided into small pieces. If an interrupt occurs that makes a high priority task ready during the insertion of a low priority task, that high priority task can be inserted and run immediately before the low priority task is inserted.

The critical response time, sometimes called the flyback time, is the time it takes to queue a new ready task and restore the state of the highest priority task to running. In a well-designed RTOS, readying a new task will take 3 to 20 instructions per ready-queue entry, and restoration of the highest-priority ready task will take 5 to 30 instructions.

In more advanced systems, real-time tasks share computing resources with many non-real-time tasks, and the ready list can be arbitrarily long. In such systems, a scheduler ready list implemented as a linked list would be inadequate.

Algorithms

Some commonly used RTOS scheduling algorithms are:

- Cooperative scheduling

- Preemptive scheduling

  o Rate-monotonic scheduling

  o Round-robin scheduling

  o Fixed priority pre-emptive scheduling, an implementation of preemptive time slicing

- o Fixed-Priority Scheduling with Deferred Preemption

- o Fixed-Priority Non-preemptive Scheduling

- o Critical section preemptive scheduling

- o Static time scheduling

- Earliest Deadline First approach

- Stochastic digraphs with multi-threaded graph traversal

Intertask Communication and Resource Sharing

A multitasking operating system like Unix is poor at real-time tasks. The scheduler gives the highest priority to jobs with the lowest demand on the computer, so there is no way to ensure that a time-critical job will have access to enough resources. Multitasking systems must manage sharing data and hardware resources among multiple tasks. It is usually unsafe for two tasks to access the same specific data or hardware resource simultaneously. There are three common approaches to resolve this problem:

Temporarily Masking/disabling Interrupts

General-purpose operating systems usually do not allow user programs to mask (disable) interrupts, because the user program could control the CPU for as long as it wishes. Some modern CPUs don't allow user mode code to disable interrupts as such control is considered a key operating system resource. Many embedded systems and RTOSs, however, allow the application itself to run in kernel mode for greater system call efficiency and also to permit the application to have greater control of the operating environment without requiring OS intervention.

On single-processor systems, an application running in kernel mode and masking interrupts is the lowest overhead method to prevent simultaneous access to a shared resource. While interrupts are masked and the current task does not make a blocking OS call, the current task has *exclusive* use of the CPU since no other task or interrupt can take control, so the critical section is protected. When the task exits its critical section, it must unmask interrupts; pending interrupts, if any, will then execute. Temporarily masking interrupts should only be done when the longest path through the critical section is shorter than the desired maximum interrupt latency. Typically this method of protection is used only when the critical section is just a few instructions and contains no loops. This method is ideal for protecting hardware bit-mapped registers when the bits are controlled by different tasks.

Binary Semaphores

When the shared resource must be reserved without blocking all other tasks (such as waiting for Flash memory to be written), it is better to use mechanisms also available on general-purpose operating systems, such as semaphores and OS-supervised interprocess messaging. Such mechanisms involve system calls, and usually invoke the OS's dispatcher code on exit, so they typically take hundreds of CPU instructions to execute, while masking interrupts may take as few as one instruction on some processors.

A binary semaphore is either locked or unlocked. When it is locked, tasks must wait for the semaphore to unlock. A binary semaphore is therefore equivalent to a mutex. Typically a task will set a timeout on its wait for a semaphore. There are several well-known problems with semaphore based designs such as priority inversion and deadlocks.

In priority inversion a high priority task waits because a low priority task has a semaphore, but the lower priority task is not given CPU time to finish its work. A typical solution is to have the task that owns a semaphore run at, or 'inherit,' the priority of the highest waiting task. But this simple approach fails when there are multiple levels of waiting: task A waits for a binary semaphore locked by task B, which waits for a binary semaphore locked by task C. Handling multiple levels of inheritance without introducing instability in cycles is complex and problematic.

In a deadlock, two or more tasks lock semaphores without timeouts and then wait forever for the other task's semaphore, creating a cyclic dependency. The simplest deadlock scenario occurs when two tasks alternately lock two semaphores, but in the opposite order. Deadlock is prevented by careful design or by having floored semaphores, which pass control of a semaphore to the higher priority task on defined conditions.

Message Passing

The other approach to resource sharing is for tasks to send messages in an organized message passing scheme. In this paradigm, the resource is managed directly by only one task. When another task wants to interrogate or manipulate the resource, it sends a message to the managing task. Although their real-time behavior is less crisp than semaphore systems, simple message-based systems avoid most protocol deadlock hazards, and are generally better-behaved than semaphore systems. However, problems like those of semaphores are possible. Priority inversion can occur when a task is working on a low-priority message and ignores a higher-priority message (or a message originating indirectly from a high priority task) in its incoming message queue. Protocol deadlocks can occur when two or more tasks wait for each other to send response messages.

Interrupt Handlers and the Scheduler

Since an interrupt handler blocks the highest priority task from running, and since real time operating systems are designed to keep thread latency to a minimum, interrupt handlers are typically kept as short as possible. The interrupt handler defers all interaction with the hardware if possible; typically all that is necessary is to acknowledge or disable the interrupt (so that it won't occur again when the interrupt handler returns) and notify a task that work needs to be done. This can be done by unblocking a driver task through releasing a semaphore, setting a flag or sending a message. A scheduler often provides the ability to unblock a task from interrupt handler context.

An OS maintains catalogues of objects it manages such as threads, mutexes, memory, and so on. Updates to this catalogue must be strictly controlled. For this reason it can be problematic when an interrupt handler calls an OS function while the application is in the act of also doing so. The OS function called from an interrupt handler could find the object database to be in an inconsistent state because of the application's update. There are two major approaches to deal with this problem: the unified architecture and the segmented architecture. RTOSs implementing the unified architecture solve the problem by simply disabling interrupts while the internal catalogue is updated. The downside of this is that interrupt latency increases, potentially losing interrupts. The segmented architecture does not make direct OS calls but delegates the OS related work to a separate handler. This handler runs at a higher priority than any thread but lower than the interrupt handlers. The advantage of this architecture is that it adds very few cycles to interrupt latency. As a result, OSes which implement the segmented architecture are more predictable and can deal with higher interrupt rates compared to the unified architecture.

Memory Allocation

Memory allocation is more critical in a real-time operating system than in other operating systems.

First, for stability there cannot be memory leaks (memory that is allocated, then unused but never freed). The device should work indefinitely, without ever needing a reboot. For this reason, dynamic memory allocation is frowned upon. Whenever possible, all required memory allocation is specified statically at compile time.

Another reason to avoid dynamic memory allocation is memory fragmentation. With frequent allocation and releasing of small chunks of memory, a situation may occur when the memory is divided into several sections, in which case the RTOS cannot allocate a large continuous block of memory, although there is enough free memory. Secondly, speed of allocation is important. A standard memory allocation scheme scans a linked list of indeterminate length to find a suitable free memory block, which is unacceptable in an RTOS since memory allocation has to occur within a certain amount of time.

Because mechanical disks have much longer and more unpredictable response times, swapping to disk files is not used for the same reasons as RAM allocation.

The simple fixed-size-blocks algorithm works quite well for simple embedded systems because of its low overhead.

Characteristics of Real-time Systems

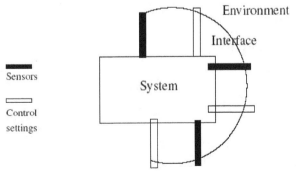

In a real-time system the events in the environment are detected by sensors and the responses to these events are generated in a timely manner. A RTOS ensures that control settings (in response to an event) are achieved in real-time.

Operation environment for RTOS

A typical real-time operating environment is shown in Figure. In this figure we note that the computer system has an interface which is embedded within its environment. The operating system achieves the desired extent of regulation as follows:

o Sense an event: The system monitors its operative environment using some sensors. These sensors keep a tab on some measurable entity. Depending upon the context of use this entity may be a measure of temperature, or a stock price fluctuation or fluid level in a reservoir. These measurements may be periodic. In that case the system would accept an input periodically. In case the measurement of inputs is taken at specified times of operation then the OS may schedule its input at these specified times or it may be interrupted to accept the input. The input may even be measured only when an unusual deviation in the value of the monitored entity occurs. In these cases the input would certainly result in an interrupt. Regardless of the input mode, the system would have an input following a sensor reading (which is an event).

o Process the data: The next important task is to process the data which has been most recently acquired. The data processing may be aimed at checking the health of the system. Usually it is to determine if some action is needed.

o Decide on an action: Usually, the processing steps involving arriving at some decisions on control settings. For instance, if the stock prices cross some threshold, then one has to decide to buy or sell or do nothing. As another example, the action may be to open a valve a little more to increase inflow in case reservoir level drops.

o Take a corrective action: In case, the settings need to be altered, the new settings are determined and control actuators are initiated. Note that the actions in turn affect the environment. It is quite possible that as a consequence, a new set of events get triggered. Also, it is possible that the corrective step requires a drastic and an immediate step. For instance, if an alarm is to be raised, then all the other tasks have to be suspended or pre-empted and an alarm raised immediately. Real- time systems quite often resort to pre-emption to prevent a catastrophe from happening.

The OS may be a bare-bone microkernel to ensure that input events are processed with minimum overhead. Usually, the sensor and monitoring instruments communicate with the rest of the system in interrupt mode. Device drivers are specifically tuned to service these inputs.We shall discuss the related design issues for micro-kernels and RTOS.

Why not use Unix or Windows? This is one very natural question to raise. Unix or Windows are operating systems that have been designed with no specific class of applications in mind. These are robust, (like all terrain vehicles), but not suitable for real- time operations (say Formula 1 cars). Their performance in real-time domain would be like that of an all terrain vehicle on a formula one race track. Note that the timeliness in response is crucial in real-time operations. General-purpose operating systems are designed to enhance throughput. Often it has considerable leeway in responding to events. Also, within a service type, the general-purpose OS cater to a very vast range of services. For example, just consider the print service. There is considerable leeway with regard to system response time. Additionally, the printer service may cater to a vast category of print devices which range from ink-jet to laser printing or from gray scale to color printing. In other words, the service rendering code is long. Additionally, it caters to a large selection in printer devices. This makes service rendering slow. Also, a few seconds of delay in printing matters very little, if at all. Real-time operative environments usually have a fixed domain of operations in which events have fairly predictable patterns, but do need monitoring and periodic checks. For instance, a vessel in a chemical process will witness fairly predictable form of rise in temperature or pressure, but needs to be monitored. This means that the scheduling strategies would be event centered or time centered. In a general-purpose computing environment the events arise from multiple, and not necessarily predictable, sources. In real-time systems, the events are fairly well known and may even have a pattern. However, there is a stipulated response time. Within this context, development of scheduling algorithms for real-time systems is a major area of research.

A natural question which may be raised is: Can one modify a general purpose OS to meet real-time requirements. Sometimes a general-purpose OS kernel is stripped down to provide for the basic IO services. This kernel is called microkernel. Microkernels do meet RTOS application specific service requirements. This is what is done in Windows CE and Embedded Linux.

Note we have made two important points above. One relates to timeliness of response and the other relates to event-centric operation. Scheduling has to be organized to ensure timeliness under event-centric operation. This may have to be done at the expense of loss of overall throughput.

Classification of Real-time Systems

The classification of real-time systems is usually based on the severity of the consequences of failing to meet time constraints. This can be understood as follows. Suppose a system requires a response to an event in time period T. Now we ask: what happens if the response is not received within the stipulated time period? The failure to meet the time constraint may result in different degrees of severity of consequences. In a life-critical or safety critical application, the failure may result in a disaster such as loss of life. A case in point is the shuttle Columbia's accident in early February 2 2003. Recall Kalpana Chawla, an aeronautics engineering Ph. D. was on board. During its descent, about 16 minutes from landing, the spacecraft temperature rose to dangerous levels resulting in a catastrophic end of the mission. Clearly, the rise in temperature as a space draft enters earth's atmosphere is anticipated. Spacecrafts have RTOS regulating the controllers to respond to such situations from developing. And yet the cooling system(s) in this case did not offer timely mitigation. Both in terms of loss of human life and the cost of mission such a failure has the highest severity of consequences. Whereas in the case of an online stock trading, or a game show, it may mean a financial loss or a missed opportunity. In the case of a dropped packet in a video streaming application it would simply mean a glitch and a perhaps a temporary drop in the picture quality. The three examples of real-time system we have given here have different levels of severity in terms of timely response. The first one has life-threatening implication; the second case refers to a missed opportunity and finally, degraded picture quality in viewing. Associated with these are the broadly accepted categories hard, firm and soft real-time systems.

Architecture of Real-time Systems: The basic architecture of such systems is simple. As shown in Figure, some sensors provide input from the operative environment and a computation determines the required control. Finally, an appropriate actuator is activated. However, since the consequence of failure to respond to events can be catastrophic, it is important to build in the following two features in the system.

1. It should be a fault tolerant design.

2. The scheduling policy must provide for pre-emptive action.

For a fault tolerant design, the strategies may include majority voting out of the faulty sensors. Systems like satellite guidance system, usually have back-up (or a hot-stand-by) system to fall back upon. This is because the cost of failure of a mission is simply too high. Designers of Airbus A-320 had pegged the figure of failure probability at lower than 10-10 for one hour period in flight As for design of scheduling policy, one first identifies the critical functions and not so critical functions within an operation. The scheduling algorithm ensures that the critical functions obtain high priority interrupts to elicit immediate responses. In Figure, we depict the priority structure for such a design.

Low priority	Not so critical application tasks	Each task represents a thread of operation
Medium priority	System tasks	
High priority tasks	Application tasks of critical nature	A thread is a light weight process. It carries the parent process's context with it

Priority structure for RTOS tasks.

A very detailed discussion on design of real-time systems is beyond the scope of this book. Yet, it is worth mentioning here that RTOS designers have two basic design orientations to consider. One is to think in terms of event-triggered operations and the other is to think of time-triggered operations. These considerations also determine its scheduling policy. The report prepared by Panzierri and his colleagues compares architectures based on these two considerations. The observation is that time-triggered architectures obtain greater predictability but end up wasting more resource cycles of operation due to more frequent pre-emptions. On the other hand, event-triggered system architectures seem to score in terms of their ability to adapt to a variety of operating scenarios. Event-triggered systems are generally better suited for asynchronous input events. The time-triggered systems are better suited for systems with periodic inputs. For now, let us examine micro-kernels which are at the heart of RTOS, event-triggered or time-triggered.

Microkernel

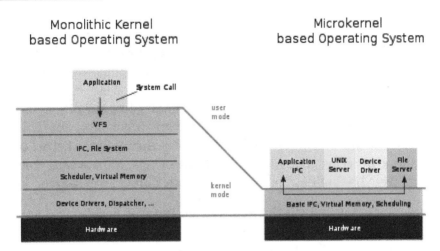

Structure of monolithic and microkernel-based operating systems, respectively

In computer science, a microkernel (also known as μ-kernel) is the near-minimum amount of software that can provide the mechanisms needed to implement an operating system (OS). These mechanisms include low-level address space management, thread management, and inter-process communication (IPC).

If the hardware provides multiple rings or CPU modes, the microkernel may be the only software executing at the most privileged level, which is generally referred to as supervisor or kernel mode. Traditional operating system functions, such as device drivers, protocol stacks and file systems, are typically removed from the microkernel itself and are instead run in user space.

In terms of the source code size, as a general rule microkernels tend to be smaller than monolithic kernels. The MINIX 3 microkernel, for example, has approximately 12,000 lines of code.

History

Microkernels trace their roots back to Danish computer pioneer Per Brinch Hansen and his tenure in Danish computer company Regnecentralen where he led software development efforts for the RC 4000 computer. In 1967, Regnecentralen was installing a RC 4000 prototype in a Polish fertilizer plant in Puławy. The computer used a small real-time operating system tailored for the needs of the plant. Brinch Hansen and his team became concerned with the lack of generality and reusability of the RC 4000 system. They feared that each installation would require a different operating system so they started to investigate novel and more general ways of creating software for the RC 4000. In 1969, their effort resulted in the completion of the RC 4000 Multiprogramming System. Its nucleus provided inter-process communication based on message-passing for up to 23 unprivileged processes, out of which 8 at a time were protected from one another. It further implemented scheduling of time slices of programs executed in parallel, initiation and control of program execution at the request of other running programs, and initiation of data transfers to or from peripherals. Besides these elementary mechanisms, it had no built-in strategy for program execution and resource allocation. This strategy was to be implemented by a hierarchy of running programs in which parent processes had complete control over child processes and acted as their operating systems.

Microkernels were first developed in the 1980s as a response to changes in the computer world, and to several challenges adapting existing "mono-kernels" to these new systems. New device drivers, protocol stacks, file systems and other low-level systems were being developed all the time. This code was normally located in the monolithic kernel, and thus required considerable work and careful code management to work on. Microkernels were developed with the idea that all of these services would be implemented as user-space programs, like any other, allowing them to be worked on monolithically and started and stopped like any other program. This would not only allow these services to be more easily worked on, but also separated the kernel code to allow it to be finely tuned without worrying about unintended side effects. Moreover, it would allow entirely new operating systems to be "built up" on a common core, aiding OS research.

Microkernels were a very hot topic in the 1980s when the first usable local area networks were being introduced. The same mechanisms that allowed the kernel to be distributed into user space also allowed the system to be distributed across network links. The first microkernels, notably Mach, proved to have disappointing performance, but the inherent advantages appeared so great that it was a major line of research into the late 1990s. However, during this time the speed of computers grew greatly in relation to networking systems, and the disadvantages in performance came to overwhelm the advantages in development terms. Many attempts were made to adapt the existing systems to have better performance, but the overhead was always considerable and most of these efforts required the user-space programs to be moved back into the kernel. By 2000, most large-scale (Mach-like) efforts had ended, although OpenStep used an adapted Mach kernel called XNU, which is used in Darwin, an operating system serving as the open source part of both macOS and iOS. As of 2012, the Mach-based GNU Hurd is also functional and included in testing versions of Arch Linux and Debian.

Although major work on microkernels had largely ended, experimenters continued development. It has since been shown that many of the performance problems of earlier designs were not a fundamental limitation of the concept, but instead due to the designer's desire to use single-purpose systems to implement as many of these services as possible. Using a more pragmatic approach to the problem, including assembly code and relying on the processor to enforce concepts normally supported in software led to a new series of microkernels with dramatically improved performance.

Microkernels are closely related to exokernels. They also have much in common with hypervisors, but the latter make no claim to minimality and are specialized to supporting virtual machines; indeed, the L4 microkernel frequently finds use in a hypervisor capacity.

Introduction

Early operating system kernels were rather small, partly because computer memory was limited. As the capability of computers grew, the number of devices the kernel had to control also grew. Throughout the early history of Unix, kernels were generally small, even though they contained various device drivers and file system implementations. When address spaces increased from 16 to 32 bits, kernel design was no longer constrained by the hardware architecture, and kernels began to grow larger.

The Berkeley Software Distribution (BSD) of Unix began the era of larger kernels. In addition to operating a basic system consisting of the CPU, disks and printers, BSD added a complete TCP/IP networking system and a number of "virtual" devices that allowed the existing programs to work 'invisibly' over the network. This growth continued for many years, resulting in kernels with millions of lines of source code. As a result of this growth, kernels were prone to bugs and became increasingly difficult to maintain.

The microkernel was intended to address this growth of kernels and the difficulties that resulted. In theory, the microkernel design allows for easier management of code due to its division into user space services. This also allows for increased security and stability resulting from the reduced amount of code running in kernel mode. For example, if a networking service crashed due to buffer overflow, only the networking service's memory would be corrupted, leaving the rest of the system still functional.

Inter-process Communication

Inter-process communication (IPC) is any mechanism which allows separate processes to communicate with each other, usually by sending messages. Shared memory is strictly speaking also an inter-process communication mechanism, but the abbreviation IPC usually only refers to message passing, and it is the latter that is particularly relevant to microkernels. IPC allows the operating system to be built from a number of small programs called servers, which are used by other programs on the system, invoked via IPC. Most or all support for peripheral hardware is handled in this fashion, with servers for device drivers, network protocol stacks, file systems, graphics, etc.

IPC can be synchronous or asynchronous. Asynchronous IPC is analogous to network communication: the sender dispatches a message and continues executing. The receiver checks (polls) for the availability of the message by attempting a receive, or is alerted to it via some notification mechanism. Asynchronous IPC requires that the kernel maintains buffers and queues for messages, and deals with buffer overflows; it also requires double copying of messages (sender to kernel and kernel to receiver). In synchronous IPC, the first party (sender or receiver) blocks until the other party is ready to perform the IPC. It does not require buffering or multiple copies, but the implicit rendezvous can make programming tricky. Most programmers prefer asynchronous send and synchronous receive.

First-generation microkernels typically supported synchronous as well as asynchronous IPC, and suffered from poor IPC performance. Jochen Liedtke assumed the design and implementation of the IPC mechanisms to be the underlying reason for this poor performance. In his L4 microkernel he pioneered methods that lowered IPC costs by an order of magnitude. These include an IPC system call that supports a send as well as a receive operation, making all IPC synchronous, and passing as much data as possible in registers. Furthermore, Liedtke introduced the concept of the *direct process switch*, where during an IPC execution an (incomplete) context switch is performed from the sender directly to the receiver. If, as in L4, part or all of the message is passed in registers, this transfers the in-register part of the message without any copying at all. Furthermore, the overhead of invoking the scheduler is avoided; this is especially beneficial in the common case where IPC is used in an RPC-type fashion by a client invoking a server. Another optimization, called *lazy scheduling*, avoids traversing scheduling queues during IPC by leaving threads that block during IPC in the ready queue. Once the scheduler is invoked, it moves such threads to the appropriate waiting queue. As in many cases a thread gets unblocked before the next scheduler invocation, this approach saves significant work. Similar approaches have since been adopted by QNX and MINIX 3.

In a series of experiments, Chen and Bershad compared memory cycles per instruction (MCPI) of monolithic Ultrix with those of microkernel Mach combined with a 4.3BSD Unix server running in user space. Their results explained Mach's poorer performance by higher MCPI and demonstrated that IPC alone is not responsible for much of the system overhead, suggesting that optimizations focused exclusively on IPC will have limited impact. Liedtke later refined Chen and Bershad's results by making an observation that the bulk of the difference between Ultrix and Mach MCPI was caused by capacity cache-misses and concluding that drastically reducing the cache working set of a microkernel will solve the problem.

In a client-server system, most communication is essentially synchronous, even if using asynchronous primitives, as the typical operation is a client invoking a server and then waiting for a reply. As it also lends itself to more efficient implementation, most microkernels generally followed L4's lead and only provided a synchronous IPC primitive. Asynchronous IPC could be implemented on top by using helper threads. However, experience has shown that the utility of synchronous IPC is dubious: synchronous IPC forces a multi-threaded design onto otherwise simple systems, with the resulting synchronization complexities. Moreover, an RPC-like server invocation sequentializes client and server, which should be avoided if they are running on separate cores. Versions of L4 deployed in commercial products have therefore found it necessary to add an asynchronous notification mechanism to better support asynchronous communication. This signal-like mechanism does not carry data and therefore does not require buffering by the kernel. By having two forms of IPC, they have nonetheless violated the principle of minimality. Other versions of L4 have switched to asynchronous IPC completely.

As synchronous IPC blocks the first party until the other is ready, unrestricted use could easily lead to deadlocks. Furthermore, a client could easily mount a denial-of-service attack on a server by sending a request and never attempting to receive the reply. Therefore, synchronous IPC must provide a means to prevent indefinite blocking. Many microkernels provide timeouts on IPC calls, which limit the blocking time. In practice, choosing sensible timeout values is difficult, and systems almost inevitably use infinite timeouts for clients and zero timeouts for servers. As a consequence, the trend is towards not providing arbitrary timeouts, but only a flag which indicates that the IPC should fail immediately if the partner is not ready. This approach effectively provides a choice of the two timeout values of zero and infinity. Recent versions of L4 and MINIX have gone down this path (older versions of L4 used timeouts, as does QNX).

Servers

Microkernel servers are essentially daemon programs like any others, except that the kernel grants some of them privileges to interact with parts of physical memory that are otherwise off limits to most programs. This allows some servers, particularly device drivers, to interact directly with hardware.

A basic set of servers for a general-purpose microkernel includes file system servers, device driver servers, networking servers, display servers, and user interface device servers. This set of servers (drawn from QNX) provides roughly the set of services offered by a Unix monolithic kernel. The necessary servers are started at system startup and provide services, such as file, network, and device access, to ordinary application programs. With such servers running in the environment of a user application, server development is similar to ordinary application development, rather than the build-and-boot process needed for kernel development.

Additionally, many "crashes" can be corrected by simply stopping and restarting the server. However, part of the system state is lost with the failing server, hence this approach requires applications to cope with failure. A good example is a server responsible for TCP/IP connections: If this server is restarted, applications will experience a "lost" connection, a normal occurrence in a networked system. For other services, failure is less expected and may require changes to application code. For QNX, restart capability is offered as the QNX High Availability Toolkit.

To make all servers restartable, some microkernels have concentrated on adding various database-like methods such as transactions, replication and checkpointing to preserve essential state across single server restarts. An example is ChorusOS, which was made for high-availability applications in the telecommunications world. Chorus included features to allow any "properly written" server to be restarted at any time, with clients using those servers being paused while the server brought itself back into its original state. However, such kernel features are incompatible with the minimality principle, and are thus not provided in modern microkernels, which instead rely on appropriate user-level protocols.

Device Drivers

Device drivers frequently perform direct memory access (DMA), and therefore can write to arbitrary locations of physical memory, including various kernel data structures. Such drivers must therefore be trusted. It is a common misconception that this means that they must be part of the kernel. In fact, a driver is not inherently more or less trustworthy by being part of the kernel.

While running a device driver in user space does not necessarily reduce the damage a misbehaving driver can cause, in practice it is beneficial for system stability in the presence of buggy (rather than malicious) drivers: memory-access violations by the driver code itself (as opposed to the device) may still be caught by the memory-management hardware. Furthermore, many devices are not DMA-capable, their drivers can be made untrusted by running them in user space. Recently, an increasing number of computers feature IOMMUs, many of which can be used to restrict a device's access to physical memory. (IBM mainframes have had IO MMUs since the IBM System/360 Model 67 and System/370). This also allows user-mode drivers to become untrusted.

User-mode drivers actually predate microkernels. The Michigan Terminal System (MTS), in 1967, supported user space drivers (including its file system support), the first operating system to be designed with that capability. Historically, drivers were less of a problem, as the number of devices was small and trusted anyway, so having them in the kernel simplified the design and avoided potential performance problems. This led to the traditional driver-in-the-kernel style of Unix, Linux, and Windows before Windows XP. With the proliferation of various kinds of peripherals, the amount of driver code escalated and in modern operating systems dominates the kernel in code size.

Essential components and minimality

As a microkernel must allow building arbitrary operating system services on top, it must provide some core functionality. At a minimum, this includes:

- some mechanisms for dealing with address spaces, required for managing memory protection

- some execution abstraction to manage CPU allocation, typically threads or scheduler activations

- inter-process communication, required to invoke servers running in their own address spaces

This minimal design was pioneered by Brinch Hansen's Nucleus and the hypervisor of IBM's VM. It has since been formalised in Liedtke's *minimality principle*:

A concept is tolerated inside the microkernel only if moving it outside the kernel, i.e., permitting competing implementations, would prevent the implementation of the system's required functionality.

Everything else can be done in a usermode program, although device drivers implemented as user programs may on some processor architectures require special privileges to access I/O hardware.

Related to the minimality principle, and equally important for microkernel design, is the separation of mechanism and policy, it is what enables the construction of arbitrary systems on top of a minimal kernel. Any policy built into the kernel cannot be overwritten at user level and therefore limits the generality of the microkernel. Policy implemented in user-level servers can be changed by replacing the servers (or letting the application choose between competing servers offering similar services).

For efficiency, most microkernels contain schedulers and manage timers, in violation of the minimality principle and the principle of policy-mechanism separation.

Start up (booting) of a microkernel-based system requires device drivers, which are not part of the kernel. Typically this means that they are packaged with the kernel in the boot image, and the kernel supports a bootstrap protocol that defines how the drivers are located and started; this is the traditional bootstrap procedure of L4 microkernels. Some microkernels simplify this by placing some key drivers inside the kernel (in violation of the minimality principle), LynxOS and the original Minix are examples. Some even include a file system in the kernel to simplify booting. A microkernel-based system may boot via multiboot compatible boot loader. Such systems usually load statically-linked servers to make an initial bootstrap or mount an OS image to continue bootstrapping.

A key component of a microkernel is a good IPC system and virtual-memory-manager design that allows implementing page-fault handling and swapping in usermode servers in a safe way. Since all services are performed by usermode programs, efficient means of communication between programs are essential, far more so than in monolithic kernels. The design of the IPC system makes or breaks a microkernel. To be effective, the IPC system must not only have low overhead, but also interact well with CPU scheduling.

Performance

On most mainstream processors, obtaining a service is inherently more expensive in a microkernel-based system than a monolithic system. In the monolithic system, the service is obtained by a single system call, which requires two *mode switches* (changes of the processor's ring or CPU mode). In the microkernel-based system, the service is obtained by sending an IPC message to a server, and obtaining the result in another IPC message from the server. This requires a context switch if the drivers are implemented as processes, or a function call if they are implemented as procedures. In addition, passing actual data to the server and back may incur extra copying overhead, while in a monolithic system the kernel can directly access the data in the client's buffers.

Performance is therefore a potential issue in microkernel systems. Indeed, the experience of first-generation microkernels such as Mach and ChorusOS showed that systems based on them performed very poorly. However, Jochen Liedtke showed that Mach's performance problems were the result of poor design and implementation, specifically Mach's excessive cache footprint. Liedtke demonstrated with his own L4 microkernel that through careful design and implementation, and especially by following the minimality principle, IPC costs could be reduced by more than an order of magnitude compared to Mach. L4's IPC performance is still unbeaten across a range of architectures.

While these results demonstrate that the poor performance of systems based on first-generation microkernels is not representative for second-generation kernels such as L4, this constitutes no proof that microkernel-based systems can be built with good performance. It has been shown that a monolithic Linux server ported to L4 exhibits only a few percent overhead over native Linux. However, such a single-server system exhibits few, if any, of the advantages microkernels are supposed to provide by structuring operating system functionality into separate servers.

A number of commercial multi-server systems exist, in particular the real-time systems QNX and Integrity. No comprehensive comparison of performance relative to monolithic systems has been published for those multiserver systems. Furthermore, performance does not seem to be the overriding concern for those commercial systems, which instead emphasize reliably quick interrupt handling response times (QNX) and simplicity for the sake of robustness. An attempt to build a high-performance multiserver operating system was the IBM Sawmill Linux project. However, this project was never completed.

It has been shown in the meantime that user-level device drivers can come close to the performance of in-kernel drivers even for such high-throughput, high-interrupt devices as Gigabit Ethernet. This seems to imply that high-performance multi-server systems are possible.

Security

The security benefits of microkernels have been frequently discussed. In the context of security the minimality principle of microkernels is, some have argued, a direct consequence of the principle of least privilege, according to which all code should have only the privileges needed to provide required functionality. Minimality requires that a system's trusted computing base (TCB) should be kept minimal. As the kernel (the code that executes in the privileged mode of the hardware) has unvetted access to any data and can thus violate its integrity or confidentiality, the kernel is always part of the TCB. Minimizing it is natural in a security-driven design.

Consequently, microkernel designs have been used for systems designed for high-security applications, including KeyKOS, EROS and military systems. In fact common criteria (CC) at the highest assurance level (Evaluation Assurance Level (EAL) 7) has an explicit requirement that the target of evaluation be "simple", an acknowledgment of the practical impossibility of establishing true trustworthiness for a complex system. Unfortunately, again, the term "simple" is misleading and ill-defined. At least the Department of Defense Trusted Computer System Evaluation Criteria introduced somewhat more precise verbiage at the B3/A1 classes:

> "The TCB shall [implement] complete, conceptually simple protection mechanisms with precisely defined semantics. Significant system engineering shall be directed toward minimizing the complexity of the TCB, as well as excluding from the TCB those modules that are not protection-critical."

> — *Department of Defense Trusted Computer System Evaluation Criteria*

Third generation

Recent work on microkernels has been focusing on formal specifications of the kernel API, and formal proofs of the API's security properties and implementation correctness. The first example of this is a mathematical proof of the confinement mechanisms in EROS, based on a simplified model of the EROS API. More recently, a comprehensive set of machine-checked proofs has been performed of the properties of the protection model of seL4, a version of L4.

This has led to what is referred to as *third-generation microkernels*, characterised by a security-oriented API with resource access controlled by capabilities, virtualization as a first-class concern, novel approaches to kernel resource management, and a design goal of suitability for formal analysis, besides the usual goal of high performance. Examples are Coyotos, seL4, Nova, and Fiasco.OC.

In the case of seL4, complete formal verification of the implementation has been achieved, i.e. a mathematical proof that the kernel's implementation is consistent with its formal specification. This provides a guarantee that the properties proved about the API actually hold for the real kernel, a degree of assurance which goes beyond even CC EAL7. It was followed by proofs of security-enforcement properties of the API, and a proof demonstrating that the executable binary code is a correct translation of the C implementation, taking the compiler out of the TCB. Taken together, these proofs establish an end-to-end proof of security properties of the kernel.

Nanokernel

The term *nanokernel* or *picokernel* historically referred to:

- A kernel where the total amount of kernel code, i.e. code executing in the privileged mode of the hardware, is very small. The term *picokernel* was sometimes used to further emphasize small size. The term *nanokernel* was coined by Jonathan S. Shapiro in the paper *The KeyKOS NanoKernel Architecture*. It was a sardonic response to Mach, which claimed to be a microkernel while Shapiro considered it monolithic, essentially unstructured, and slower than the systems it sought to replace. Subsequent reuse of and response to the term, including the picokernel coinage, suggest that the point was largely missed. Both *nanokernel* and *picokernel* have subsequently come to have the same meaning expressed by the term microkernel.

- A virtualization layer underneath an operating system, which is more correctly referred to as a hypervisor.

- A hardware abstraction layer that forms the lowest-level part of a kernel, sometimes used to provide real-time functionality to normal operating systems, like Adeos.

There is also at least one case where the term nanokernel is used to refer not to a small kernel, but one that supports a nanosecond clock resolution.

Microkernels and RTOS

As stated earlier, micro-kernels are kernels with bare-bone, minimal essentials. To understand the notion of "bare-bone minimal essentials", we shall proceed bottom up. Also, we shall take an embedded system design viewpoint.

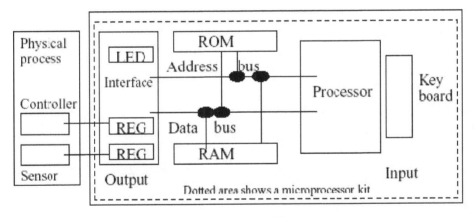

Embedded system architecture

Let us first consider a microprocessor kit. The kit is shown in figure within the dotted area. We can program the kit in machine language. The program can be directly stored in memory. On execution we observe output on LEDs. We also have some attached ROM. To simulate the operation of an embedded system input can be read from sensors and we can output to an interface to activate an actuator. We can use the timers and use these to periodically monitor a process. One can demonstrate the operation of an elevator control or a washing machine with these kits. We just write one program and may even do single steps through this program. Here there is no need to have an operating system. There is only one resident program.

Next, we move to an added level of complexity in interfaces. For an embedded system, input and output characterizations are very crucial. Many of the controls in embedded systems require a real-time clock. The need for real-time clocks arises from the requirement to periodically monitor (or regulate) process health. Also, abnormal state of any critical process variable needs to be detected. The timers, as also abnormal values of process state variables, generate interrupt. An example of process monitoring is shown in figure. As for the operational scenario, note that a serial controller is connected to two serial ports. Both the serial ports may be sending data. The system needs to regulate this traffic through the controller. For instance, in our example, regulating the operations of the serial controller is itself a task. In general, there may be more than one task each with its own priority level to initiate an interrupt, or there is a timer to interrupt. Essentially, one or more interrupts may happen. Interrupts require two actions. One to store away the context of the running process. The other is to switch to an interrupt service routine (ISR). The ROM may store ISRs. Before switching to an ISR, the context (the status of the present program) can be temporarily stored in RAM. All these requirements translate to management of multiple tasks with their own priorities. And that establishes the need for an embedded operating system.

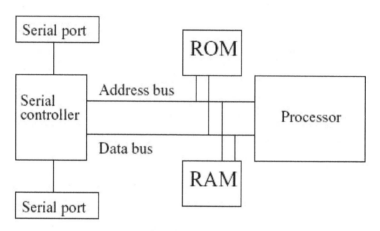

Embedded system example

In addition, to fully meet control requirements, the present level of technology supports on-chip peripherals. Also, there may be more than one timer. Multiple timers enable monitoring multiple activities, each with a different period. There are also a number of ports to support inputs from multiple sensors and outputs to multiple controllers. All this because: a process in which this system is embedded usually has several periodic measurements to be made and several levels of priority of operations. Embedded systems may be even internet enabled. For instance, hand-held devices are usually net enabled.

In Figure we show a software view. The software view is that the device drivers are closely and directly tied to the peripherals. This ensures timely IO required by various tasks. The context of the applications define the tasks.

Typically, the IO may be using polling or an interrupt based IO. The IO may also be memory mapped. If it is memory mapped then the memory space is adequately allocated to offer IO mappings. Briefly, then the embedded system OS designers shall pay attention to the device drivers and scheduling of tasks based on interrupt priority. The device driver functions in this context are the following.

- Do the initialization when started. May need to store an initial value in a register.

- Move the data from the device to the system. This is the most often performed task by the device driver.

- Bring the hardware to a safe state, if required. This may be needed when a recovery is required or the system needs to be reset.

- Respond to interrupt service routine. The interrupt service routine may need some status information. A typical embedded system OS is organized as a minimal system. Essentially, it is a system which has a microkernel at the core which is duly supported by a library of system call functions. The microkernel together with this library is capable of the following.

- Identify and create a task.

- Resource allocation and reallocation amongst tasks.

- Delete a task.

- Identify task state like running, ready-to-run, blocked for IO etc.

- To support task operations (launch, block, read-port, run etc.), i.e. should facilitate low level message passing (or signals communication).

- Memory management functions (allocation and de-allocation to processes).

- Support preemptive scheduling policy.

- Should have support to handle priority inversion3.

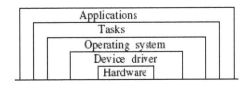 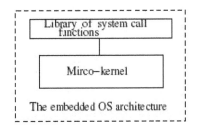

Software view of microkernel based OS.

Let us elaborate on some of these points. The allocation and de-allocation of main memory in a microkernel requires that there is a main memory management system. Also, the fact that we can schedule the operation of tasks means that it is essential to have a loader as a part of a microkernel. Usually, the micro-kernels are designed with a system all \functions" library. These calls support, creation of a task, loading of a task, and communication via ports. Also, there may be a need to either suspend or kill tasks. When tasks are de-allocated, a resource reallocation may happen. This requires support for semaphores. Also, note that a support for critical section management is needed. With semaphores this can be provided for as well. In case the system operates in a distributed environment (tele-metered or internet environment), then a network support is also required. Here again, the support could be minimal so as to be able to communicate via a port. Usually in such systems, the ports are used as "mailboxes". Finally, hardware dependent features are supported via system calls.

When a task is created (or loaded), the task parameters in the system calls, include the size (in terms of main memory required), priority of the task, point of entry for task and a few other parameters to indicate the resources, ownership, or access rights. The microkernel needs to maintain some information about tasks like the state information of each task. This again is very minimal information like, running, runnable, blocked, etc. For periodic tasks we need to support the clock-based interrupt mechanism. We also have to support multiple interrupt levels. There are many advantages of a microkernel-based OS design. In particular, a microkernel affords portability. In fact, Carsten Ditze , argues that microkernel can be designed with minimal hardware dependence. The user services can be offered as set of library of system calls or utilities. In fact, Carsten advocates configuration management by suitably tailoring the library functions to meet the requirements of a real-time system. In brief, there are two critical factors in the microkernel design. One concerns the way we may handle nested interrupts with priority. The other concerns the way we may take care of scheduling. We studied interrupts in detail in the chapter on IO. Here, we focus on the consideration in the design of schedulers for real-time systems. An embedded OS veers around the device drivers and a microkernel with a library of system calls which supports real-time operations. One category of embedded systems are the hand-held devices. Next, we shall see the nature of operations of hand-held devices.

OS for Hand-held Devices

The first noticeable characteristic of hand-held devices is their size. Hand-held devices can be carried in person; this means that these device offer mobility. Mobile devices may be put in the category of phones, pagers, and personal digital assistants (PDAs). Each of these devices have evolved from different needs and in different ways. Mobile phones came about as the people became more mobile themselves. There was this felt need to extend the capabilities of land-line communication. Clearly, the way was to go over air and support common phone capabilities for voice. The mobile phone today supports text via SMS and even offers internet connectivity. The pagers are ideal for text transmission and PDAs offer many of the personal productivity tools. Now a days there are devices which capture one or more of these capabilities in various combinations. In Figure we depict architecture of a typical hand-held device. Typically, the hand-held devices have the following hard-ware base.

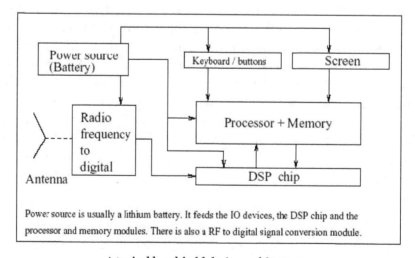

Power source is usually a lithium battery. It feeds the IO devices, the DSP chip and the processor and memory modules. There is also a RF to digital signal conversion module.

A typical hand-held derive architecture.

Microprocessor * Memory (persistent + volatile) * RF communication capability

* IO units (keys + buttons / small screen (LCD)) * Power source (battery)

Today's enabling technologies offer sophisticated add-ons. For instance, the DSP (digital signal processing) chips allow MP3 players and digital cameras to be attached with PDAs and mobiles. This means that there are embedded and real-time applications being developed for hand-held devices. The signal processing capabilities are easily several MIPS (million instructions per second) and beyond. The IO may also allow use of stylus and touch screen capabilities. Now let us look at some of the design concerns for OS on hand-held devices. One of the main considerations in hand-held devices is to be able to operate while conserving power. Even though the lithium batteries are rechargeable, these batteries drain in about 2 hours time. Another consideration is the flexibility in terms of IO.

These devices should be able to communicate using serial ports (or USB ports), infrared ports as well as modems. The OS should be able to service file transfer protocols. Also, the OS should have a small footprint, typically about 100K bytes with plug-in modules. Other design requirements include very low boot time and robustness. Another important facet of the operations is that hand-held devices hold a large amount of personal and enterprise information. This requires that the OS should have some minimal individual authentication before giving access to the device.

In some of the OSs, a memory management unit (MMU) is used to offer virtual memory operation. The MMU also determines if the data is in RAM. The usual architecture is microkernel supported by a library of functions. An embedded Linux or similar capability OS is used in these devices. Microsoft too has some offerings around the Windows CE kernel.

The main consideration in scheduling for real-time systems is the associated predictability of response. To ensure the predictability of response, real-time systems resort to pre-emptive policies. This ensures that an event receives its due attention. So, one basic premise in real-time systems is that the scheduling must permit pre-emption. The obvious price is: throughput. The predictability requirement is regardless of the nature of input from the environment, which may be synchronous or asynchronous. Also, note that predictability does not require that the inputs be strictly periodic in nature (it does not rule out that case though). Predictability does tolerate some known extent of variability. The required adjustment to the variability is akin to the task of a wicket- keeper in the game of cricket. A bowler brings in certain variabilities in his bowling. The wicket-keeper is generally aware of the nature of variability the bowler beguiles. The wicket-keeper operates like a real-time system, where the input generator is the bowler, who has the freedom to choose his ball line, length, and flight. Clearly, one has to bear the worst case in mind. In real-time systems too, the predictable situations require to cater for the worst case schedulability of tasks. Let us first understand this concept. Schedulability of a task is influenced by all the higher priority tasks that are awaiting scheduling. We can explain this as follows. Suppose we identify our current task as tc and the other higher priority tasks as t1; ::::; tn where ti identifies the i-th task having priority higher than tc. Now let us sum up the upper bounds for time of completion for all the higher priority tasks t1; ::::; tn and to it add the time required for tc. If the total time is less than the period by which task tc must be completed, then we say that task tc meets the worst case schedulability consideration. Note that schedulability ensures predictability and offers an upper bound on acceptable time of completion for task tc. Above, we have emphasized pre-emption and predictability for real-time systems. We shall next examine some popular scheduling policies. The following three major scheduling policies are quite popular.

1. Rate monotonic (or RM for short) scheduling policy.

2. The earliest deadline first (or EDF for short) scheduling policy.

3. The least laxity first (or LLF) scheduling policy.

A curious reader may wonder if the predictability (in terms of schedulability for timely response) could be guaranteed under all conditions. In fact, predictability does get affected when a lower priority task holds a mutually shared resource and blocks a higher priority task. This is termed as a case of priority inversion. The phenomenon of priority inversion may happen both under RM and EDF schedules. We shall discuss the priority inversion in section We shall also describe strategies to overcome this problem.

Rate Monotonic Scheduling

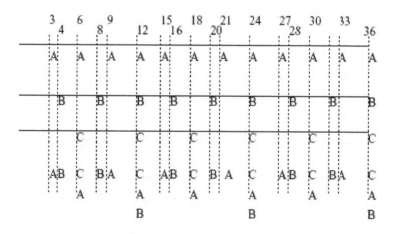

Rate monotonic scheduling for tasks.

Some real-time systems have tasks that require periodic monitoring and regulation. So the events are cyclic in nature. This cyclicity requires predictable event detection and consequent decision on control settings. For this category of real-time systems thepopular scheduling strategy is rate monotonic scheduling. Let us now examine it in some detail. The rate monotonic scheduling stipulates that all the tasks are known apriori. Also, known is their relative importance. This means that we know their orders of priority. Tasks with highest priority have the shortest periodicity. The tasks may be independent of each other. Armed with this information, and the known times of completion for each task, we find the least common multiple lcm of the task completion times. Let us denote the lcm as Trm. Now a schedule is drawn for the entire time period Trm such that each task satisfies the schedulability condition. The schedule so generated is the RM schedule. This schedule is then repeated with period Trm. As an example, consider that events A;B; and C happen with time periods 3, 4, and 6, and when an event occurs the system must respond to these. Then we need to draw up a schedule as shown in Figure. Note that at times 12, 24, and 36 all the three tasks need to be attended to while at time 21 only task A needs to be attended. This particular schedule is drawn taking its predictability into account. To that extent the RM policy ensures predictable performance. In theory, the rate monotonic scheduling is known to be an optimal policy when priorities are statically defined tasks.

Earliest Deadline First Policy

The EDF scheduling handles the tasks with dynamic priorities. The priorities are determined by the proximity of the deadline for task completion. Lower priorities are assigned when deadlines are further away. The highest priority is accorded to the task with the earliest deadline. Clearly, the tasks can be put in a queue like data-structure with the entries in the ascending order of the deadlines for completion. In case the inputs are periodic in nature, schedulability analysis is possible. However, in general the EDF policy can not guarantee optimal performance for the environment with periodic inputs. Some improvement can be seen when one incorporates some variations in EDF policy. For instance, one may account for the possibility of distinguishing the mandatory tasks from those that may be optional. Clearly, the mandatory tasks obtain schedules for execution by pre-emption whenever necessary. The EDF is known to utilize the processor better than the RM policy option.

Earliest Least Laxity First Policy

This is a policy option in which we try to see the slack time that may be available to start a task. This slack time is measured as follows:

slack time = dead line i remaining processing time

The slack defines the laxity of the task. This policy has more overhead in general but has been found to be very useful for multi-media applications in multiprocessor environment.

Priority Inversion

Often priority inversion happens when a higher priority task gets blocked due to the fact that a mutually exclusive resource R is currently being held by a lower priority task. This may happen as follows. Suppose we have three tasks t1; t2, and t3 with priorities in the order of their index with task t1 having the highest priority. Now suppose there is a shared resource R which task t3 and task t1 share. Suppose t3 has obtained resource R and it is to now execute. Priority inversion occurs with the following plausible sequence of events.

1. Resource R is free and t3 seeks to execute. It gets resource R and t3 is executing.

2. Task t3 is executing. However, before it completes task t1 seeks to execute.

3. Task t3 is suspended and task t1 begins to execute till it needs resource R. It gets suspended as the mutually exclusive resource R is not available.

4. Task t3 is resumed. However, before it completes task t2 seeks to be scheduled.

5. Task t3 is suspended and task t2 begins executing.

6. Task t2 is completed. Task t1 still cannot begin executing as resource R is not available (held by task t3).

7. Task t3 resumes to finish its execution and releases resource R.

8. Blocked task t1 now runs to completion.

The main point to be noted in the above sequence is: even though the highest priority task t1 gets scheduled using a pre-emptive strategy, it completes later than the lower priority tasks t2 and t3! Now that is priority inversion.

How to handle priority inversion: To ensure that priority inversion does not lead to missing deadlines, the following strategy is adopted . In the steps described above, the task t1 blocks when it needs resource R which is with task t3. At that stage, we raise the priority of task t3, albeit temporarily to the level of task t1. This ensures that task t2 cannot get scheduled now. Task t3 is bound to complete and release the resource R. That would enable scheduling of the task t1 before task t2. This preserves the priority order and avoids the priority inversion. Consequently, the deadlines for task t1 can be adhered to with predictability.

References

- Tanenbaum, Andrew (2008). Modern Operating Systems. Upper Saddle River, NJ: Pearson/Prentice Hall. p. 160. ISBN 978-0-13-600663-3

- Denning, Peter J. (December 1976). "Fault tolerant operating systems". ACM Computing Surveys. 8 (4): 359–389. ISSN 0360-0300. doi:10.1145/356678.356680

- Baiardi, F.; A. Tomasi; M. Vanneschi (1988). Architettura dei Sistemi di Elaborazione, volume 1 (in Italian). Franco Angeli. ISBN 88-204-2746-X

- Roch, Benjamin (2004). "Monolithic kernel vs. Microkernel" (PDF). Archived from the original (PDF) on 2006-11-01. Retrieved 2006-10-12

- Schroeder, Michael D.; Jerome H. Saltzer (March 1972). "A hardware architecture for implementing protection rings". Communications of the ACM. 15 (3): 157–170. ISSN 0001-0782. doi:10.1145/361268.361275

- Tanenbaum, Andrew S. (1979). Structured Computer Organization. Englewood Cliffs, New Jersey: Prentice-Hall. ISBN 0-13-148521-0

- Hansen, Per Brinch (April 1970). "The nucleus of a Multiprogramming System". Communications of the ACM. 13 (4): 238–241. ISSN 0001-0782. doi:10.1145/362258.362278

- "Improving the reliability of commodity operating systems". Doi.acm.org. doi:10.1002/spe.4380201404. Retrieved 2010-06-19

Computer Security: An Overview

In the age where the Internet has become a part of the daily human lives catering to many needs such as booking tickets, socializing, buying and selling products, etc., information needs to be protected. Since the operating system is the resource regulator of a computer system, it should also be the security service provider. This section elucidates the crucial theories and principles related to computer security.

Computer Security

Computer security, also known as cyber security or IT security, is the protection of computer systems from the theft or damage to their hardware, software or information, as well as from disruption or misdirection of the services they provide.

Cyber security includes controlling physical access to the hardware, as well as protecting against harm that may come via network access, data and code injection. Also, due to malpractice by operators, whether intentional, accidental, IT security is susceptible to being tricked into deviating from secure procedures.

The field is of growing importance due to the increasing reliance on computer systems and the Internet in most societies, wireless networks such as Bluetooth and Wi-Fi – and the growth of "smart" devices, including smartphones, televisions and tiny devices as part of the Internet of Things.

Vulnerabilities and Attacks

A vulnerability is a system susceptibility or flaw. Many vulnerabilities are documented in the Common Vulnerabilities and Exposures (CVE) database. An *exploitable* vulnerability is one for which at least one working attack or "exploit" exists.

To secure a computer system, it is important to understand the attacks that can be made against it, and these threats can typically be classified into one of the categories below:

Backdoor

A backdoor in a computer system, a cryptosystem or an algorithm, is any secret method of bypassing normal authentication or security controls. They may exist for a number of reasons, including by original design or from poor configuration. They may have been added by an authorized party to allow some legitimate access, or by an attacker for malicious reasons; but regardless of the motives for their existence, they create a vulnerability.

Denial-of-service Attack

Denial of service attacks (DoS) are designed to make a machine or network resource unavailable to its intended users. Attackers can deny service to individual victims, such as by deliberately entering a wrong password enough consecutive times to cause the victim account to be locked, or they may overload the capabilities of a machine or network and block all users at once. While a network attack from a single IP address can be blocked by adding a new firewall rule, many forms of Distributed denial of service (DDoS) attacks are possible, where the attack comes from a large number of points – and defending is much more difficult. Such attacks can originate from the zombie computers of a botnet, but a range of other techniques are possible including reflection and amplification attacks, where innocent systems are fooled into sending traffic to the victim.

Direct-access Attacks

An unauthorized user gaining physical access to a computer is most likely able to directly copy data from it. They may also compromise security by making operating system modifications, installing software worms, keyloggers, covert listening devices or using wireless mice. Even when the system is protected by standard security measures, these may be able to be by-passed by booting another operating system or tool from a CD-ROM or other bootable media. Disk encryption and Trusted Platform Module are designed to prevent these attacks.

Eavesdropping

Eavesdropping is the act of surreptitiously listening to a private conversation, typically between hosts on a network. For instance, programs such as Carnivore and NarusInsight have been used by the FBI and NSA to eavesdrop on the systems of internet service providers. Even machines that operate as a closed system (i.e., with no contact to the outside world) can be eavesdropped upon via monitoring the faint electro-magnetic transmissions generated by the hardware; TEMPEST is a specification by the NSA referring to these attacks.

Spoofing

Spoofing, in general, is a fraudulent or malicious practice in which communication is sent from an unknown source disguised as a source known to the receiver. Spoofing is most prevalent in communication mechanisms that lack a high level of security.

Tampering

Tampering describes a malicious modification of products. So-called "Evil Maid" attacks and security services planting of surveillance capability into routers are examples.

Privilege Escalation

Privilege escalation describes a situation where an attacker with some level of restricted access is able to, without authorization, elevate their privileges or access level. So for example a standard computer user may be able to fool the system into giving them access to restricted data; or even to "become root" and have full unrestricted access to a system.

Phishing

Phishing is the attempt to acquire sensitive information such as usernames, passwords, and credit card details directly from users. Phishing is typically carried out by email spoofing or instant messaging, and it often directs users to enter details at a fake website whose look and feel are almost identical to the legitimate one. Preying on a victim's trust, phishing can be classified as a form of social engineering.

Clickjacking

Clickjacking, also known as "UI redress attack" or "User Interface redress attack", is a malicious technique in which an attacker tricks a user into clicking on a button or link on another webpage while the user intended to click on the top level page. This is done using multiple transparent or opaque layers. The attacker is basically "hijacking" the clicks meant for the top level page and routing them to some other irrelevant page, most likely owned by someone else. A similar technique can be used to hijack keystrokes. Carefully drafting a combination of stylesheets, iframes, buttons and text boxes, a user can be led into believing that they are typing the password or other information on some authentic webpage while it is being channeled into an invisible frame controlled by the attacker.

Social Engineering

Social engineering aims to convince a user to disclose secrets such as passwords, card numbers, etc. by, for example, impersonating a bank, a contractor, or a customer.

A common scam involves fake CEO emails sent to accounting and finance departments. In early 2016, the FBI reported that the scam has cost US businesses more than $2bn in about two years.

In May 2016, the Milwaukee Bucks NBA team was the victim of this type of cyber scam with a perpetrator impersonating the team's president Peter Feigin, resulting in the handover of all the team's employees' 2015 W-2 tax forms.

Systems at Risk

Computer security is critical in almost any industry which uses computers. Currently, most electronic devices such as computers, laptops and cellphones come with built in firewall security software, but despite this, computers are not 100 percent accurate and dependable to protect our data (Smith, Grabosky & Urbas, 2004.) There are many different ways of hacking into computers. It can be done through a network system, clicking into unknown links, connecting to unfamiliar Wi-Fi, downloading software and files from unsafe sites, power consumption, electromagnetic radiation waves, and many more. However, computers can be protected through well built software and hardware. By having strong internal interactions of properties, software complexity can prevent software crash and security failure.

Financial Systems

Web sites and apps that accept or store credit card numbers, brokerage accounts, and bank account information are prominent hacking targets, because of the potential for immediate financial gain from transferring money, making purchases, or selling the information on the black market. In-store payment systems and ATMs have also been tampered with in order to gather customer account data and PINs.

Utilities and Industrial Equipment

Computers control functions at many utilities, including coordination of telecommunications, the power grid, nuclear power plants, and valve opening and closing in water and gas networks. The Internet is a potential attack vector for such machines if connected, but the Stuxnet worm demonstrated that even equipment controlled by computers not connected to the Internet can be vulnerable to physical damage caused by malicious commands sent to industrial equipment (in that case uranium enrichment centrifuges) which are infected via removable media. In 2014, the Computer Emergency Readiness Team, a division of the Department of Homeland Security, investigated 79 hacking incidents at energy companies. Vulnerabilities in smart meters (many of which use local radio or cellular communications) can cause problems with billing fraud.

Aviation

The aviation industry is very reliant on a series of complex system which could be attacked. A simple power outage at one airport can cause repercussions worldwide, much of the system relies on radio transmissions which could be disrupted, and controlling aircraft over oceans is especially dangerous because radar surveillance only extends 175 to 225 miles offshore. There is also potential for attack from within an aircraft.

In Europe, with the (Pan-European Network Service) and NewPENS, and in the US with the NextGen program, air navigation service providers are moving to create their own dedicated networks.

The consequences of a successful attack range from loss of confidentiality to loss of system integrity, which may lead to more serious concerns such as exfiltration of data, network and air traffic control outages, which in turn can lead to airport closures, loss of aircraft, loss of passenger life, damages on the ground and to transportation infrastructure. A successful attack on a military aviation system that controls munitions could have even more serious consequences.

Consumer Devices

Desktop computers and laptops are commonly infected with malware either to gather passwords or financial account information, or to construct a botnet to attack another target. Smart phones, tablet computers, smart watches, and other mobile devices such as Quantified Self devices like activity trackers have also become targets and many of these have sensors such as cameras, microphones, GPS receivers, compasses, and accelerometers which could be exploited, and may collect personal information, including sensitive health information. Wifi, Bluetooth, and cell phone networks on any of these devices could be used as attack vectors, and sensors might be remotely activated after a successful breach.

Home automation devices such as the Nest thermostat are also potential targets.

Large Corporations

Large corporations are common targets. In many cases this is aimed at financial gain through identity theft and involves data breaches such as the loss of millions of clients' credit card details by Home Depot, Staples, and Target Corporation. Medical records have been targeted for use in general identify theft, health insurance fraud, and impersonating patients to obtain prescription drugs for recreational purposes or resale.

Not all attacks are financially motivated however; for example security firm HBGary Federal suffered a serious series of attacks in 2011 from hacktivist group Anonymous in retaliation for the firm's CEO claiming to have infiltrated their group, and Sony Pictures was attacked in 2014 where the motive appears to have been to embarrass with data leaks, and cripple the company by wiping workstations and servers.

Automobiles

If access is gained to a car's internal controller area network, it is possible to disable the brakes and turn the steering wheel. Computerized engine timing, cruise control, anti-lock brakes, seat belt tensioners, door locks, airbags and advanced driver assistance systems make these disruptions possible, and self-driving cars go even further. Connected cars may use wifi and bluetooth to communicate with onboard consumer devices, and the cell phone network to contact concierge and emergency assistance services or get navigational or entertainment information; each of these networks is a potential entry point for malware or an attacker. Researchers in 2011 were even able to use a malicious compact disc in a car's stereo system as a successful attack vector, and cars with built-in voice recognition or remote assistance features have onboard microphones which could be used for eavesdropping. In 2015 hackers remotely carjacked a Jeep from 10 miles away and drove it into a ditch.

A 2015 report by U.S. Senator Edward Markey criticized manufacturers' security measures as inadequate, and also highlighted privacy concerns about driving, location, and diagnostic data being collected, which is vulnerable to abuse by both manufacturers and hackers.

In September 2016 the United States Department of Transportation announced some safety standards for the design and development of autonomous vehicles, called states to come up with uniform policies applying to driverless cars, clarified how current regulations can be applied to driverless cars and opened the door for new similar regulations.

Marshall Heilman notes that "the government has to have some type of legislation and mandate to secure [the] environment" of self-driving cars as hackers otherwise could be able to take over cars and notes that "some type of event [...] is going to have to occur before the government actually gets involved and sets those particular standards".

Cybersecurity of automobiles doesn't just involve the production but also the discovery, proactive measures and patching of vulnerabilities. In 2016 Tesla pushed out security fixes "over the air" and into its cars' computer systems after a Chinese whitehat hacking group disclosed it with an apparent altruistic and/or reputation incentive.

Government

Government and military computer systems are commonly attacked by activists and foreign powers. Local and regional government infrastructure such as traffic light controls, police and intelligence agency communications, personnel records, student records, and financial systems are also potential targets as they are now all largely computerized. Passports and government ID cards that control access to facilities which use RFID can be vulnerable to cloning.

Internet of Things and Physical Vulnerabilities

The Internet of Things (IoT) is the network of physical objects such as devices, vehicles, and buildings that are embedded with electronics, software, sensors, and network connectivity that enables them to collect and exchange data – and concerns have been raised that this is being developed without appropriate consideration of the security challenges involved.

While the IoT creates opportunities for more direct integration of the physical world into computer-based systems, it also provides opportunities for misuse. In particular, as the Internet of Things spreads widely, cyber attacks are likely to become an increasingly physical (rather than simply virtual) threat. If a front door's lock is connected to the Internet, and can be locked/unlocked from a phone, then a criminal could enter the home at the press of a button from a stolen or hacked phone. People could stand to lose much more than their credit card numbers in a world controlled by IoT-enabled devices. Thieves have also used electronic means to circumvent non-Internet-connected hotel door locks.

Medical Systems

Medical devices have either been successfully attacked or had potentially deadly vulnerabilities demonstrated, including both in-hospital diagnostic equipment and implanted devices including pacemakers and insulin pumps. There are many reports of hospitals and hospital organizations getting hacked, including ransomware attacks, Windows XP exploits, viruses, and data breaches of sensitive data stored on hospital servers. On 28 December 2016 the US Food and Drug Administration released its recommendations that are not legally enforceable for how medical device manufacturers should maintain the security of Internet-connected devices.

Impact of Security Breaches

Serious financial damage has been caused by security breaches, but because there is no standard model for estimating the cost of an incident, the only data available is that which is made public by the organizations involved. "Several computer security consulting firms produce estimates of total worldwide losses attributable to virus and worm attacks and to hostile digital acts in general. The 2003 loss estimates by these firms range from $13 billion (worms and viruses only) to $226 billion (for all forms of covert attacks). The reliability of these estimates is often challenged; the underlying methodology is basically anecdotal."

However, reasonable estimates of the financial cost of security breaches can actually help organizations make rational investment decisions. According to the classic Gordon-Loeb Model analyzing the optimal investment level in information security, one can conclude that the amount a firm spends to protect information should generally be only a small fraction of the expected loss (i.e., the expected value of the loss resulting from a cyber/information security breach).

Attacker Motivation

As with physical security, the motivations for breaches of computer security vary between attackers. Some are thrill-seekers or vandals, others are activists or criminals looking for financial gain. State-sponsored attackers are now common and well resourced, but started with amateurs such as

Markus Hess who hacked for the KGB, as recounted by Clifford Stoll, in *The Cuckoo's Egg*.

A standard part of threat modelling for any particular system is to identify what might motivate an attack on that system, and who might be motivated to breach it. The level and detail of precautions will vary depending on the system to be secured. A home personal computer, bank, and classified military network face very different threats, even when the underlying technologies in use are similar.

Computer Protection (Countermeasures)

In computer security a countermeasure is an action, device, procedure, or technique that reduces a threat, a vulnerability, or an attack by eliminating or preventing it, by minimizing the harm it can cause, or by discovering and reporting it so that corrective action can be taken.

Some common countermeasures are listed in the following sections:

Security by Design

Security by design, or alternately secure by design, means that the software has been designed from the ground up to be secure. In this case, security is considered as a main feature.

Some of the techniques in this approach include:

- The principle of least privilege, where each part of the system has only the privileges that are needed for its function. That way even if an attacker gains access to that part, they have only limited access to the whole system.

- Automated theorem proving to prove the correctness of crucial software subsystems.

- Code reviews and unit testing, approaches to make modules more secure where formal correctness proofs are not possible.

- Defense in depth, where the design is such that more than one subsystem needs to be violated to compromise the integrity of the system and the information it holds.

- Default secure settings, and design to "fail secure" rather than "fail insecure". Ideally, a secure system should require a deliberate, conscious, knowledgeable and free decision on the part of legitimate authorities in order to make it insecure.

- Audit trails tracking system activity, so that when a security breach occurs, the mechanism and extent of the breach can be determined. Storing audit trails remotely, where they can only be appended to, can keep intruders from covering their tracks.

- Full disclosure of all vulnerabilities, to ensure that the "window of vulnerability" is kept as short as possible when bugs are discovered.

Security Architecture

The Open Security Architecture organization defines IT security architecture as "the design artifacts that describe how the security controls (security countermeasures) are positioned, and how they relate to the overall information technology architecture. These controls serve the purpose to maintain the system's quality attributes: confidentiality, integrity, availability, accountability and assurance services".

Techopedia defines security architecture as "a unified security design that addresses the necessities and potential risks involved in a certain scenario or environment. It also specifies when and where to apply security controls. The design process is generally reproducible." The key attributes of security architecture are:

- the relationship of different components and how they depend on each other.

- the determination of controls based on risk assessment, good practice, finances, and legal matters.

- the standardization of controls.

Security Measures

A state of computer "security" is the conceptual ideal, attained by the use of the three processes: threat prevention, detection, and response. These processes are based on various policies and system components, which include the following:

- User account access controls and cryptography can protect systems files and data, respectively.

- Firewalls are by far the most common prevention systems from a network security perspective as they can (if properly configured) shield access to internal network services, and block certain kinds of attacks through packet filtering. Firewalls can be both hardware- or software-based.

- Intrusion Detection System (IDS) products are designed to detect network attacks in-progress and assist in post-attack forensics, while audit trails and logs serve a similar function for individual systems.

- "Response" is necessarily defined by the assessed security requirements of an individual system and may cover the range from simple upgrade of protections to notification of legal authorities, counter-attacks, and the like. In some special cases, a complete destruction of the compromised system is favored, as it may happen that not all the compromised resources are detected.

Today, computer security comprises mainly "preventive" measures, like firewalls or an exit procedure. A firewall can be defined as a way of filtering network data between a host or a network and another network, such as the Internet, and can be implemented as software running on the machine, hooking into the network stack (or, in the case of most UNIX-based operating systems such as Linux, built into the operating system kernel) to provide real time filtering and blocking. Another implementation is a so-called "physical firewall", which consists of a separate machine filtering network traffic. Firewalls are common amongst machines that are permanently connected to the Internet.

Some organizations are turning to big data platforms, such as Apache Hadoop, to extend data accessibility and machine learning to detect advanced persistent threats.

However, relatively few organisations maintain computer systems with effective detection systems, and fewer still have organised response mechanisms in place. As result, as Reuters points out: "Companies for the first time report they are losing more through electronic theft of data than physical stealing of assets". The primary obstacle to effective eradication of cyber crime could be traced to excessive reliance on firewalls and other automated "detection" systems. Yet it is basic evidence gathering by using packet capture appliances that puts criminals behind bars.

Vulnerability Management

Vulnerability management is the cycle of identifying, and remediating or mitigating vulnerabilities", especially in software and firmware. Vulnerability management is integral to computer security and network security.

Vulnerabilities can be discovered with a vulnerability scanner, which analyzes a computer system in search of known vulnerabilities, such as open ports, insecure software configuration, and susceptibility to malware

Beyond vulnerability scanning, many organisations contract outside security auditors to run regular penetration tests against their systems to identify vulnerabilities. In some sectors this is a contractual requirement.

Reducing Vulnerabilities

While formal verification of the correctness of computer systems is possible, it is not yet common. Operating systems formally verified include seL4, and SYSGO's PikeOS – but these make up a very small percentage of the market.

Cryptography properly implemented is now virtually impossible to directly break. Breaking them requires some non-cryptographic input, such as a stolen key, stolen plaintext (at either end of the transmission), or some other extra cryptanalytic information.

Two factor authentication is a method for mitigating unauthorized access to a system or sensitive information. It requires "something you know"; a password or PIN, and "something you have"; a card, dongle, cellphone, or other piece of hardware. This increases security as an unauthorized person needs both of these to gain access.

Social engineering and direct computer access (physical) attacks can only be prevented by non-computer means, which can be difficult to enforce, relative to the sensitivity of the information. Training is often involved to help mitigate this risk, but even in a highly disciplined environments (e.g. military organizations), social engineering attacks can still be difficult to foresee and prevent.

It is possible to reduce an attacker's chances by keeping systems up to date with security patches and updates, using a security scanner or/and hiring competent people responsible for security. The effects of data loss/damage can be reduced by careful backing up and insurance.

Hardware Protection Mechanisms

While hardware may be a source of insecurity, such as with microchip vulnerabilities maliciously introduced during the manufacturing process, hardware-based or assisted computer security also offers an alternative to software-only computer security. Using devices and methods such as dongles, trusted platform modules, intrusion-aware cases, drive locks, disabling USB ports, and mobile-enabled access may be considered more secure due to the physical access (or sophisticated backdoor access) required in order to be compromised. Each of these is covered in more detail below.

- USB dongles are typically used in software licensing schemes to unlock software capabilities, but they can also be seen as a way to prevent unauthorized access to a computer or other device's software. The dongle, or key, essentially creates a secure encrypted tunnel between the software application and the key. The principle is that an encryption scheme on the dongle, such as Advanced Encryption Standard (AES) provides a stronger measure of security, since it is harder to hack and replicate the dongle than to simply copy the native software to another machine and use it. Another security application for dongles is to use them for accessing web-based content such as cloud software or Virtual Private Networks (VPNs). In addition, a USB dongle can be configured to lock or unlock a computer.

- Trusted platform modules (TPMs) secure devices by integrating cryptographic capabilities onto access devices, through the use of microprocessors, or so-called computers-on-a-chip. TPMs used in conjunction with server-side software offer a way to detect and authenticate hardware devices, preventing unauthorized network and data access.

- Computer case intrusion detection refers to a push-button switch which is triggered when a computer case is opened. The firmware or BIOS is programmed to show an alert to the operator when the computer is booted up the next time.

- Drive locks are essentially software tools to encrypt hard drives, making them inaccessible to thieves. Tools exist specifically for encrypting external drives as well.

- Disabling USB ports is a security option for preventing unauthorized and malicious access to an otherwise secure computer. Infected USB dongles connected to a network from a computer inside the firewall are considered by the magazine Network World as the most common hardware threat facing computer networks.

- Mobile-enabled access devices are growing in popularity due to the ubiquitous nature of cell phones. Built-in capabilities such as Bluetooth, the newer Bluetooth low energy (LE), Near field communication (NFC) on non-iOS devices and biometric validation such as thumb print readers, as well as QR code reader software designed for mobile devices, offer new, secure ways for mobile phones to connect to access control systems. These control systems provide computer security and can also be used for controlling access to secure buildings.

Secure Operating Systems

One use of the term "computer security" refers to technology that is used to implement secure operating systems. In the 1980s the United States Department of Defense (DoD) used the "Orange Book" standards, but the current international standard ISO/IEC 15408, "Common Criteria" defines a number of progressively more stringent Evaluation Assurance Levels. Many common operating systems meet the EAL4 standard of being "Methodically Designed, Tested and Reviewed", but the formal verification required for the highest levels means that they are uncommon. An example of an EAL6 ("Semiformally Verified Design and Tested") system is Integrity-178B, which is used in the Airbus A380 and several military jets.

Secure Coding

In software engineering, secure coding aims to guard against the accidental introduction of security vulnerabilities. It is also possible to create software designed from the ground up to be secure. Such systems are "secure by design". Beyond this, formal verification aims to prove the correctness of the algorithms underlying a system; important for cryptographic protocols for example.

Capabilities and Access Control Lists

Within computer systems, two of many security models capable of enforcing privilege separation are access control lists (ACLs) and capability-based security. Using ACLs to confine programs has been proven to be insecure in many situations, such as if the host computer can be tricked into indirectly allowing restricted file access, an issue known as the confused deputy problem. It has also been shown that the promise of ACLs of giving access to an object to only one person can never be guaranteed in practice. Both of these problems are resolved by capabilities. This does not mean practical flaws exist in all ACL-based systems, but only that the designers of certain utilities must take responsibility to ensure that they do not introduce flaws.

Capabilities have been mostly restricted to research operating systems, while commercial OSs still use ACLs. Capabilities can, however, also be implemented at the language level, leading to a style of programming that is essentially a refinement of standard object-oriented design. An open source project in the area is the E language.

The most secure computers are those not connected to the Internet and shielded from any interference. In the real world, the most secure systems are operating systems where security is not an add-on.

Response to Breaches

Responding forcefully to attempted security breaches (in the manner that one would for attempted physical security breaches) is often very difficult for a variety of reasons:

- Identifying attackers is difficult, as they are often in a different jurisdiction to the systems they attempt to breach, and operate through proxies, temporary anonymous dial-up accounts, wireless connections, and other anonymising procedures which make backtracing difficult and are often located in yet another jurisdiction. If they successfully breach security, they are often able to delete logs to cover their tracks.

- The sheer number of attempted attacks is so large that organisations cannot spend time pursuing each attacker (a typical home user with a permanent. Note however, that most of the sheer bulk of these attacks are made by automated vulnerability scanners and computer worms.

- Law enforcement officers are often unfamiliar with information technology, and so lack the skills and interest in pursuing attackers. There are also budgetary constraints. It has been argued that the high cost of technology, such as DNA testing, and improved forensics mean less money for other kinds of law enforcement, so the overall rate of criminals not getting dealt with goes up as the cost of the technology increases. In addition, the identification of attackers across a network may require logs from various points in the network and in many countries, the release of these records to law enforcement (with the exception of being voluntarily surrendered by a network administrator or a system administrator) requires a search warrant and, depending on the circumstances, the legal proceedings required can be drawn out to the point where the records are either regularly destroyed, or the information is no longer relevant.

Notable Attacks and Breaches

Some illustrative examples of different types of computer security breaches are given below.

Robert Morris and the First Computer Worm

In 1988, only 60,000 computers were connected to the Internet, and most were mainframes, minicomputers and professional workstations. On November 2, 1988, many started to slow down, because they were running a malicious code that demanded processor time and that spread itself to other computers – the first internet "computer worm". The software was traced back to 23-year-old Cornell University graduate student Robert Tappan Morris, Jr. who said 'he wanted to count how many machines were connected to the Internet'.

Rome Laboratory

In 1994, over a hundred intrusions were made by unidentified crackers into the Rome Laboratory, the US Air Force's main command and research facility. Using trojan horses, hackers were able to obtain unrestricted access to Rome's networking systems and remove traces of their activities. The intruders were able to obtain classified files, such as air tasking order systems data and furthermore able to penetrate connected networks of National Aeronautics and Space Administration's Goddard Space Flight Center, Wright-Patterson Air Force Base, some Defense contractors, and other private sector organizations, by posing as a trusted Rome center user.

TJX Customer Credit Card Details

In early 2007, American apparel and home goods company TJX announced that it was the victim of an unauthorized computer systems intrusion and that the hackers had accessed a system that stored data on credit card, debit card, check, and merchandise return transactions.

Stuxnet Attack

The computer worm known as Stuxnet reportedly ruined almost one-fifth of Iran's nuclear centrifuges by disrupting industrial programmable logic controllers (PLCs) in a targeted attack generally believed to have been launched by Israel and the United States although neither has publicly acknowledged this.

Global Surveillance Disclosures

In early 2013, massive breaches of computer security by the NSA were revealed, including deliberately inserting a backdoor in a NIST standard for encryption and tapping the links between Google's data centres. These were disclosed by NSA contractor Edward Snowden.

Target and Home Depot Breaches

In 2013 and 2014, a Russian/Ukrainian hacking ring known as "Rescator" broke into Target Corporation computers in 2013, stealing roughly 40 million credit cards, and then Home Depot computers in 2014, stealing between 53 and 56 million credit card numbers. Warnings were delivered at both corporations, but ignored; physical security breaches using self checkout machines are believed to have played a large role. "The malware utilized is absolutely unsophisticated and uninteresting," says Jim Walter, director of threat intelligence operations at security technology company McAfee – meaning that the heists could have easily been stopped by existing antivirus software had administrators responded to the warnings. The size of the thefts has resulted in major attention from state and Federal United States authorities and the investigation is ongoing.

Office of Personnel Management Data Breach

In April 2015, the Office of Personnel Management discovered it had been hacked more than a year earlier in a data breach, resulting in the theft of approximately 21.5 million personnel records handled by the office. The Office of Personnel Management hack has been described by federal officials as among the largest breaches of government data in the history of the United States. Data targeted in the breach included personally identifiable information such as Social Security Numbers, names, dates and places of birth, addresses, and fingerprints of current and former government employees as well as anyone who had undergone a government background check. It is believed the hack was perpetrated by Chinese hackers but the motivation remains unclear.

Ashley Madison Breach

In July 2015, a hacker group known as "The Impact Team" successfully breached the extramarital relationship website Ashley Madison. The group claimed that they had taken not only company data but user data as well. After the breach, The Impact Team dumped emails from the company's CEO, to prove their point, and threatened to dump customer data unless the website was taken down permanently. With this initial data release, the group stated "Avid Life Media has been instructed to take Ashley Madison and Established Men offline permanently in all forms, or we will release all customer records, including profiles with all the customers' secret sexual fantasies and matching credit card transactions, real names and addresses, and employee documents and emails. The other websites may stay online." When Avid Life Media, the parent company that created the Ashley Madison website, did not take the site offline, The Impact Group released two more compressed files, one 9.7GB and the second 20GB. After the second data dump, Avid Life Media CEO Noel Biderman resigned, but the website remained functional.

Legal Issues and Global Regulation

Conflict of laws in cyberspace has become a major cause of concern for computer security community. Some of the main challenges and complaints about the antivirus industry are the lack of global web regulations, a global base of common rules to judge, and eventually punish, cyber crimes and cyber criminals. There is no global cyber law and cybersecurity treaty that can be invoked for enforcing global cybersecurity issues.

International legal issues of cyber attacks are complicated in nature. Even if an antivirus firm locates the cyber criminal behind the creation of a particular virus or piece of malware or form of cyber attack, often the local authorities cannot take action due to lack of laws under which to prosecute. Authorship attribution for cyber crimes and cyber attacks is a major problem for all law enforcement agencies.

"[Computer viruses] switch from one country to another, from one jurisdiction to another – moving around the world, using the fact that we don't have the capability to globally police operations like this. So the Internet is as if someone [had] given free plane tickets to all the online criminals of the world." Use of dynamic DNS, fast flux and bullet proof servers have added own complexities to this situation.

Role of Government

The role of the government is to make regulations to force companies and organizations to protect their systems, infrastructure and information from any cyber-attacks, but also to protect its own national infrastructure such as the national power-grid.

The question of whether the government should intervene or not in the regulation of the cyberspace is a very polemical one. Indeed, for as long as it has existed and by definition, the cyberspace is a virtual space free of any government intervention. Where everyone agree that an improvement on cybersecurity is more than vital, is the government the best actor to solve this issue? Many government officials and experts think that the government should step in and that there is a crucial need for regulation, mainly due to the failure of the private sector to solve efficiently the cybersecurity problem. R. Clarke said during a panel discussion at the RSA Security Conference in San Francisco, he believes that the "industry only responds when you threaten regulation. If industry doesn't respond (to the threat), you have to follow through." On the other hand, executives from the private sector agree that improvements are necessary, but think that the government intervention would affect their ability to innovate efficiently.

International Actions

Many different teams and organisations exist, including:

- The Forum of Incident Response and Security Teams (FIRST) is the global association of CSIRTs. The US-CERT, AT&T, Apple, Cisco, McAfee, Microsoft are all members of this international team.

- The Council of Europe helps protect societies worldwide from the threat of cybercrime through the Convention on Cybercrime.

- The purpose of the Messaging Anti-Abuse Working Group (MAAWG) is to bring the messaging industry together to work collaboratively and to successfully address the various forms of messaging abuse, such as spam, viruses, denial-of-service attacks and other messaging exploitations. France Telecom, Facebook, AT&T, Apple, Cisco, Sprint are some of the members of the MAAWG.

- ENISA : The European Network and Information Security Agency (ENISA) is an agency of the European Union with the objective to improve network and information security in the European Union.

Europe

CSIRTs in Europe collaborate in the TERENA task force TF-CSIRT. TERENA's Trusted Introducer service provides an accreditation and certification scheme for CSIRTs in Europe. A full list of known CSIRTs in Europe is available from the Trusted Introducer website.

National Actions

Computer Emergency Response Teams

Most countries have their own computer emergency response team to protect network security.

Canada

On October 3, 2010, Public Safety Canada unveiled Canada's Cyber Security Strategy, following a Speech from the Throne commitment to boost the security of Canadian cyberspace. The aim of the strategy is to strengthen Canada's "cyber systems and critical infrastructure sectors, support economic growth and protect Canadians as they connect to each other and to the world." Three main pillars define the strategy: securing government systems, partnering to secure vital cyber systems outside the federal government, and helping Canadians to be secure online. The strategy involves multiple departments and agencies across the Government of Canada. The Cyber Incident Management Framework for Canada outlines these responsibilities, and provides a plan for coordinated response between government and other partners in the event of a cyber incident. The Action Plan 2010–2015 for Canada's Cyber Security Strategy outlines the ongoing implementation of the strategy.

Public Safety Canada's Canadian Cyber Incident Response Centre (CCIRC) is responsible for mitigating and responding to threats to Canada's critical infrastructure and cyber systems. The CCIRC provides support to mitigate cyber threats, technical support to respond and recover from targeted cyber attacks, and provides online tools for members of Canada's critical infrastructure sectors. The CCIRC posts regular cyber security bulletins on the Public Safety Canada website. The CCIRC also operates an online reporting tool where individuals and organizations can report a cyber incident. Canada's Cyber Security Strategy is part of a larger, integrated approach to critical infrastructure protection, and functions as a counterpart document to the National Strategy and Action Plan for Critical Infrastructure.

On September 27, 2010, Public Safety Canada partnered with STOP.THINK.CONNECT, a coalition of non-profit, private sector, and government organizations dedicated to informing the general public on how to protect themselves online. On February 4, 2014, the Government of Canada launched the Cyber Security Cooperation Program. The program is a $1.5 million five-year initiative aimed at improving Canada's cyber systems through grants and contributions to projects in support of this objective. Public Safety Canada aims to begin an evaluation of Canada's Cyber Security Strategy in early 2015. Public Safety Canada administers and routinely updates the GetCyberSafe portal for Canadian citizens, and carries out Cyber Security Awareness Month during October.

China

China's network security and information technology leadership team was established February 27, 2014. The leadership team is tasked with national security and long-term development and co-ordination of major issues related to network security and information technology. Economic, political, cultural, social and military fields as related to network security and information technology strategy, planning and major macroeconomic policy are being researched. The promotion of national network security and information technology law are constantly under study for enhanced national security capabilities.

Germany

Berlin starts National Cyber Defense Initiative: On June 16, 2011, the German Minister for Home Affairs, officially opened the new German NCAZ (National Center for Cyber Defense) Nationales Cyber-Abwehrzentrum located in Bonn. The NCAZ closely cooperates with BSI (Federal Office for Information Security) Bundesamt für Sicherheit in der Informationstechnik, BKA (Federal Police Organisation) Bundeskriminalamt (Deutschland), BND (Federal Intelligence Service) Bundesnachrichtendienst, MAD (Military Intelligence Service) Amt für den Militärischen Abschirmdienst and other national organisations in Germany taking care of national security aspects. According to the Minister the primary task of the new organisation founded on February 23, 2011, is to detect and prevent attacks against the national infrastructure and mentioned incidents like Stuxnet.

India

Some provisions for cybersecurity have been incorporated into rules framed under the Information Technology Act 2000.

The National Cyber Security Policy 2013 is a policy framework by Ministry of Electronics and Information Technology (MeitY) which aims to protect the public and private infrastructure from cyber attacks, and safeguard "information, such as personal information (of web users), financial and banking information and sovereign data".

The Indian Companies Act 2013 has also introduced cyber law and cyber security obligations on the part of Indian directors.

Pakistan

Cyber-crime has risen rapidly in Pakistan. There are about 34 million Internet users with 133.4 million mobile subscribers in Pakistan. According to Cyber Crime Unit (CCU), a branch of Federal Investigation Agency, only 62 cases were reported to the unit in 2007, 287 cases in 2008, ratio dropped in 2009 but in 2010, more than 312 cases were registered. However, there are many unreported incidents of cyber-crime.

"Pakistan's Cyber Crime Bill 2007", the first pertinent law, focuses on electronic crimes, for example cyber-terrorism, criminal access, electronic system fraud, electronic forgery, and misuse of encryption.

National Response Centre for Cyber Crime (NR3C) – FIA is a law enforcement agency dedicated to fight cybercrime. Inception of this Hi-Tech crime fighting unit transpired in 2007 to identify and curb the phenomenon of technological abuse in society. However, certain private firms are also working in cohesion with the government to improve cyber security and curb cyberattacks.

People in Pakistan can now report terrorist and extremist online-content on Surfsafe® Pakistan web portal. Surfsafe® is an initiative by CODEPAK. Tier3 Cyber Security Pakistan led the development of the Surfsafe® e-system which includes reporting portal and Surfsafe® e-Scouts system. The National Counter Terrorism Authority (NACTA) of Pakistan provides the leadership for the Surfsafe® Campaign.

South Korea

Following cyberattacks in the first half of 2013, when government, news-media, television station, and bank websites were compromised, the national government committed to the training of 5,000 new cybersecurity experts by 2017. The South Korean government blamed its northern counterpart for these attacks, as well as incidents that occurred in 2009, 2011, and 2012, but Pyongyang denies the accusations.

United States

Legislation

The 1986 18 U.S.C. 1030, more commonly known as the Computer Fraud and Abuse Act is the key legislation. It prohibits unauthorized access or damage of "protected computers" as defined in 18 U.S.C. 1030(e)(2).

Although various other measures have been proposed, such as the "Cybersecurity Act of 2010 – S. 773" in 2009, the "International Cybercrime Reporting and Cooperation Act – H.R.4962" and "Protecting Cyberspace as a National Asset Act of 2010 – S.3480" in 2010 – none of these has succeeded.

Executive order 13636 *Improving Critical Infrastructure Cybersecurity* was signed February 12, 2013.

Agencies

The Department of Homeland Security has a dedicated division responsible for the response system, risk management program and requirements for cybersecurity in the United States called the National Cyber Security Division. The division is home to US-CERT operations and the National Cyber Alert System. The National Cybersecurity and Communications Integration Center brings together government organizations responsible for protecting computer networks and networked infrastructure.

The third priority of the Federal Bureau of Investigation (FBI) is to: *"Protect the United States against cyber-based attacks and high-technology crimes"*, and they, along with the National White Collar Crime Center (NW3C), and the Bureau of Justice Assistance (BJA) are part of the multi-agency task force, The Internet Crime Complaint Center, also known as IC3.

In addition to its own specific duties, the FBI participates alongside non-profit organizations such as InfraGard.

In the criminal division of the United States Department of Justice operates a section called the Computer Crime and Intellectual Property Section. The CCIPS is in charge of investigating computer crime and intellectual property crime and is specialized in the search and seizure of digital evidence in computers and networks.

The United States Cyber Command, also known as USCYBERCOM, is tasked with the defense of specified Department of Defense information networks and *"ensure US/Allied freedom of action in cyberspace and deny the same to our adversaries."* It has no role in the protection of civilian networks.

The U.S. Federal Communications Commission's role in cybersecurity is to strengthen the protection of critical communications infrastructure, to assist in maintaining the reliability of networks during disasters, to aid in swift recovery after, and to ensure that first responders have access to effective communications services.

The Food and Drug Administration has issued guidance for medical devices, and the National Highway Traffic Safety Administration is concerned with automotive cybersecurity. After being criticized by the Government Accountability Office, and following successful attacks on airports and claimed attacks on airplanes, the Federal Aviation Administration has devoted funding to securing systems on board the planes of private manufacturers, and the Aircraft Communications Addressing and Reporting System. Concerns have also been raised about the future Next Generation Air Transportation System.

Computer Emergency Readiness Team

"Computer emergency response team" is a name given to expert groups that handle computer security incidents. In the US, two distinct organization exist, although they do work closely together.

- US-CERT: part of the National Cyber Security Division of the United States Department of Homeland Security.

- CERT/CC: created by the Defense Advanced Research Projects Agency (DARPA) and run by the Software Engineering Institute (SEI).

Modern Warfare

Cybersecurity is becoming increasingly important as more information and technology is being made available on cyberspace. There is growing concern among governments that cyberspace will become the next theatre of warfare. As Mark Clayton from the *Christian Science Monitor* described in an section titled "The New Cyber Arms Race":

In the future, wars will not just be fought by soldiers with guns or with planes that drop bombs. They will also be fought with the click of a mouse a half a world away that unleashes carefully weaponized computer programs that disrupt or destroy critical industries like utilities, transportation, communications, and energy. Such attacks could also disable military networks that control the movement of troops, the path of jet fighters, the command and control of warships.

This has led to new terms such as *cyberwarfare* and *cyberterrorism*. More and more critical infrastructure is being controlled via computer programs that, while increasing efficiency, exposes new vulnerabilities. The test will be to see if governments and corporations that control critical systems such as energy, communications and other information will be able to prevent attacks before they occur. As Jay Cross, the chief scientist of the Internet Time Group, remarked, "Connectedness begets vulnerability."

Job Market

Cybersecurity is a fast-growing field of IT concerned with reducing organizations' risk of hack or data breach. According to research from the Enterprise Strategy Group, 46% of organizations say that they have a "problematic shortage" of cybersecurity skills in 2016, up from 28% in 2015. Commercial, government and non-governmental organizations all employ cybersecurity professionals. The fastest increases in demand for cybersecurity workers are in industries managing increasing volumes of consumer data such as finance, health care, and retail. However, the use of the term "cybersecurity" is more prevalent in government job descriptions.

Typical cybersecurity job titles and descriptions include:

Security analyst

> Analyzes and assesses vulnerabilities in the infrastructure (software, hardware, networks), investigates using available tools and countermeasures to remedy the detected vulnerabilities, and recommends solutions and best practices. Analyzes and assesses damage to the data/infrastructure as a result of security incidents, examines available recovery tools and processes, and recommends solutions. Tests for compliance with security policies and procedures. May assist in the creation, implementation, and/or management of security solutions.

Security engineer

> Performs security monitoring, security and data/logs analysis, and forensic analysis, to detect security incidents, and mounts incident response. Investigates and utilizes new technologies and processes to enhance security capabilities and implement improvements. May also review code or perform other security engineering methodologies.

Security architect

Designs a security system or major components of a security system, and may head a security design team building a new security system.

Security administrator

Installs and manages organization-wide security systems. May also take on some of the tasks of a security analyst in smaller organizations.

Chief Information Security Officer (CISO)

A high-level management position responsible for the entire information security division/ staff. The position may include hands-on technical work.

Chief Security Officer (CSO)

A high-level management position responsible for the entire security division/staff. A newer position now deemed needed as security risks grow.

Security Consultant/Specialist/Intelligence

Broad titles that encompass any one or all of the other roles/titles, tasked with protecting computers, networks, software, data, and/or information systems against viruses, worms, spyware, malware, intrusion detection, unauthorized access, denial-of-service attacks, and an ever increasing list of attacks by hackers acting as individuals or as part of organized crime or foreign governments.

Student programs are also available to people interested in beginning a career in cybersecurity. Meanwhile, a flexible and effective option for information security professionals of all experience levels to keep studying is online security training, including webcasts.

Terminology

The following terms used with regards to engineering secure systems are explained below.

- Access authorization restricts access to a computer to group of users through the use of authentication systems. These systems can protect either the whole computer – such as through an interactive login screen – or individual services, such as an FTP server. There are many methods for identifying and authenticating users, such as passwords, identification cards, and, more recently, smart cards and biometric systems.

- Anti-virus software consists of computer programs that attempt to identify, thwart and eliminate computer viruses and other malicious software (malware).

- Applications with known security flaws should not be run. Either leave it turned off until it can be patched or otherwise fixed, or delete it and replace it with some other application. Publicly known flaws are the main entry used by worms to automatically break into a system and then spread to other systems connected to it. The security website Secunia provides a search tool for unpatched known flaws in popular products.

- Authentication techniques can be used to ensure that communication end-points are who they say they are.

- Automated theorem proving and other verification tools can enable critical algorithms and code used in secure systems to be mathematically proven to meet their specifications.

- Backups are a way of securing information; they are another copy of all the important computer files kept in another location. These files are kept on hard disks, CD-Rs, CD-RWs, tapes and more recently on the cloud. Suggested locations for backups are a fireproof, waterproof, and heat proof safe, or in a separate, offsite location than that in which the original files are contained. Some individuals and companies also keep their backups in safe deposit boxes inside bank vaults. There is also a fourth option, which involves using one of the file hosting services that backs up files over the Internet for both business and individuals, known as the cloud.

  o Backups are also important for reasons other than security. Natural disasters, such as earthquakes, hurricanes, or tornadoes, may strike the building where the computer is located. The building can be on fire, or an explosion may occur. There needs to be a recent backup at an alternate secure location, in case of such kind of disaster. Further, it is recommended that the alternate location be placed where the same disaster would not affect both locations. Examples of alternate disaster recovery sites being compromised by the same disaster that affected the primary site include having had a primary site in World Trade Center I and the recovery site in 7 World Trade Center, both of which were destroyed in the 9/11 attack, and having one's primary site and recovery site in the same coastal region, which leads to both being vulnerable to hurricane damage (for example, primary site in New Orleans and recovery site in Jefferson Parish, both of which were hit by Hurricane Katrina in 2005). The backup media should be moved between the geographic sites in a secure manner, in order to prevent them from being stolen.

- Capability and access control list techniques can be used to ensure privilege separation and mandatory access control.

- Chain of trust techniques can be used to attempt to ensure that all software loaded has been certified as authentic by the system's designers.

- Confidentiality is the nondisclosure of information except to another authorized person.

- Cryptographic techniques can be used to defend data in transit between systems, reducing the probability that data exchanged between systems can be intercepted or modified.

- Cyberwarfare is an internet-based conflict that involves politically motivated attacks on information and information systems. Such attacks can, for example, disable official websites and networks, disrupt or disable essential services, steal or alter classified data, and cripple financial systems.

- Data integrity is the accuracy and consistency of stored data, indicated by an absence of any alteration in data between two updates of a data record.

This is secret stuff, PSE do not...

5a0 (k$hQ% ...

This is secret stuff, PSE do not...

Cryptographic techniques involve transforming information, scrambling it so it becomes unreadable during transmission. The intended recipient can unscramble the message; ideally, eavesdroppers cannot.

- Encryption is used to protect the message from the eyes of others. Cryptographically secure ciphers are designed to make any practical attempt of breaking infeasible. Symmetric-key ciphers are suitable for bulk encryption using shared keys, and public-key encryption using digital certificates can provide a practical solution for the problem of securely communicating when no key is shared in advance.

- Endpoint security software helps networks to prevent exfiltration (data theft) and virus infection at network entry points made vulnerable by the prevalence of potentially infected portable computing devices, such as laptops and mobile devices, and external storage devices, such as USB drives.

- Firewalls are an important method for control and security on the Internet and other networks. A network firewall can be a communications processor, typically a router, or a dedicated server, along with firewall software. A firewall serves as a gatekeeper system that protects a company's intranets and other computer networks from intrusion by providing a filter and safe transfer point for access to and from the Internet and other networks. It screens all network traffic for proper passwords or other security codes and only allows authorized transmission in and out of the network. Firewalls can deter, but not completely prevent, unauthorized access (hacking) into computer networks; they can also provide some protection from online intrusion.

- Honey pots are computers that are either intentionally or unintentionally left vulnerable to attack by crackers. They can be used to catch crackers or fix vulnerabilities.

- Intrusion-detection systems can scan a network for people that are on the network but who should not be there or are doing things that they should not be doing, for example trying a lot of passwords to gain access to the network.

- A microkernel is the near-minimum amount of software that can provide the mechanisms to implement an operating system. It is used solely to provide very low-level, very precisely defined machine code upon which an operating system can be developed. A simple example is the early '90s GEMSOS (Gemini Computers), which provided extremely low-level machine code, such as "segment" management, atop which an operating system could be built. The theory (in the case of "segments") was that—rather than have the operating system itself worry about mandatory access separation by means of military-style labeling—it is safer if a low-level, independently scrutinized module can be charged solely with the management of individually labeled segments, be they memory "segments" or file system "segments" or executable text "segments." If software below the visibility of the operating system is (as in this case) charged with labeling, there is no theoretically viable means for a clever hacker to subvert the labeling scheme, since the operating system *per se* does not provide mechanisms for interfering with labeling: the operating system is, essentially, a client (an "application," arguably) atop the microkernel and, as such, subject to its restrictions.

- Pinging The ping application can be used by potential crackers to find if an IP address is reachable. If a cracker finds a computer, they can try a port scan to detect and attack services on that computer.

- Social engineering awareness keeps employees aware of the dangers of social engineering and/or having a policy in place to prevent social engineering can reduce successful breaches of the network and servers.

Vulnerability (Computing)

In computer security, a vulnerability is a weakness which allows an attacker to reduce a system's information assurance. Vulnerability is the intersection of three elements: a system susceptibility or flaw, attacker access to the flaw, and attacker capability to exploit the flaw. To exploit a vulnerability, an attacker must have at least one applicable tool or technique that can connect to a system weakness. In this frame, vulnerability is also known as the attack surface.

Vulnerability management is the cyclical practice of identifying, classifying, remediating, and mitigating vulnerabilities. This practice generally refers to software vulnerabilities in computing systems.

A security risk may be classified as a vulnerability. The use of vulnerability with the same meaning of risk can lead to confusion. The risk is tied to the potential of a significant loss. Then there are vulnerabilities without risk: for example when the affected asset has no value. A vulnerability with one or more known instances of working and fully implemented attacks is classified as an exploitable vulnerability — a vulnerability for which an exploit exists. The window of vulnerability is the time from when the security hole was introduced or manifested in deployed software, to when access was removed, a security fix was available/deployed, or the attacker was disabled.

Security bug (security defect) is a narrower concept: there are vulnerabilities that are not related to software: hardware, site, personnel vulnerabilities are examples of vulnerabilities that are not software security bugs.

Constructs in programming languages that are difficult to use properly can be a large source of vulnerabilities.

Definitions

ISO 27005 defines vulnerability as:

> *A weakness of an asset or group of assets that can be exploited by one or more threats*

where an *asset is anything that has value to the organization, its business operations and their continuity, including information resources that support the organization's mission*

IETF RFC 2828 define vulnerability as:

> *A flaw or weakness in a system's design, implementation, or operation and management that could be exploited to violate the system's security policy.*

The Committee on National Security Systems of United States of America defined vulnerability in CNSS Instruction No. 4009 dated 26 April 2010 National Information Assurance Glossary:

> *Vulnerability — Weakness in an IS, system security procedures, internal controls, or implementation that could be exploited.*

Many NIST publications define vulnerability in IT contest in different publications: FISMApedia term provide a list. Between them SP 800-30, give a broader one:

> *A flaw or weakness in system security procedures, design, implementation, or internal controls that could be exercised (accidentally triggered or intentionally exploited) and result in a security breach or a violation of the system's security policy.*

ENISA defines vulnerability in as:

> *The existence of a weakness, design, or implementation error that can lead to an unexpected, undesirable event [G.11] compromising the security of the computer system, network, application, or protocol involved (ITSEC).*

The Open Group defines vulnerability in as:

> *The probability that threat capability exceeds the ability to resist the threat.*

Factor Analysis of Information Risk (FAIR) defines vulnerability as:

> *The probability that an asset will be unable to resist the actions of a threat agent*

According FAIR vulnerability is related to Control Strength, i.e. the strength of a control as compared to a standard measure of force and the threat Capabilities, i.e. the probable level of force that a threat agent is capable of applying against an asset.

ISACA defines vulnerability in Risk It framework as:

> *A weakness in design, implementation, operation or internal control.*

Data and Computer Security: Dictionary of standards concepts and terms, authors Dennis Longley and Michael Shain, Stockton Press, ISBN 0-935859-17-9, defines vulnerability as:

> *1) In computer security, a weakness in automated systems security procedures, administrative controls, Internet controls, etc., that could be exploited by a threat to gain unauthorized access to information or to disrupt critical processing. 2) In computer security, a weakness in the physical layout, organization, procedures, personnel, management, administration, hardware or softwarethat may be exploited to cause harm to the ADP system or activity. 3) In computer security, any weakness or flaw existing in a system. The attack or harmful event, or the opportunity available to a threat agent to mount that attack.*

Matt Bishop and Dave Bailey give the following definition of computer vulnerability:

> *A computer system is composed of states describing the current configuration of the entities that make up the computer system. The system computes through the application of state transitions that change the state of the system. All states reachable from a given initial state using a set of state transitions fall into the class of authorized or unauthorized, as defined by a security policy. In this paper, the definitions of these classes and transitions is considered axiomatic. A vulnerable state is an authorized state from which an unauthorized state can be reached using authorized state transitions. A compromised state is the state so reached. An attack is a sequence of authorized state transitions which end in a compromised state. By definition, an attack begins in a vulnerable state. A vulnerability is a characterization of a vulnerable state which distinguishes it from all non-vulnerable states. If generic, the vulnerability may characterize many vulnerable states; if specific, it may characterize only one...*

National Information Assurance Training and Education Center defines vulnerability:

> *A weakness in automated system security procedures, administrative controls, internal controls, and so forth, that could be exploited by a threat to gain unauthorized access to information or disrupt critical processing. 2. A weakness in system security procedures, hardware design, internal controls, etc. , which could be exploited to gain unauthorized access to classified or sensitive information. 3. A weakness in the physical layout, organization, procedures, personnel, management, administration, hardware, or software that may be exploited to cause harm to the ADP system or activity. The presence of a vulnerability does not in itself cause harm; a vulnerability is merely a condition or set of conditions that may allow the ADP system or activity to be harmed by an attack. 4. An assertion primarily concerning entities of the internal environment (assets); we say that an asset (or class of assets) is vulnerable (in some way, possibly involving an agent or collection of agents); we write: V(i,e) where: e may be an empty set. 5. Susceptibility to various threats. 6. A set of properties of a specific internal entity that, in union with a set of properties of a specific external entity, implies a risk. 7. The characteristics of a system which cause it to suffer a definite degradation (incapability to perform the designated mission) as a result of having been subjected to a certain level of effects in an unnatural (manmade) hostile environment.*

Vulnerability and Risk Factor Models

A resource (either physical or logical) may have one or more vulnerabilities that can be exploited by a threat agent in a threat action. The result can potentially compromise the confidentiality, integrity or availability of resources (not necessarily the vulnerable one) belonging to an organization and/or other parties involved (customers, suppliers). The so-called CIA triad is the basis of Information Security.

An attack can be *active* when it attempts to alter system resources or affect their operation, compromising integrity or availability. A *"passive attack"* attempts to learn or make use of information from the system but does not affect system resources, compromising confidentiality.

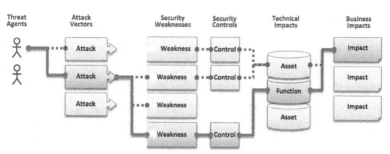

OWASP: relationship between threat agent and business impact

OWASP depicts the same phenomenon in slightly different terms: a threat agent through an attack vector exploits a weakness (vulnerability) of the system and the related security controls, causing a technical impact on an IT resource (asset) connected to a business impact.

The overall picture represents the risk factors of the risk scenario.

Information Security Management System

A set of policies concerned with information security management, the information security management system (ISMS), has been developed to manage, according to Risk management principles, the countermeasures in order to ensure the security strategy is set up following the rules and regulations applicable in a country. These countermeasures are also called Security controls, but when applied to the transmission of information they are called security services.

Classification

Vulnerabilities are classified according to the asset class they are related to:

- hardware
    - susceptibility to humidity
    - susceptibility to dust
    - susceptibility to soiling
    - susceptibility to unprotected storage
- software
    - insufficient testing
    - lack of audit trail
- network
    - unprotected communication lines
    - insecure network architecture
- personnel

- o   inadequate recruiting process

- o   inadequate security awareness

- physical site

    - o   area subject to flood

    - o   unreliable power source

- organizational

    - o   lack of regular audits

    - o   lack of continuity plans

    - o   lack of security.

Causes

- Complexity: Large, complex systems increase the probability of flaws and unintended access points

- Familiarity: Using common, well-known code, software, operating systems, and/or hardware increases the probability an attacker has or can find the knowledge and tools to exploit the flaw

- Connectivity: More physical connections, privileges, ports, protocols, and services and time each of those are accessible increase vulnerability

- Password management flaws: The computer user uses weak passwords that could be discovered by brute force. The computer user stores the password on the computer where a program can access it. Users re-use passwords between many programs and websites

- Fundamental operating system design flaws: The operating system designer chooses to enforce suboptimal policies on user/program management. For example, operating systems with policies such as default permit grant every program and every user full access to the entire computer. This operating system flaw allows viruses and malware to execute commands on behalf of the administrator

- Internet Website Browsing: Some internet websites may contain harmful Spyware or Adware that can be installed automatically on the computer systems. After visiting those websites, the computer systems become infected and personal information will be collected and passed on to third party individuals

- Software bugs: The programmer leaves an exploitable bug in a software program. The software bug may allow an attacker to misuse an application

- Unchecked user input: The program assumes that all user input is safe. Programs that do not check user input can allow unintended direct execution of commands or SQL statements (known as Buffer overflows, SQL injection or other non-validated inputs)

- Not learning from past mistakes: for example most vulnerabilities discovered in IPv4 protocol software were discovered in the new IPv6 implementations.

The research has shown that the most vulnerable point in most information systems is the human user, operator, designer, or other human: so humans should be considered in their different roles as asset, threat, information resources. Social engineering is an increasing security concern.

Vulnerability Consequences

The impact of a security breach can be very high. The fact that IT managers, or upper management, can (easily) know that IT systems and applications have vulnerabilities and do not perform any action to manage the IT risk is seen as a misconduct in most legislations. Privacy law forces managers to act to reduce the impact or likelihood of that security risk. Information technology security audit is a way to let other independent people certify that the IT environment is managed properly and lessen the responsibilities, at least having demonstrated the good faith. Penetration test is a form of verification of the weakness and countermeasures adopted by an organization: a White hat hacker tries to attack an organization's information technology assets, to find out how easy or difficult it is to compromise the IT security. The proper way to professionally manage the IT risk is to adopt an Information Security Management System, such as ISO/IEC 27002 or Risk IT and follow them, according to the security strategy set forth by the upper management.

One of the key concept of information security is the principle of defence in depth: i.e. to set up a multilayer defence system that can:

- prevent the exploit

- detect and intercept the attack

- find out the threat agents and prosecute them

Intrusion detection system is an example of a class of systems used to detect attacks.

Physical security is a set of measures to protect physically the information asset: if somebody can get physical access to the information asset, it is quite easy to make resources unavailable to its legitimate users.

Some sets of criteria to be satisfied by a computer, its operating system and applications in order to meet a good security level have been developed: ITSEC and Common criteria are two examples.

Vulnerability Disclosure

Responsible disclosure (many now refer to it as 'coordinated disclosure' because the first is a biased word) of vulnerabilities is a topic of great debate. As reported by The Tech Herald in August 2010, "Google, Microsoft, TippingPoint, and Rapid7 have recently issued guidelines and statements addressing how they will deal with disclosure going forward."

A responsible disclosure first alerts the affected vendors confidentially before alerting CERT two weeks later, which grants the vendors another 45-day grace period before publishing a security advisory.

Full disclosure is done when all the details of vulnerability is publicized, perhaps with the intent to put pressure on the software or procedure authors to find a fix urgently.

Well respected authors have published books on vulnerabilities and how to exploit them: Hacking: The Art of Exploitation Second Edition is a good example.

Security researchers catering to the needs of the cyberwarfare or cybercrime industry have stated that this approach does not provide them with adequate income for their efforts. Instead, they offer their exploits privately to enable Zero day attacks.

The never ending effort to find new vulnerabilities and to fix them is called Computer insecurity.

In January 2014 when Google revealed a Microsoft vulnerability before Microsoft released a patch to fix it, a Microsoft representative called for coordinated practices among software companies in revealing disclosures.

Vulnerability Inventory

Mitre Corporation maintains a list of disclosed vulnerabilities in a system called Common Vulnerabilities and Exposures, where vulnerability are classified (scored) using Common Vulnerability Scoring System (CVSS).

OWASP collects a list of potential vulnerabilities with the aim of educating system designers and programmers, therefore reducing the likelihood of vulnerabilities being written unintentionally into the software.

Vulnerability Disclosure Date

The time of disclosure of a vulnerability is defined differently in the security community and industry. It is most commonly referred to as "a kind of public disclosure of security information by a certain party". Usually, vulnerability information is discussed on a mailing list or published on a security web site and results in a security advisory afterward.

The time of disclosure is the first date a security vulnerability is described on a channel where the disclosed information on the vulnerability has to fulfill the following requirement:

- The information is freely available to the public

- The vulnerability information is published by a trusted and independent channel/source

- The vulnerability has undergone analysis by experts such that risk rating information is included upon disclosure

Identifying and Removing Vulnerabilities

Many software tools exist that can aid in the discovery (and sometimes removal) of vulnerabilities in a computer system. Though these tools can provide an auditor with a good overview of possible vulnerabilities present, they can not replace human judgment. Relying solely on scanners will yield false positives and a limited-scope view of the problems present in the system.

Vulnerabilities have been found in every major operating system including Windows, macOS, various forms of Unix and Linux, OpenVMS, and others. The only way to reduce the chance of a vulnerability being used against a system is through constant vigilance, including careful system maintenance (e.g. applying software patches), best practices in deployment (e.g. the use of firewalls and access controls) and auditing (both during development and throughout the deployment lifecycle).

Examples of Vulnerabilities

Vulnerabilities are related to:

- physical environment of the system
- the personnel
- management
- administration procedures and security measures within the organization
- business operation and service delivery
- hardware
- software
- communication equipment and facilities
- and their combinations.

It is evident that a pure technical approach cannot even protect physical assets: one should have administrative procedure to let maintenance personnel to enter the facilities and people with adequate knowledge of the procedures, motivated to follow it with proper care.

Four examples of vulnerability exploits:

- an attacker finds and uses an overflow weakness to install malware to export sensitive data;
- an attacker convinces a user to open an email message with attached malware;
- an insider copies a hardened, encrypted program onto a thumb drive and cracks it at home;
- a flood damages one's computer systems installed at ground floor.

Software Vulnerabilities

Common types of software flaws that lead to vulnerabilities include:

- Memory safety violations, such as:
    - Buffer overflows and over-reads
    - Dangling pointers
- Input validation errors, such as:
    - Format string attacks

- o   SQL injection
- o   Code injection
- o   E-mail injection
- o   Directory traversal
- o   Cross-site scripting in web applications
- o   HTTP header injection
- o   HTTP response splitting
- Race conditions, such as:
  - o   Time-of-check-to-time-of-use bugs
  - o   Symlink races
- Privilege-confusion bugs, such as:
  - o   Cross-site request forgery in web applications
  - o   Clickjacking
  - o   FTP bounce attack
- Privilege escalation
- User interface failures, such as:
  - o   Warning fatigue or user conditioning.
  - o   Blaming the Victim Prompting a user to make a security decision without giving the user enough information to answer it
  - o   Race Conditions
- Side-channel attack
  - o   Timing attack

Some set of coding guidelines have been developed and a large number of static code analysers has been used to verify that the code follows the guidelines.

OS and Security

Computers, with their ubiquitous presence, have ceased to be a wonder they once were. Their usage is pervasive. Information access and delivery from, and to, a remote location via internet is common. Today many societal services like railway time-table or election results are rendered through computers. The notion of electronic commerce has given fillip to provisioning commercial services as well. Most individuals use computers to store private information at home and critical professional information at work. They also use computers to access information from other computers anywhere on the net. In this kind of scenario, information is the key resource and needs to be protected.

The OS, being the system's resource regulator, must provide for security mechanisms. It must not only secure the information to protect the privacy but also prevent misuse of system resources. Unix designers had aimed to support large-scale program development and team work. The main plank of design was flexibility and support tools. The idea was to promote creation of large programs through cooperative team efforts. All this was long before 9/11. Security has become a bigger issue now. Much of Unix provisioning of services was with the premise that there are hardly, if any, abuses of system. So, Unix leaves much to be desired in respect of security. And yet, Unix has the flexibility to augment mechanisms that primarily protect users resources like files and programs. Unix incorporates security through two mechanisms, user authentication and access control. We shall elaborate on both these aspects and study what could be adequate security measures. We begin with some known security breaches. That helps to put security measures in proper perspective.

- Security Breaches

We first need to comprehend the types of security breaches that may happen. Breaches may happen with malicious intent or may be initiated by users inadvertently, or accidentally. They may end up committing a security breach through a mis-typed command or ill understood interpretation of some command. In both these instances the OS must protect the interest of legitimate users of the system. Unix also does not rule out a malicious access with the intent to abuse the system. It is well known that former disgruntled employees often attempt access to systems to inflict damages or simply corrupt some critical information. Some malicious users' actions may result in one of the following three kinds of security breaches:

o   Disclosure of information.

o   Compromising integrity of data.

o   Denial of service to legitimate users of the system.

To launch an attack, an attacker may correctly guess a weak password of a legitimate user. He can then access the machine and all HW and SW resources made available to that user. Note that a password is an intended control (a means to authenticate a user) to permit legitimate access to system resources. Clearly, a malicious user may employ password racking methods with the explicit intent to bypass the intended controls. He may access classified information and may also misuse the system resources. An un authorized access ay be launched to steal precious processor cycles resulting in denial of service. Or, he may be able to acquire privileged access to modify critical files corrupting sensitive data. This would be an act of active misuse. Some activities like watching the traffic on a system or browsing without modifying files may be regarded as an act of passive misuse. Even this is a breach of security as it does lead to disclosure. It may result in some deterioration, albeit not noticeable, in the overall services as well.

Examples of Security Breaches

Here we shall discuss a few well known attacks that have happened and have been recorded. Study of these examples helps us to understand how security holes get created. Besides, it helps us to determine strategies to plug security holes as they manifest. Next we describe a few attack scenarios. Not all of these scenarios can be handled by OS control mechanisms. Nonetheless, it is very revealing to see how the attacks happen.

- External Masquerading: This is the case of unauthorized access. The access may be via a communication media tap, recording and playback. For instance, a login session may be played back to masquerade another user. The measures require a network-based security solution.

- Pest Programs: A malicious user may use a pest program to cause a subsequent harm. Its effect may manifest at some specified time or event. The Trojan horse and virus attacks fall in this category. The main difference between a Trojan horse and a virus is that, a virus is a self reproducing program. Some virus writers have used the Terminate and Stay Resident (TSR) program facility in Micro-soft environments to launch such attacks. The pest programs require internal controls to counter. Generally, the time lag helps the attacker to cover the tracks. Typically, a virus propagation involves the following steps:

- Remote copy: In this step a program is copied to a remote machine.

- Remote execute: The copied program is instructed to execute. The step requires repeating the previous step on the other connected machine, thereby propagating the virus.

- Bypassing internal controls: This is achieved usually by cracking passwords, or using compiler generated attack to hog or deny resources.

- Use a given facility for a different purpose: This form of attack involves use of a given facility for a purpose other than it was intended for. For example, in Unix we can list files in any directory. This can be used to communicate secret information without being detected. Suppose 'userB' is not permitted to communicate or access files of 'userA'. When 'userB' access files of 'userA' he will always get a message permission denied. However, 'userA' may name his files as atnine, tonight, wemeet. When 'userB' lists the files in the directory of 'userA' he gets the message "at nine tonight we meet", thereby defeating the access controls.

- Active authority misuse: This happens when an administrator (or an individual) abuses his user privileges. A user may misuse the resources advanced to him in good faith and trust. An administrator may falsify book keeping data or a user may manipulate accounts data or some unauthorized person may be granted an access to sensitive information.

- Abuse through inaction: An administrator may choose to be sloppy (as he may be disgruntled) in his duties and that can result in degraded services.

- Indirect abuse: This does not quite appear like an attack and yet it may be. For instance, one may work on machine `A' to crack a protection key on machine `B'. It may appear as a perfectly legal study on machine `A' while the intent is to break the machine `B' internal controls.

We next discuss the commonly used methods of attacks. It is recommended to try a few of these in off-line mode. With that no damage to the operating environment occurs nor is the operation of an organization affected.

- The Password spoof program: We consider the following Trojan horse and the effect it generates. It is written in a Unix like command language.

  B1='ORIGIN: NODE whdl MODULE 66 PORT 12' B2='DESTINATION:'

  FILE=$HOME/CRYPT/SPOOFS/TEST

  trap " 1 2 3 5 15 echo $B1

  sleep 1 echo " echo $B2 read dest

  echo 'login: read login stty -echo

  echo 'password: read password stty echo

  echo "

  echo $login $passwd >> spooffile echo 'login incorrect'

  exec login

The idea is quite simple. The program on execution leaves a login prompt on the terminal. To an unsuspecting user it seems the terminal is available for use. A user would login and his login session with password shall be simply copied on to spooffile. The attacker can later retrieve the login name and password from the spooffile and now impersonate the user.

- Password theft by clever reasoning: In the early days passwords in Unix systems were stored in an encrypted form under /etc/password. The current practice of using a shadow file will be discussed later. So, in early days, the safety of password lay in the difficulty associated with decrypting just this file. So attackers used to resort to a clever way of detecting passwords. One such attack was through an attempt to match commonly used mnemonics, or use of convenient word patterns. Usually, these are words that are easy to type or recall. The attacker generated these and used the encrypting function to encrypt them. Once the encrypted pattern matched, the corresponding password was compromised.

- Logic Bomb: A logic bomb is usually a set-up like the login spoof described earlier. The attacker sets it up to go off when some conditions combine to happen. It may be long after the attacker (a disgruntled employee for instance) has quit the organization. This may leave no trail. Suppose we use an editor that allows setting of parameters to OS shell, the command interpreter. Now suppose one sets up a Unix command rm *.* and puts it in a file called EditMe and sends it over to the system administrator. If the system administrator opens the file and tries to edit the file, it may actually remove all the files unless he opens it in a secure environment.

  Also, if the administrator attempts opening this as a user, damage would be less, compared to when he opens it as a root.

- Scheduled File Removal: One of the facilities available on most OSs is scheduled execution of a program or a shell script. Under Unix this is done by using at command. A simple command like : *rm -f /usr* at 0400 saturday attack This can result in havoc. The program may be kept in a write protected directory and then executed at some specified time. The program recursively removes files without diagnostic messages from all users under *usr*.

- Field Separator Attack: The attack utilizes some OS features. The following steps describe the attack :

   1   The attacker redefines the field separator to include backslash character so that path names such as /coo/koo are indistinguishable from coo koo.

   2   The attacker knowing that some system program, say *sysprog,* uses administrative privilege to open a file called /coo/koo creates a program coo and places it in an accessible directory. The program is coded to transfer privileges from the system to the user via a copied OS shell.

   3   The attacker invokes *sysprog* which will try to open /coo/koo with the administrative privileges but will actually open the file coo since the field separator has been redefined. This will have the desired effect of transferring privileges to the user, just as the attacker intended.

- Insertion of Compiler Trojan Horse: To launch an attack with a very widely distributed effect an attacker may choose a popular filtering program based Trojan horse. A compiler is a good candidate for such an attack. To understand an attack via a compiler Trojan horse, let us first describe how a compiler works:

Compile: get (line); Translate (line);

A real compiler is usually more complex than the above description. Even this models a lexical analysis followed by the translating phases in a compiler. The objective of the Trojan horse would be to look for some patterns in the input programs and replace these with some trap door that will allow the attacker to attack the system at a later time. Thus the operation gets modified to:

Compile : get (line);

if line == "readpwd(p)" then translate (Trojan horse insertion) else

translate (line);

- The Race Condition Attack: A race condition occurs when two or more operations occur in an undefined manner. Specifically, the attacker attempts to change the state of the file system between two file system operations. Usually, the program expects these two operations to apply to the same file, or expects the information retrieved to be the same. If the file operations are not atomic, or do not reference the same file this cannot be guaranteed without proper care.

In Solaris 2.x's ps utility had a security hole that was caused by a race condition. The utility would open a temporary file, and then use the *chown()* system call with the file's full path to change its ownership to root. This sequence of events was easily exploitable. All that an attacker now had to do was to first slow down the system, and find the file so created, delete it, and then slip in a new SUID world writable file. Once the new file was created with that mode and with the ownership changed by *chown* to root by the insecure process, the attacker simply copies a shell into the file. The attacker gets a root shell.

The problem was that the second operation used the file name and not the file descriptor. If a call to *fchown()* would have been used on the file descriptor returned from the original *open()* operation, the security hole would have been avoided. File names are not unique. The file name /tmp/foo is really just an entry in the directory /tmp. Directories are special files. If an attacker can create, and delete files from a directory the program cannot trust file names taken from it. Or, to look at it in a more critical way, because the directory is modifiable by the attacker, a program cannot trust it as a source of valid input. Instead it should use file descriptors to perform its operations. One solution is to use the sticky bit. This will prevent the attacker from removing the file, but not prevent the attacker from creating files in the directory.

An Aside: Only directories can have sticky bit set. When a directory has the sticky bit turned on, anyone with the write permission can write (create a file) to the directory, but he cannot delete a file created by other users.

- The Symlink Attack: A security hole reported for SUN's license manager stemmed from the creation of a file without checking for symbolic links (or soft links). An *open()* call was made to either create the file if it did not exist, or open it if it did exist. The problem with a symbolic link is that an open call will follow it and not consider the link to constitute a created file. So if one had /tmp/foo. symlinked to /.rhosts or "/root/.rhosts), the latter file would be transparently opened. The license manager seemed to have used the O_CREAT flag with the open call making it create the file if it did not exist. To make matters worse, it created the file with world writable permissions. Since it ran as root, the .rhosts file could be created, written to, and root privileges attained.

Attack Prevention Methods

Attack prevention may be attempted at several levels. These include individual screening and physical controls in operations. Individual screening would require that users are screened to authenticate themselves and be responsible individuals. Physical controls involve use of physical access control. Finally, there are methods that may require configuration controls. We shall begin the discussion on the basic attack prevention with the defenses that are built in Unix. These measures are directed at user authentication and file access control.

User Authentication

First let us consider how a legitimate user establishes his identity to the system to access permitted resources. This is achieved typically by username/password pair. When the system finishes booting, the user is prompted for a username and then a password in succession. The password typed is not echoed to the screen for obvious reasons. Once the password is verified the user is given an interactive shell from where he can start issuing commands to the system. Clearly, choosing a clever password is important. Too simple a password would be an easy give away and too complex would be hard to remember. So how can we choose a nice password?

Choosing a good password: A malicious user usually aims at obtaining a complete control over the system. For this he must acquire the superuser or root status. Usually, he attacks vulnerable points like using badly installed software, bugs in some system software or human errors. There are several ways to hack a computer, but most ways require extensive knowledge. A relatively easier way is to log in as a normal user and search the system for bugs to become superuser. To do this, the attacker will have to have a valid user code and password combination to start with. Therefore, it is of utmost importance that all users on a system choose a password which is quite difficult to guess. The security of each individual user is closely related to the security of the whole system. Users often have no idea how a multi-user system works and do not realize that by choosing an easy to remember password, they indirectly make it possible for an attacker to manipulate the entire system. It is essential to educate the users well to avoid lackadaisical attitudes. For instance, if some one uses a certain facility for printing or reading some mails only, he may think that security is unimportant. The problem arises when someone assumes his identity. Therefore, the users should feel involved with the security of the system. It also means that it is important to notify the users of the security guidelines. Or at least make them understand why good passwords are essential.

Picking good passwords: We will look at some methods for choosing good passwords. A typical good password may consist up to eight characters. This means passwords like `members only' and `members and guests' may be mutually inter-changeable. A password should be hard to guess but easy to remember. If a password is not easy to remember then users will be tempted to write down their password on yellow stickers which makes it futile. So, it is recommended that a password should not only have upper or lowercase alphabets, but also has a few non-alphanumeric characters in it. The non-alphanumeric characters may be like (%,,*, =) etc. The use of control characters is possible, but not all control characters can be used, as that can create problems with some networking protocols. We next describe a few simple methods to generate good passwords.

- Concatenate two words that together consist of seven characters and that have no connection to each other. Concatenate them with a punctuation mark in the middle and convert some characters to uppercase like in 'abLe+pIG'.

- Use the first characters of the words of not too common a sentence. From the sentence "My pet writers are Wodehouse and Ustinov", as an example, we can create password "MpwaW+U!". Note in this case we have an eight-character password with uppercase characters as well as punctuation marks.

- Alternatively, pick a consonant and one or two vowels resulting in a pronounceable (and therefore easy to remember) word like 'koDuPaNi'.

This username/password information is kept traditionally in the /etc/passwd file, commonly referred to simply as the password file. A typical entry in the password file is shown below:

user:x:504:504::/home/user:/bin/bash

There are nine colon separated fields in the above line. They respectively refer to the user name, password x (explained later), UID, GID, the GECOS field 1, home directory and users' default shell. In the early implementations of the Unix, the password information was kept in the passwd file in plain text. The passwd file has to be world readable as many programs require to authenticate themselves against this file. As the expected trust level enhanced, it became imperative to encrypt the password as well. So, the password field is stored in an encrypted format. Initially, the crypt function was used extensively to do this. As the speed of the machines increased the encrypted passwords were rendered useless by the brute force techniques. All a potential attacker needed to do is to get the passwd file and then do a dictionary match of the encrypted password. This has led to another innovation in the form of the shadow suite of programs. In modern systems compatible with the shadow suite the password information is now kept in the /etc/shadow file and the password field in the passwd file is filled with an x (as indicated above). The actual encrypted password is kept in the /etc/shadow file in the following format :

user:1UaV6PunD$vpZUg1REKpHrtJrVi12HP.:11781:0:99999:7:::

The second field here is the password in an md5 hash 2. The other fields relate to special features which the shadow suite offers. It offers facilities like aging of the passwords, enforcing the length of the passwords etc. The largest downside to using the shadow passwords is the difficulty of modifying all of the programs that require passwords from the appropriate file to use /etc/shadow instead. Implementing other new security mechanisms presents the same difficulty. It would be ideal if all of these programs used a common framework for authentication and other security related measures, such as checking for weak passwords and printing the message of the day.

Pluggable authentication modules Red Hat and Debian Linux distributions ship with "Pluggable Authentication Modules" (PAM for short) and PAM-aware applications. PAM offers a flexible framework which may be customized as well. The basic PAM- based security model is shown in Figure. Essentially, the figure shows that one may have multiple levels of authentication, each invoked by a separate library module. PAM aware applications use these library modules to authenticate. Using PAM modules, the administrator can control exactly how authentication may proceed upon login. Such authentications go beyond the traditional /etc/passwd file checks. For instance, a certain application may require the pass-word as well as a form of bio-metric authentication. The basic strategy is to incorporate a file (usually called /etc/pam.d/login) which initiates a series of authentication checks for every login attempt. This file ensures that a certain authentication check sequence is observed. Technically, the library modules may be selectable. These selections may depend upon the severity of the authentication required. The administrator can customize the needed choices in the script. At the next level, we may even have an object based security model in which every object access would require authentication for access, as well as methods invocation.

For now we shall examine some typical security policies and how Unix translates security policies in terms of access control mechanisms.

```
$ldd /bin/login
libcrypt.so.1 => /lib/libcrypt.so.1
libpam.so.0 => /lib/libpam.so.0
libpam_misc.so.0 => /lib/libpam_misc.so.0



Other similar lines to link up library modules
/lib/ld-linux.so.2 => /lib/ld-linux.so.2
```

Each line above helps to authenticate in a different way.

Calls to different modules may be selectable for customisation.

Pluggable authentication.

Security Policy and Access Control

Most access control mechanisms emanate from a stated security policy. It is important to learn to design a security policy and offer suitable access mechanisms that can support security policies. Security policy models have evolved from many real-life operating scenarios. For instance, if we were to follow a regime of defense forces, we may resort to a hierarchy based policy. In such a policy, the access to resources shall be determined by associating ranks with users. This requires a security-related labeling on information to permit access. The access is regulated by examining the rank of the user in relation to the security label of the information being sought. For a more detailed discussion the reader may refer where there is a discussion on how to specify security policies as well.

If we were to model the security policies based on commercial and business practices or the financial services model, then data integrity would take a very high precedence. This like, the accounts and audit practices, preserves the integrity of data at all times. In practice, however, we may have to let the access be governed by ownership (who own the information) and role definitions of the users. For instance, in an organization, an individual user may own some information but some critical information may be owned by the institution. Also, its integrity should be impregnable. And yet the role of a system manager may require that he has access privileges which may allow him a free reign in running the system smoothly.

Almost all OSs provide for creating system logs of usage. These logs are extremely useful in the design of Intrusion Detection Systems (IDS). The idea is quite simple. All usages of resources are tracked by the OS and recorded. On analysis of the recorded logs it is possible to determine if there has been any misuse. The IDS helps to detect if a breach has occurred. Often this is after the event has taken place. To that extent the IDS provides a lot of input in designing security tools. With IDS in place one can trace how the attack happened. One can prevent attacks from happening in future. A full study and implementation of IDS is beyond the scope of this book. We would refer the reader to Amoroso's recent book on the subject.

Defenses in Unix: Defenses in Unix are built around the access control 3. Unix's access control is implemented through its file system. Each file (or directory) has a number of attributes, including a file name, permission bits, a UID and a GID. The UID of a file specifies its owner. In Chapter 2, we had explained that the permission bits are used to specify permissions to read (r), write (w), and execute (x). These permissions are associated with every file of every user, for the members of the user's group, and for all other users of that system. For instance, the permission string rwxr-x--x specifies that the owner may read, write and execute, the user's group members are allowed to read and execute it, while all the other users of the system may be permitted to only execute this file. A dash (`-`) in the permission set indicates that the access rights are not permitted. Furthermore, each process in Unix has an effective and a real UID as well as an effective and a real GID associated with it. The real UID (and GID) are the primary identifications that Unix systems continually maintain based on the identifications assigned at the time of accounts creation. However, access rights and privileges evolve over time. The effective identifications precisely reflect that. A process's effective identification indicates the access privileges. Whenever a process attempts to access a file, the kernel will use the process's effective UID and GID to compare them with the UID and the GID associated with the file to decide whether or not to grant the request.

As we stated earlier, Unix logs the systems' usage. Unix kernel, and system processes, store pertinent information in the log files. The logs may be kept either locally, or centrally, on an network server. Sometimes logs are prepared for a fixed duration of time (like for 1 to 30 days) or archived. The logs may be analyzed on-line or off-line on a secured isolated system. An analysis on a secured isolated system has the advantage that it cannot be modified by an attacker (to erase his trace). Also, the analysis can be very detailed as this is the only purpose of such a system.

With the security concerns coming into focus, security standards have emerged. Usually the security standards recommend achieving minimal assured levels of security through some form of configuration management. Most OSs, Unix included, permit a degree of flexibility in operations by appropriately configuring the system resources. In addition, modern Unix systems support a fairly comprehensive type of auditing known as C2 audit. This is so named because it fulfils the audit requirements for the TCSEC C2 security level.

Networking concerns: Realistically speaking almost all machines are networked. In any case every machine has built-in network (NW) support. The default NW support is TCP/IP or its variant. This is very assuring from the point of compatibility. The range of NW services support includes remote terminal access and remote command execution using *rsh, rlogin* commands and remote file transfer using *ftp* command. The remote service soliciting commands are collectively known as the r commands. The NW File System (NFS) is designed to offer transparency to determine the location of the file. This is done by supporting mounting of a remote file as if it was on the local file system. In fact, NFS technically supports multiple hosts to share files over a local area network (LAN). The Network Information System (NIS), formally known as the Sun Yellow Pages, enables hosts to share systems and NW databases. The NW databases contain data concerning user account information, group membership, mail aliases etc. The NFS facilitates centralized administration of the file system. Basically, the r commands are not secure. There are many reasons why these are insecure operations. We delineate some of these below.

- The primary one being that Unix was designed to facilitate usage with a view to cooperating in flexible ways. The initial design did not visualize a climate of suspicion. So, they assumed that all hosts in the network are trusted to play by the rules, e.g. any request arising out of a TCP/IP port below 1024 is considered to be trusted.

- These commands require a simple address-based authentication, i.e. the source address of a request is used to decide whether or not to grant an access or offer a service.

- They send clear text passwords over the network.

Now a days there are other better alternatives to the r commands, namely *ssh, slogin* and *scp*, respectively, which use strong *ssl* public key infrastructure to encrypt their traffic. Before an NFS client can access files on a file system exported by an NFS server, it needs to mount the file system. If a mount operation succeeds, the server will respond with a file handle, which is later used in all accesses to that file system in order to verify that the request is coming from a legitimate client. Only clients that are trusted by the server are allowed to mount a file system. The primary problem with NFS is the weak authentication of the mount request. Usually the authentication is based on IP address of the client machine. Note that it is not difficult to fake an IP address. So, one may configure NIS to operate with an added security protocol as described below.

- Ensure minimally traditional Unix authentication based on machine identification and UID.

- Augment data encryption standard (DES) authentication .

The DES authentication provides quite strong security. The authentication based on machine identification or UID is used by default while using NFS. Yet another authentication method based on Kerberos is also supported by NIS. The servers as well as the clients are sensitive to attacks, but some are of the opinion that the real security problem with NIS lies in the client side. It is easy for an intruder to fake a reply from the NIS server. There are more secure replacements for the NIS as well (like LDAP), and other directory services.

Unix security mechanisms rely heavily on its access control mechanisms. We shall study the access control in more detail a little later. However, before we do that within the broad framework of network concerns we shall briefly indicate what roles the regulatory agencies play. This is because NWs are seen as a basic infrastructure.

Internet security concerns and role of security agencies: In USA, a federally funded Computer Emergency Response Team (CERT) continuously monitors the types of attacks that happen. On its site it offers a lot of advisory information. It even helps organizations whose systems may be under attack. Also, there is critical infrastructure protection board within whose mandate it is to protect internet from attack. The National Security Agency (NSA) acts as a watchdog body and influences such decisions as to what level of security products may be shipped out of USA. The NSA is also responsible to recommend acceptable security protocols and standards in USA. NSA is the major security research agency in USA. For instance, it was NSA that made the recommendation on product export restriction beyond a certain level of DES security (in terms of number of bits).

In India too, we have a board that regulates IT infrastructure security. For instance, it has identified the nature of Public Key Infrastructure. Also, it has identified organizations that may offer security-related certification services. These services assure of authentication and support non-repudiation in financial and legal transactions. It has set standards for acceptable kind of digital signatures.

File permissions: The file permissions model presents some practical difficulties. This is because Unix generally operates with none or all for group permissions. Now consider the following scenario:

There are three users with usernames Bhatt, Kulish, and Srimati and they belong to the group users. Is there anyway for Bhatt to give access to a file that he owns to Kulish alone. Unfortunately it is not possible unless Bhatt and Kulish belong to an identifiable group (and only these two must be members of that group) of which Srimati is not a member. To allow users to create their own groups and share files, there are programs like sudo which the administrator can use to give limited superuser privileges to ordinary users. But it is cumbersome to say the least. There is another option in the BSD family of Unix versions, where a user must belong to the Wheel group to run programs like *sudo* or *su*. This is where the Access Control Lists (ACLs) and the extended attributes come into picture. Since access control is a major means of securing in Unix we next discuss that.

More on access control in Unix: Note that in Unix all information is finally in the form of a file. So everything in Unix is a file. All the devices are files (one notable exception being the network devices and that too for historical reasons). All data is kept in the form of files. The configuration for the servers running on the system is kept in files. Also, the authentication information itself is stored as files. So, the file system's security is the most important aspect in Unix security model. Unix provides access control of the resources using the two mechanisms:

1. The file permissions, uid, gid.

2. User-name and password authentication.

The file access permissions determine whether a user has access permissions to seek requested services. Username and password authentication is required to ensure that the user is who he claims to be. Now consider the following *rwx* permissions for user, group and others.

$ ls -l

drwxrwxr-x 3 user group 4096 Apr 12 08:03 directory

-rw-rw-r-- 1 user group 159 Apr 20 07:59 sample2e.aux

The first line above shows the file permissions associated with the file identified as a directory. It has read, write and execute permission for the user and his group and read and execute for others. The first letter 'd' shows that it is a directory which is a file containing information about other files. In the second line the first character is empty which indicates that it is a regular file. Occasionally, one gets to see two other characters in that field. These are 's' and 'l', where 's' indicates a socket and 'l' indicates that the file is a link. There are two kinds of links in Unix. The hard link and the soft link (also known as symbolic links). A hard link is just an entry in the directory pointing to the same file on the hard disk. On the other hand, the symbolic link is another separate file pointing to the original file. The practical difference is that a hard link has to be on the same device as the original but the symbolic link can be on a different device. Also, if we remove a file, the hard link for the file will also be removed. In the case of a symbolic link, it will still exist pointing no where.

In Unix every legitimate user is given a user account which is associated with a user id (Unix only knows and understands user ids here to in referred as UIDs).The mapping of the users is maintained in the file /etc/passwd. The UID 0 is reserved. This user id is a special superuser id and is assigned to the user ROOT. The SU ROOT has unlimited privileges on the system. Only SU ROOT can create new user accounts on a system. All other UIDs and GIDs are basically equal.

A user may belong to one or more groups up to 16. A user may be enjoined to other groups or leave some groups as long as the number remains below the number permitted by the system. At anytime the user must belong to at least one group. Different flavors of Unix follow different conventions. Linux follows the convention of creating one group with the same name as the username whenever a new user id is created. BSDs follow the convention of having all the ordinary users belong to a group called users.

It is to be noted that the permissions are matched from left to right. As a consequence, the following may happen. Suppose a user owns a file and he does not have some permission. However, suppose the group (of which he also is a member) has the permission. In this situation because of the left to right matching, he still cannot have permission to operate on the file. This is more of a quirk as the user can always change the permissions whichever way he desires if he owns the file.

The user of the system must be able to perform certain security critical functions on the system normally exclusive to the system administrator, without having access to the same security permissions. One way of giving users' a controlled access to a limited set of system privileges is for the system to allow the execution of a specified process by an ordinary user, with the same permissions as another user, i.e. system privileges. This specified process can then perform application level checks to insure that the process does not perform actions that the user was not intended to be able to perform. This of course places stringent requirements on the process in terms of correctness of execution, lest the user be able to circumvent the security checks, and perform arbitrary actions, with system privileges.

Two separate but similar mechanisms handle impersonation in Unix, the so called set UID, (SUID), and set-GID (SGID) mechanisms. Every executable file on a file system so configured, can be marked for SUID/SGID execution. Such a file is executed with the permissions of the owner/ group of the file, instead of the current user. Typically, certain services that require superuser privileges are wrapped in a SUID superuser program, and the users of the system are given permission to execute this program. If the program can be subverted into performing some action that it was not originally intended to perform, serious breaches of security can result.

The above system works well in a surprising number of situations. But we will illustrate a few situations where it fails to protect or even facilitates the attacker. Most systems today also support some form of access control list (ACL) based schemes.

Access control lists: On Unix systems, file permissions define the file mode as well. The file mode contains nine bits that determine access permissions to the file plus three special bits. This mechanism allows to define access permissions for three classes of users: the file owner, the owning group, and the rest of the world. These permission bits are modified using the *chmod* utility. The main advantage of this mechanism is its simplicity. With a couple of bits, many permission scenarios can be modeled. However, there often is a need to specify relatively fine-grained access permissions.

Access Control Lists (ACLs) support more fine grained permissions. Arbitrary users and groups can be granted or denied access in addition to the three traditional classes of users. The three classes of users can be regarded as three entries of an Access Control List. Additional entries can be added that define the permissions which the specific users or groups are granted.

An example of the use of ACLs: Let's assume a small company producing soaps for all usages. We shall call it Soaps4All. Soaps4All runs a Linux system as its main file server. The system administrator of Soaps4All is called Damu. One particular team of users, the Toileteers, deals with the development of new toilet accessories. They keep all their shared data in the sub-directory /home/ toileteers/shared. Kalyan is the administrator of the Toileteers team. Other members are Ritu, Vivek, and Ulhas.

Username Groups Function

Damu users System administrator

Kalyan toileteers, jumboT, perfumedT administrator ritu toileteers, jumboT vivek toileteers, perfumedT

ulhas toileteers, jumboT, perfumedT

Inside the shared directory, all Toileteers shall have read access. Kalyan, being the Toileteers administrator, shall have full access to all the sub-directories as well as to files in those sub-directories. Everybody who is working on a project shall have full access to the project's sub-directory in /home/toileteers/shared.

Suppose two brand new soaps are under development at the moment. These are called Jumbo and Perfumed. Ritu is working on Jumbo. Vivek is working on Perfumed. Ulhas is working on both the projects. This is clearly reflected by the users' group membership in the table.

We have the following directory structure:

$ ls -l

drwx------ 2 Kalyan toileteers 1024 Apr 12 12:47 Kalyan

drwx------ 2 ritu toileteers 1024 Apr 12 12:47 ritu

drwxr-x--- 2 Kalyan toileteers 1024 Apr 12 12:48 shared

drwx------ 2 ulhas toileteers 1024 Apr 12 13:23 ulhas

drwx------ 2 vivek toileteers 1024 Apr 12 12:48 vivek

/shared$ls -l

drwxrwx--- 2 Kalyan jumbo 1024 Sep 25 14:09 jumbo

drwxrwx--- 2 Kalyan perfumed 1024 Sep 25 14:09 perfumed Now note the following:

Y   Ritu does not have a read access to /home/toileteers/shared/perfumed.

Y   Vivek does not have read access to /home/toileteers/shared/jumbo.

Y   Kalyan does not have write access to files which others create in any project sub- directory.

The first two problems could be solved by granting everyone read access to the /home/toileteers/shared/ directory tree using the others permission bits (making the directory tree world readable). Since nobody else but Toileteers have access to the /home/toileteers directory, this is safe. However, we would need to take great care of the other permissions of the /home/toileteers directory.

Adding anything to the toileteers directory tree later that is world readable is impossible. With ACLs, there is a better solution. The third problem has no clean solution within the traditional permission system.

The solution using ACLs: The /home/toileteers/shared/ sub-directories can be made readable for Toileteers, and fully accessible for the respective project group. For Kalyan's administrative rights, a separate ACL entry is needed. This is the command to grant read access to the Toileteers. This is in addition to the existing permissions of other users and groups:

$setfacl -m g:toileteers:rx *

$getfacl *

file: jumbo

owner: Kalyan

group: jumbo user::rwx group::rwx group:toileteers:r-x mask:rwx

other:---

file: perfumed

owner: Kalyan

group: perfumed user::rwx group::rwx group:toileteers:r-x mask:rwx

other:---

Incidentally, AFS(Andrew File System), and XFS (SGI's eXtended File System) support ACLs.

References

- Gasser, Morrie (1988). Building a Secure Computer System (PDF). Van Nostrand Reinhold. p. 3. ISBN 0-442-23022-2. Retrieved 6 September 2015

- Schlienger, Thomas; Teufel, Stephanie (2003). "Information security culture-from analysis to change". South African Computer Journal. 31: 46–52

- James Cook (December 16, 2014). "Sony Hackers Have Over 100 Terabytes Of Documents. Only Released 200 Gigabytes So Far". Business Insider. Retrieved December 18, 2014

- Gordon, Lawrence; Loeb, Martin (November 2002). "The Economics of Information Security Investment". ACM Transactions on Information and System Security. 5 (4): 438–457. doi:10.1145/581271.581274

- Kiountouzis, E. A.; Kokolakis, S. A. Information systems security: facing the information society of the 21st century. London: Chapman & Hall, Ltd. ISBN 0-412-78120-4

- "Target security breach affects up to 40M cards". Associated Press via Milwaukee Journal Sentinel. 19 December 2013. Retrieved 21 December 2013

- Ovidiu Vermesan; Peter Friess. "Internet of Things: Converging Technologies for Smart Environments and Integrated Ecosystems" (PDF). River Publishers. Retrieved 4 November 2016

- Bavisi, Sanjay (2009). "22". In Vacca, John. Computer and Information Security Handbook. Morgan Kaufmann Publications. Elsevier Inc. p. 375. ISBN 978-0-12-374354-1

- Barrett, Devlin. "U.S. Suspects Hackers in China Breached About four (4) Million People's Records, Officials Say". The Wall Street Journal

- Lipner, Steve (2015). "The Birth and Death of the Orange Book". IEEE Annals of the History of Computing. 37 (2): 19–31. doi:10.1109/MAHC.2015.27

- "Abstract Formal Specification of the seL4/ARMv6 API" (PDF). Archived from the original (PDF) on 21 May 2015. Retrieved May 19, 2015

- Wright, Joe; Harmening, Jim (2009). "15". In Vacca, John. Computer and Information Security Handbook. Morgan Kaufmann Publications. Elsevier Inc. p. 257. ISBN 978-0-12-374354-1

- Kwanwoo Jun (23 September 2013). "Seoul Puts a Price on Cyberdefense". Wall Street Journal. Dow Jones & Company, Inc. Retrieved 24 September 2013

- "Action Plan 2010–2015 for Canada's Cyber Security Strategy". Public Safety Canada. Government of Canada. Retrieved 3 November 2014

- Mansfield-Devine, Steve (2015-09-01). "The Ashley Madison affair". Network Security. 2015 (9): 8–16. doi:10.1016/S1353-4858(15)30080-5

- Kakareka, Almantas (2009). "23". In Vacca, John. Computer and Information Security Handbook. Morgan Kaufmann Publications. Elsevier Inc. p. 393. ISBN 978-0-12-374354-1

- De Silva, Richard (11 Oct 2011). "Government vs. Commerce: The Cyber Security Industry and You (Part One)". Defence IQ. Retrieved 24 Apr 2014

Permissions

Index